LEGENDARY LOCALS

OF

AMBLER

PENNSYLVANIA

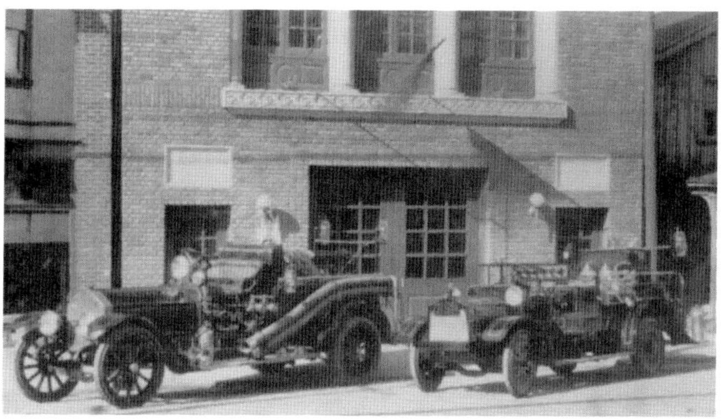

I0805743

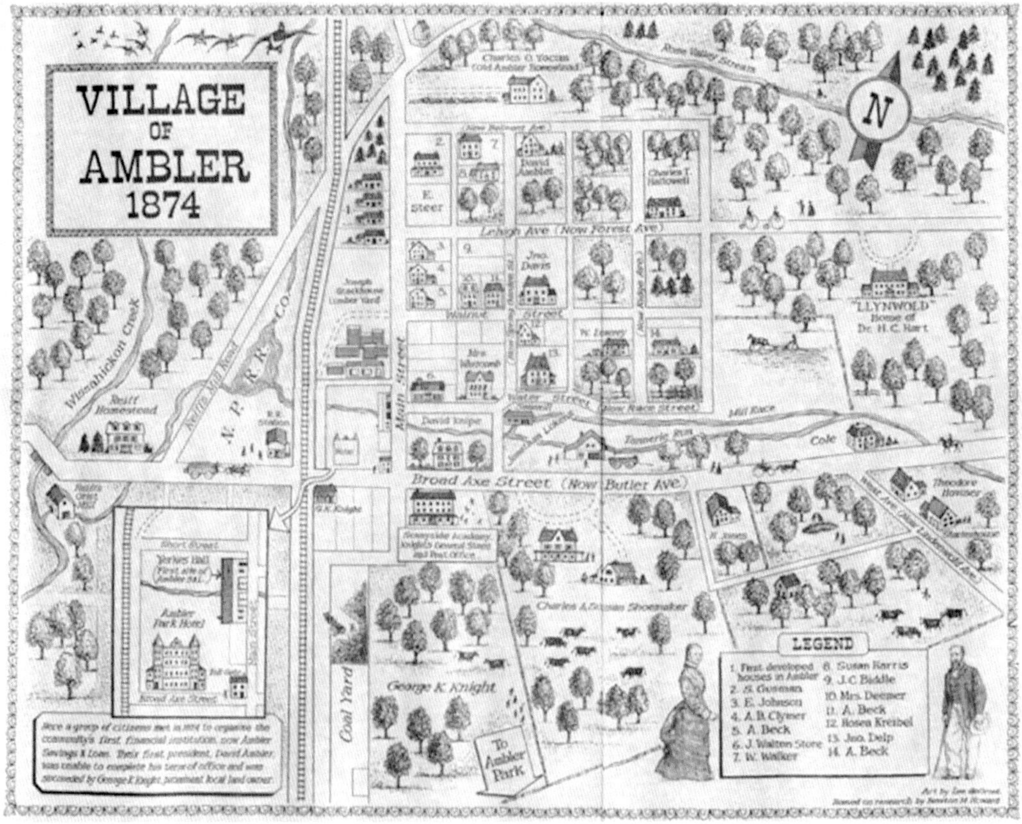

Ambler in 1874

Before the borough was incorporated in 1888 and its name was officially changed to Ambler, the rural village was known in 1874 as Wissahickon. But as the mills began to fade along the Wissahickon Creek and other industries grew alongside the Northern Pennsylvania Railroad tracks, the character of the village began to change. This map, which shows the highlights of Ambler at the century's three-quarter mark, could be seen in the Ambler Savings Bank until 2014. (Courtesy of Historical Society of Fort Washington.)

Page 1: Old Meets New

Purchased by the Wissahickon Fire Company in 1916, the first American motorized La France fire truck, capable of pouring 1,275 gallons of water per minute, sits proudly on the left, next to the horse-drawn chemical wagon mounted on a second-hand Packard truck to the left. (Courtesy of Buck Amey.)

LEGENDARY LOCALS

OF

AMBLER

PENNSYLVANIA

FRANK D. QUATTRONE

LEGENDARY LOCALS

ISBN 978-1-4671-0195-0

Legendary Locals is an imprint of Arcadia Publishing
Charleston, South Carolina

Printed in the United States of America

Library of Congress Control Number: 2014948300

For all general information, please contact Arcadia Publishing:
Telephone 843-853-2070
Fax 843-853-0044
E-mail sales@arcadiapublishing.com
For customer service and orders:
Toll-Free 1-888-313-2665

Visit us on the Internet at www.arcadiapublishing.com

Dedication

To my beloved wife and best friend, Eve, without whose sunshine my world would grow dark, and to my six wonderful granddaughters—Melissa, 20; Allison, 16; the twins Jenni and Sammy, 14; Sarah, 9; and precocious little Katie, 6—without whose curiosity and laughter the world would become far too serious

On the Front Cover: Clockwise from top left:
Hardware store owners the Deck brothers (Photograph by Newt Howard; courtesy of Buck Amey; see page 56), high-flying Rotarians Bob Deen and Thomas J. Morrison (Photograph by George Fray; courtesy of Thomas J. Morrison; see page 120), Ambler's namesake Mary Ambler (Courtesy of Buck Amey; see page 32), horticulturalist Jane Bownes Haines (Courtesy of Temple University Ambler Campus; see page 28), Ambler's Canine Corps (Photograph by Walter Free; courtesy of William E. Strasburg; see page 13), state representative George E. Saurman (Photograph by Walter Free; courtesy of George E. Saurman; see page 11), renowned restaurateur Michael Wei (Photograph by Eve M. Quattrone; see page 108), police officer Edward "Eagle" Johnson (Courtesy of Edward "Eagle" Johnson; see page 14), president of National Foundation for Celiac Awareness Alice Bast (Courtesy of National Foundation for Celiac Awareness; see page 116).

On the Back Cover: From left to right:
Ambler mayor Charles T. "Bud" Wahl (Courtesy of the Wahl family; see page 16), Costa's Delicatessen owner Rocco Costa (Courtesy of the Costa family; see page 104).

CONTENTS

ACKNOWLEDGMENTS

Without the encouragement, patience, love, and support of my dear wife, Eve, this book would not have been possible. The constant inquiries and excited chatter of our six granddaughters—Melissa, Allison, Jenni and Sammy, Sarah, and Katie—also helped keep me on track, as did their wonderful parents, Barbara and David Greenberg, Danny and Stacey Henken, and Marylou Galyo.

My heart also goes out to Peggy Dolan, executive director of the Kelly Anne Dolan Memorial Fund, who hired me as communications director once the dust had settled from my departure from Montgomery Media. She gave me time, space, and support, in the midst of my regular responsibilities, to complete this book.

I also learned much about journalism and life from my mentors at Montgomery Media, Fred D. Behringer and Mike Morsch, and the paper's longtime publisher, William E. Strasburg, especially inspired me. And I cannot thank former colleague Linda Finarelli enough for the great article she wrote on my book in the *Ambler Gazette*.

For photographs and story ideas, I am truly grateful for fellow historians Buck Amey and Ross Gordon Gerhart III. For great suggestions and contacts, I thank Bernadette Dougherty, Martin Brown, Dan Ritter, Rick Denzien and Debra Lee, George E. Saurman, Ambler police chief William F. Foley Jr., the Costa family, Elena and Chuck Giannasio, Sharon Cooke-Vargas, the elegant Ditter family, KC Biedlingmaier, the good people at the Ambler and Blue Bell Rotaries, my old Villanova University friend Berne Siergiej, the principal, front office staff, and librarians of Wissahickon High School—and yes, my new friend—celebrated actress Melanie Mayron!

For excellent scanning services, I owe much to Heather Christein and her staff at the Willow Grove Staples. And some of the best interviews I have done for this book took place at my favorite restaurant in the Ambler area, Zakes Café, where my friends and chefs par excellence, the siblings Marlene Zakes and Joe McFadden, plied us with delectable savory and sweet treats and respectful, unobtrusive service.

And where would I be without the patience, guidance, and professional expertise of my wonderful editor at Arcadia Publishing, Erin Vosgien, whose constant encouragement kept my finger off the panic button. And yes—thank you, Ambler, for giving me ample reason to write this book. Because there are so many more unsung heroes not covered here, do not be surprised if there is a second volume!

INTRODUCTION

When he speaks of the community spirit he finds in Ambler, the bustling borough he covered with such gentlemanly zeal for nearly four decades, Montgomery Newspapers' longtime publisher William E. Strasburg likes to invoke Plato's *The Republic*, Thomas More's *Utopia*, and James Hilton's *Lost Horizon*. Not surprising for a man who coauthored (with James P. Cooney) the philosophical book *In Search of Community: Reversing the Course of a Nation in Conflict*. Strasburg founded Montgomery Newspapers in 1952, when he purchased the *Ambler Gazette* from Joseph Haywood. He soon added the *Public Spirit*, the *Times Chronicle*, and other papers to the mix.

Horace Lukens had founded the *Gazette*, soon to become the borough's award-winning newspaper, in 1883. Reporting all the news that was fit to print, it got the word out about available jobs, the upwardly spiraling economy and the new spirit of optimism in the burgeoning community.

Like his predecessor nearly 70 years earlier, Strasburg was determined to have the *Gazette* reflect and direct the mind and soul of the community it served. The *Gazette*, under the watchful leadership of executive editors like Fred D. Behringer and Mike Morsch, especially at a time of diminishing revenues and a shrinking staff, provided awareness and support of public projects and important issues like the need for housing for the less advantaged.

If Strasburg helped set the standard for award-winning suburban journalism—and we are not talking about the relatively recent upsurge in so-called "community journalism" mocked in the November 9, 2014, episode of HBO's acclaimed series *The Newsroom*—he says it would not have been possible without the great-hearted, committed citizens who were more than willing to live and work in harmony. That was something he had not experienced in all the years he covered the world's hot spots, from the underprivileged villages of Nigeria and the shocking Soviet invasion of Czechoslovakia in 1968 to the Pentagon.

So he worked with the resilient blue-collar workers, the visionary professionals, the Ambler Rotary, the borough council, Ambler Main Street, even the state legislature, to help revitalize, and publicize, the little borough that could.

Like many communities in America's early years, Ambler had slowly come alive because its main marine thoroughfare, the scenic, rushing Wissahickon Creek, had provided the means to power its nine mills, which produced flour, lumber, and cloth for the little town then called Wissahickon. By 1855, when the single-track North Penn Railroad arrived, the town's center of gravity had shifted from the original crossroads where Bethlehem and Butler Pikes met, to the western end of town. The very next year, as fate would have it, the railroad would also bring Ambler's greatest moment of infamy, when the northbound Shackamaxon collided head-on with the southbound Aramingo around the dew-laden curve near Camp Hill station. The impact caused three cars to pile up on the engine of the outbound train. The sickening din could be heard for miles around.

To the tangled remains of mangled metal, wooden coaches, and human bodies (eventually, there were 59 fatalities and nearly 100 injured) rushed volunteer firefighters from the Congress Engine and Hose Co. of Chestnut Hill four miles away, pulling their primitive hand-drawn hand-pumper for the rescue effort and physicians from as far off as Germantown and Philadelphia.

As history and legend merge, it seemed even more significant that a frail, kindly Quaker woman named Mary Ambler had also arrived on the scene. Some accounts report that she drove to the site in her wagon, stuffed with bed sheets and medical supplies, but the more enduring legend has it that she walked the two miles from her home in nearby Wissahickon to tend to the maimed victims of the crash. She was said to have the healing touch. So whether she laid on hands to minister to the wounded or simply helped direct the rescue work with her calming influence, Mary Ambler's efforts in the Great Train Accident of 1856 made history.

When the town of Wissahickon was incorporated as a borough in 1888, it was renamed Ambler in honor of its "Angel of Mercy," one of the few towns in America named after a woman.

Commerce boomed again when a second set of tracks was laid in 1873. Within 10 years, in 1882, as the mills were beginning to fail, Ambler's economy and growth received a significant boost when the Keasbey & Mattison (K&M) Company relocated from Philadelphia to Ambler. With the visionary chemist Richard V. Mattison directing operations, K&M soon switched from producing pharmaceuticals to manufacturing asbestos products. By the turn of the century, Ambler had become, in effect, "the asbestos capital of the world," and many residents who worked at the plant eventually became ill from breathing in asbestos dust.

A weakened K&M folded during the Great Depression, but Ambler did not. Because of its community spirit and the strength of its many fine churches, schools, and civic institutions—from the Wissahickon police and fire departments to a proactive borough council and Ambler Main Street—Ambler has survived economic downturns and the devastating effect of suburban malls on its many mom-and-pop shops.

Better yet, revitalized Ambler, a comfortable working-class town, a great place to live that few residents like to leave, has become a destination for people from miles around, people who love its professional theater and art movie house, its lively and internationally diverse dining scene, and the many festivals hosted by the borough each year. Ambler is as close to that idealized vision of community that William E. Strasburg envisions in his book as one could imagine.

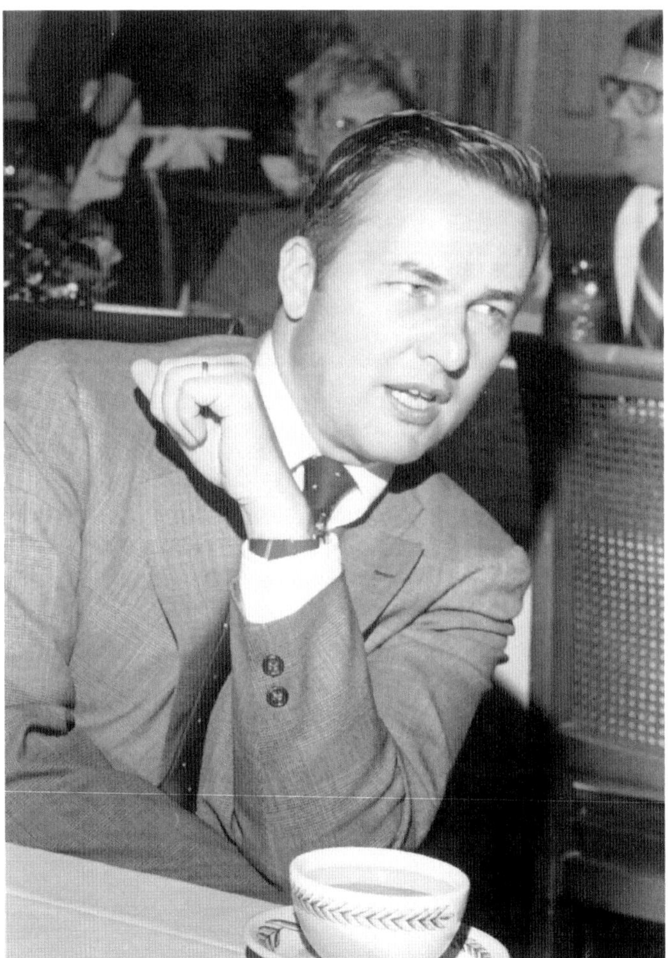

In Search of Community
Some call William E. Strasburg "Mr. Ambler" because of his longtime commitment to the borough. But his reach extended far beyond the borough. When he purchased the *Ambler Gazette* in 1952, his mission as publisher was for the paper "to reflect and direct the new spirit of the community." (Courtesy of William E. Strasburg.)

CHAPTER ONE

Political and Civil Servants

Beloved is a term one seldom hears with regard to political and civil servants—the legislators, mayors, and council members, who debate and make the laws, and the police and firefighters, who put their lives on the line to keep public gathering spaces, streets, and homes safe.

Perhaps it is because only 6,500 people reside within the compact borough, located just 16 miles north of Philadelphia. Perhaps, it is because it is a working-class enclave in the midst of the more affluent municipalities in Montgomery County. But there is a palpable warmth that residents and visitors alike feel whenever they shop, dine, or take care of their daily business in the borough.

Maybe, it is because US congressmen like J. William Ditter and state legislators like George E. Saurman set such splendid examples for leadership. A friendly sort, Saurman literally "knocked on every door" before running for mayor to be sure he knew what his future constituency needed and wanted. When beloved three-term Mayor Charles T. "Bud" Wahl, perhaps revitalized Ambler's biggest booster, passed away in August 2014, the whole town came out to mourn him and tell heartwarming stories about his gregariousness, perpetual smile and generosity to anyone in need.

Congressman Ditter's son, the Hon. J. William Ditter Jr. is still serving as a federal judge early into his nineties, and his staff and the public adore him. Police chief William F. Foley Jr. speaks warmly of growing up in a borough where practically all his neighbors and friends loved being volunteer firemen. It was like an extended family. Former police officer Edward "Eagle" Johnson reflects fondly on growing up African American in a predominantly Italian American neighborhood. He says he never felt like an outsider because everyone treated him with kindness and respect.

This seems to be the prevailing mood in Ambler—hardworking people who actually seem to grow up liking each other, helping each other out, and working together for the greater good.

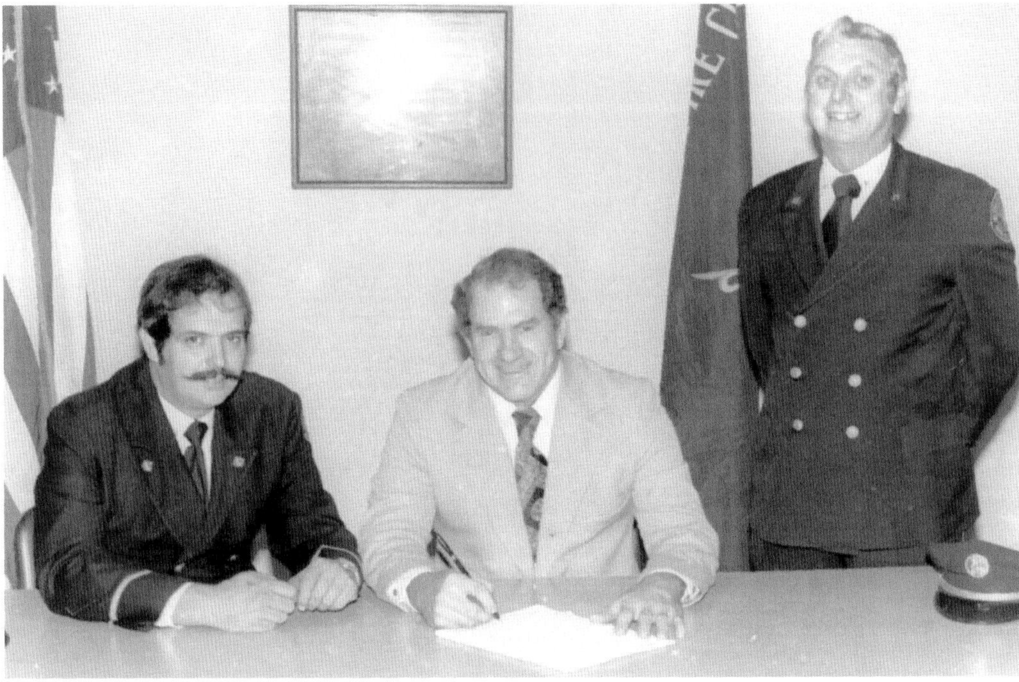

MADD about Service

As mayor of Ambler, George E. Saurman (center, with John Snyder, left, and unidentified, right) discovered that his major role was to run the police department. Inexperienced with police work, he took police science, juvenile delinquency, and drug abuse courses at Montgomery County Community College, all of which fueled 11 successful years in office, which saw significant decreases in juvenile delinquency and drug abuse and an expansion of the police force. With strong support from Marie Tursi (left), a Horsham mother whose son was killed by a drunk driver in 1980, and Gov. Dick Thornburgh (center), Pennsylvania state representative George E. Saurman (right) helped establish the first affiliate chapter of MADD (Mothers Against Drunk Driving) in Pennsylvania. In his 14 years as a legislator (1981–1994), Saurman also worked on bills regarding nursing, autism, drug and alcohol abuse on college campuses, health, welfare, and aging. (Both, courtesy of George E. Saurman.)

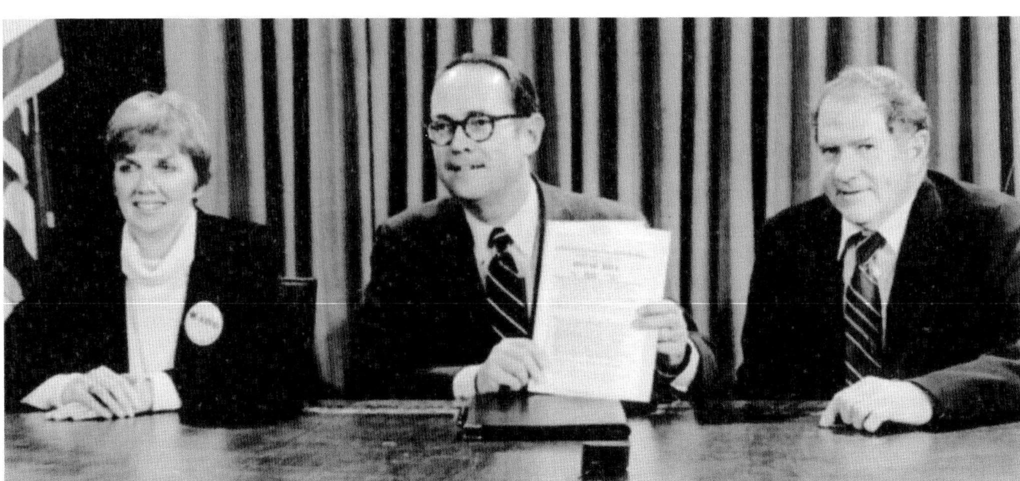

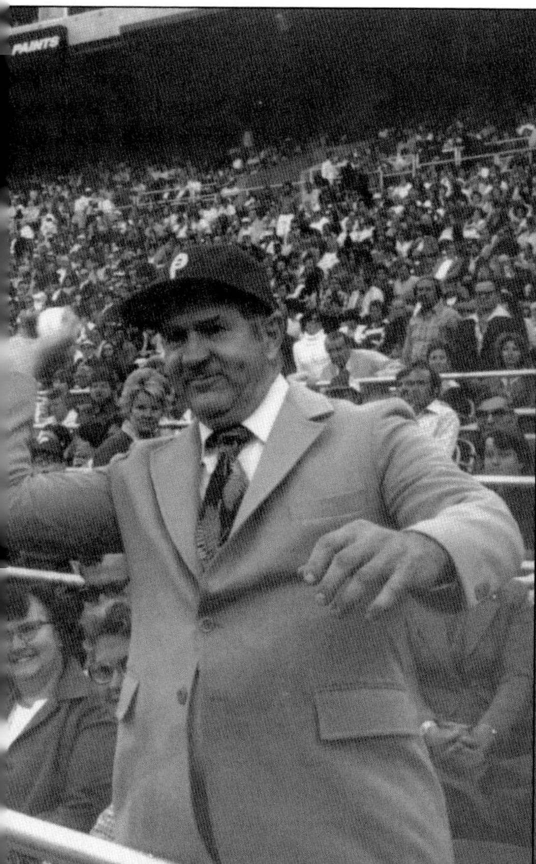

First Pitch

Tossing out the first pitch at Ambler Night at Veterans Stadium before a Philadelphia Phillies game in the 1970s is popular Ambler mayor George E. Saurman, who helped organize the event. He served as mayor for 11 years (1970–1981) and on the Ambler Borough Council (1966–1970, 1995–1999). A consummate diplomat who successfully worked both sides of the aisle, he was also a businessman. Because his Ambler company imported cocoa to make chocolate milk, Saurman became known as "the Chocolate Mayor." As mayor, Saurman also brought the Canine Corps to the police force and initiated programs to engage disaffected youth. The Texas-born civil servant and World War II veteran has also written two books: *We've Done Them Wrong*, on the US mistreatment of Native Americans, and the political fantasy novel *A Story of Two Trees*. Pictured in 1974 with unidentified members of Ambler Borough Council, police officers, the crossing guard, and members of the Canine Corps are Ambler mayor George E. Saurman (second row, third from left), Chief Lester Carpenter (fourth from left), and borough president Doc Signore (fifth from left). (Left, courtesy of George E. Saurman; below, photograph by Walter Free; courtesy of George E. Saurman.)

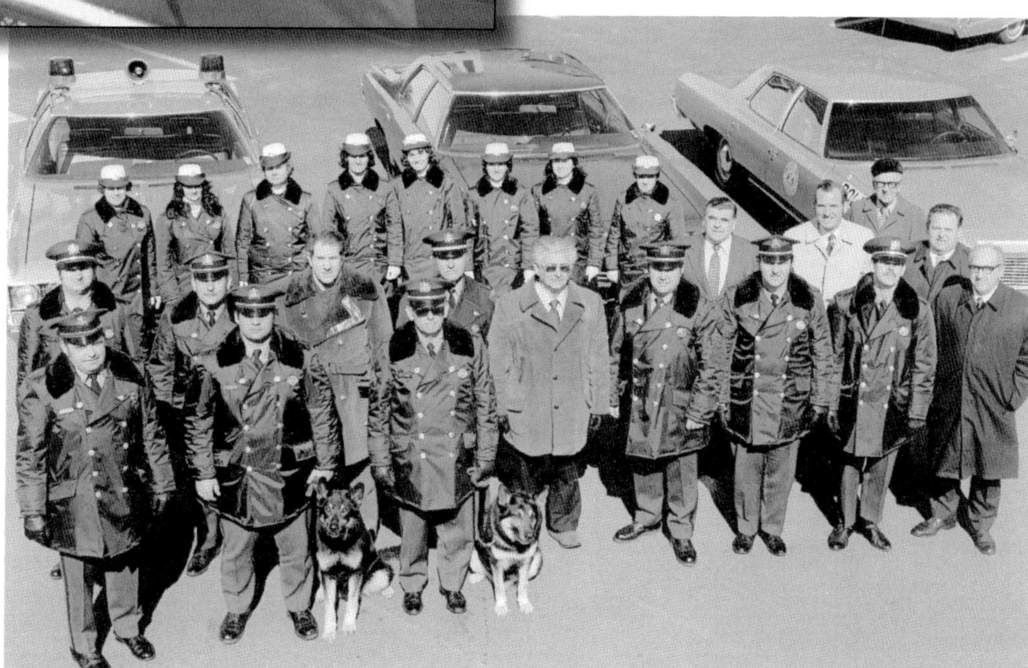

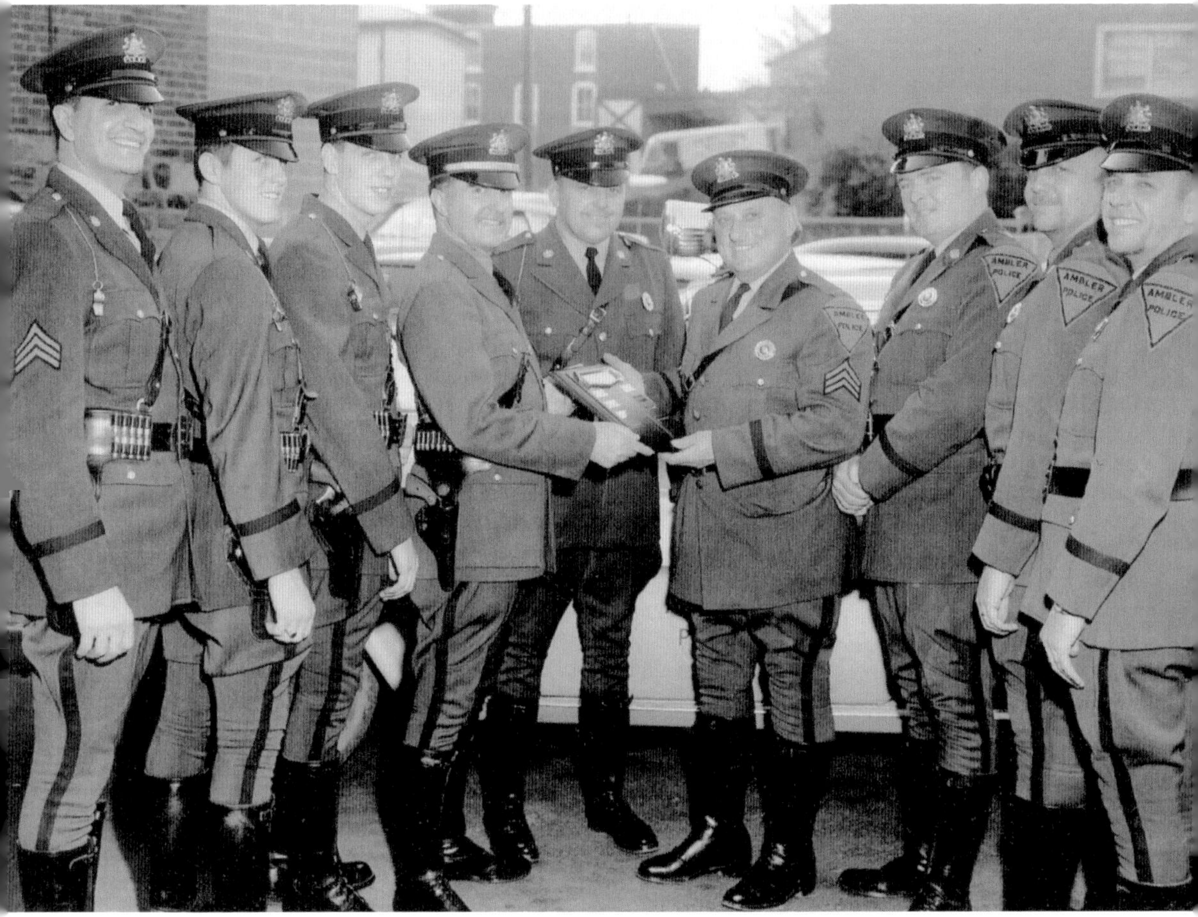

Ambler's Finest

Ambler's police department has worked tirelessly to keep the bustling borough relatively crime-free. Establishing close contact with the community in the 1970s are, from left to right, Sgt. Leon Angelichio, Ofcs. Charles "Mickey" Hopwood and Tom Brewster, Chief Lester Carpenter, future chief Frank Wack, Sgt. Francis Hildman, and Ofcs. George Heller, Claude Whery, and Woody Wagner. (Photograph by Edward H. Maguire; courtesy of *Norristown Times Herald* and George E. Saurman.)

Canine Corps

Posing proudly with the newly established Canine Corps are, from left to right, (first row) future chief Rocco Wack and Ofcs. Ray Moscardelli, Woody Wagner, and Hank Pishock; (second row) Ofcs. Pete Conway and Mike Galardi, future chief Frank Wack, Chief Lester Carpenter, unidentified, and Ofcs. Tony Tumolo and Anthony Lapore. Chief Carpenter, known for being out on the street where he would always be available to help his neighbors, was on the force from 1938 to 1976. His son Craig Carpenter said that his father had no hobbies: "The [police] force was all that he knew." (Photograph by Walter Free; courtesy of George E. Saurman.)

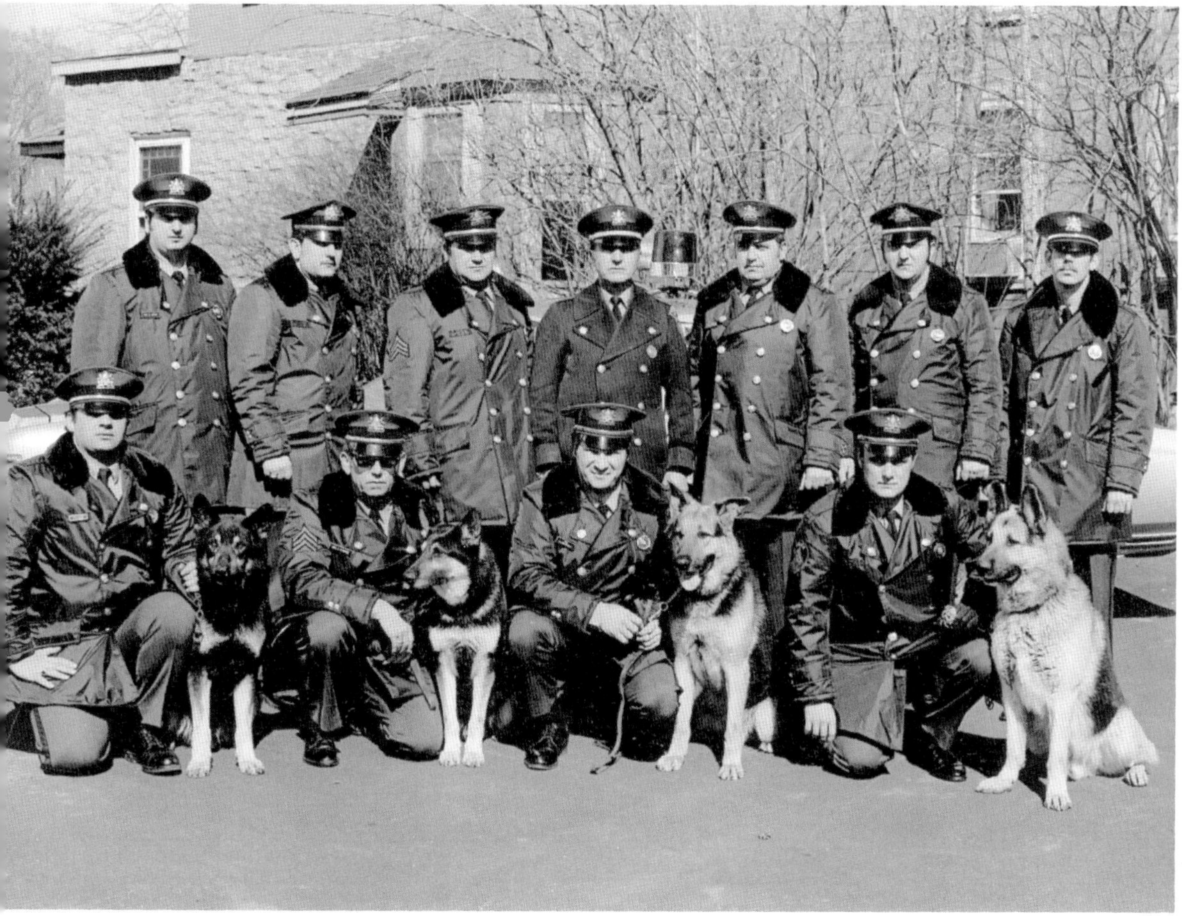

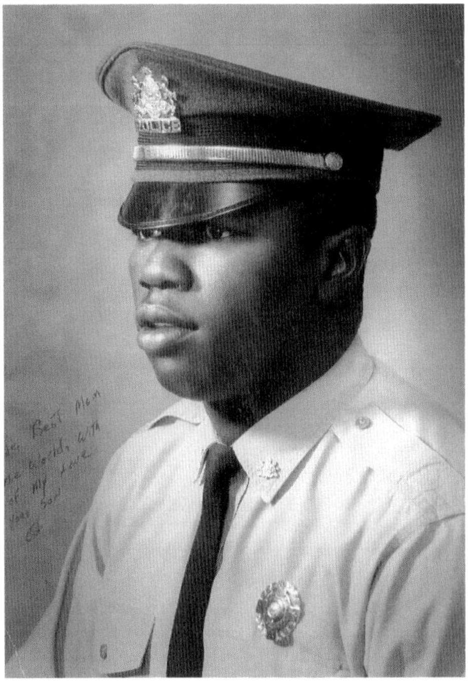

The Eagle Flies

The second African American hired by the Ambler police department, one of the first municipalities to do so, Edward "Eagle" Johnson was once a star tackle for Ambler High's football team. Known for his devastating flying tackles (no longer legal), as well as his receding hairline, Johnson soon earned the sobriquet "Eagle" and endeared himself to his teammates (the team's record was 23-0 during his years there) and, later, to Ambler's police force and community. He loved growing up in Ambler, where he found little prejudice against blacks and a friendly, outgoing Italian American community. After graduation, Eagle joined the Air Force (he obviously loved to fly). Some years later, while still an officer on the force, after meeting his dear wife and surviving a serious cancer scare, he turned his thoughts and soul to a higher power. He is now the first African American pastor at Holmesburg Baptist Church, a white bastion in Northeast Philadelphia, where he is revered for his challenging messages from the pulpit as well as his Bible study classes. (Both, courtesy of Edward "Eagle" Johnson.)

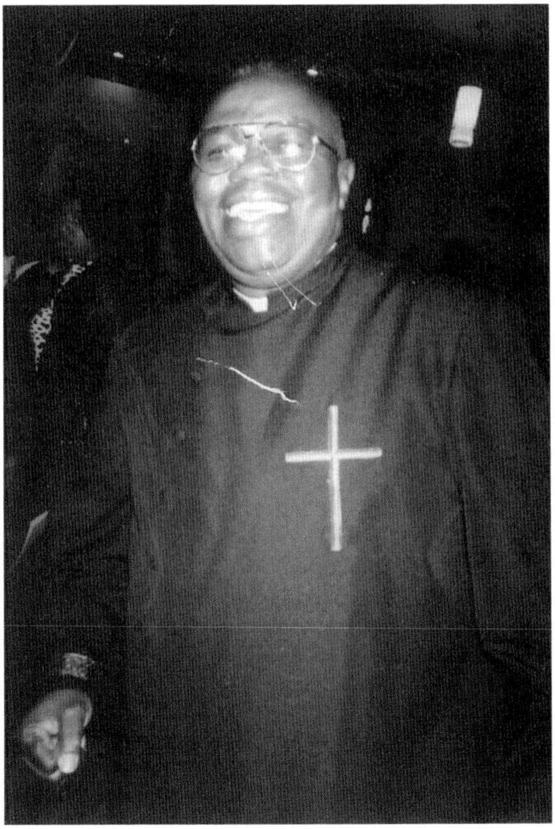

New Look Police

William F. Foley Jr., chief of the Ambler Borough Police Department since 2008, acknowledges that the force has come a long way since it first began serving the community at the end of the 19th century. At that time, very little crime beset the bustling borough. A common sight along Butler Avenue, Ambler's principal thoroughfare, was High Constable Dick Ford atop his trusty steed, tipping his cap as he made his rounds, eyes sharpened for any sign of misconduct (think bar fights or horse thievery). Today, the force has grown to 10 officers patrolling the streets in three state-of-the-art squad cars, plus three manning the station, located in what Foley nicknamed "the lower bedroom" of the present borough building. Much better, he said, than "the closet," which was in the basement of the previous borough building at 31 East Butler Avenue. Foley said that when he was growing up in his Southern Avenue neighborhood, there were about eight volunteer firemen living nearby, including his two best friends. All their families were friends. "It was like having 30 sets of parents," Foley reflected. "You had to help each other out." Naturally, inspired by his pal and next-door neighbor Jesse Hayden, whose granddad, Arthur R. Hayden, had served as chief of the Wissahickon Fire Company from 1907 to 1913 and 1916 to 1920 (Jesse himself was fire chief in 1976), he became a volunteer fireman in 1970 while he was still in high school.

Seven years later, inspired by his friends Rocco and Frank Wack (each of whom had served previously as chief of police), he became a full-time police officer. As societal mores have changed—from Vietnam-era demonstrations in his youth to the drug issues that began plaguing the country in the late 1970s, through the usual weekend fracases in the bars—Foley has also seen the department evolve. "Today, we're dealing more with cyber-crime, identity theft, and the like, much of it affecting our senior citizens." So the department is trying to keep pace with the new technology to protect its community. And that should become even easier in the foreseeable future, as the department is moving into new headquarters, the abandoned Mattison Avenue Elementary School building, in 2015. Foley says that the police department has made a significant impact on the community, allowing Ambler's longtime residents to work, sleep, shop, and enjoy life in peace, even as more and more visitors from outside the borough pour in to indulge in professional theater, art-house cinema, exceptional restaurant choices, and exciting street festivals that have made Ambler such an attractive destination in the past two decades. (Photograph by Michael W. Heayn; courtesy of Chief William F. Foley Jr.)

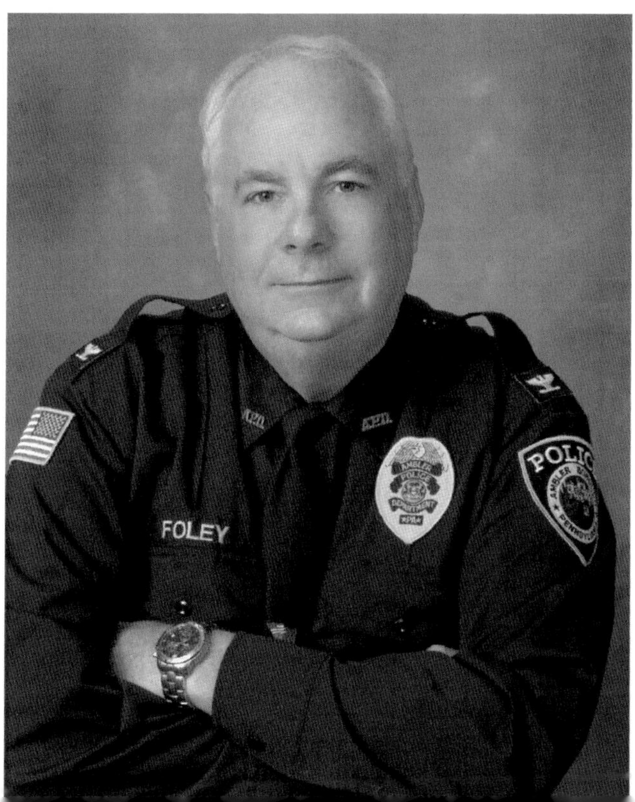

Mr. Mayor

Shortly after his death on August 9, 2014, Mary Jane Wahl explained, quite simply, her husband Charles T. "Bud" Wahl's universal appeal: "Bud was a worker bee, moving chairs for the Christmas Parade [he is the smiling, white-haired gentleman sitting tall in the mayor's car]; he helped with Meals on Wheels. He was so personable and sincere that he could always find someone to help. He always tried to do the best for all involved—from his loving family to the community he loved so well." Mayor of Ambler for three consecutive terms (2001 to 2013), Bud Wahl had the vision and energy to help shepherd the revitalization of the borough, by personally visiting the owners of each of the business establishments, by arranging for videos and local promos on regional television, and by making Ambler Main Street his second home. (Courtesy of the Wahl family.)

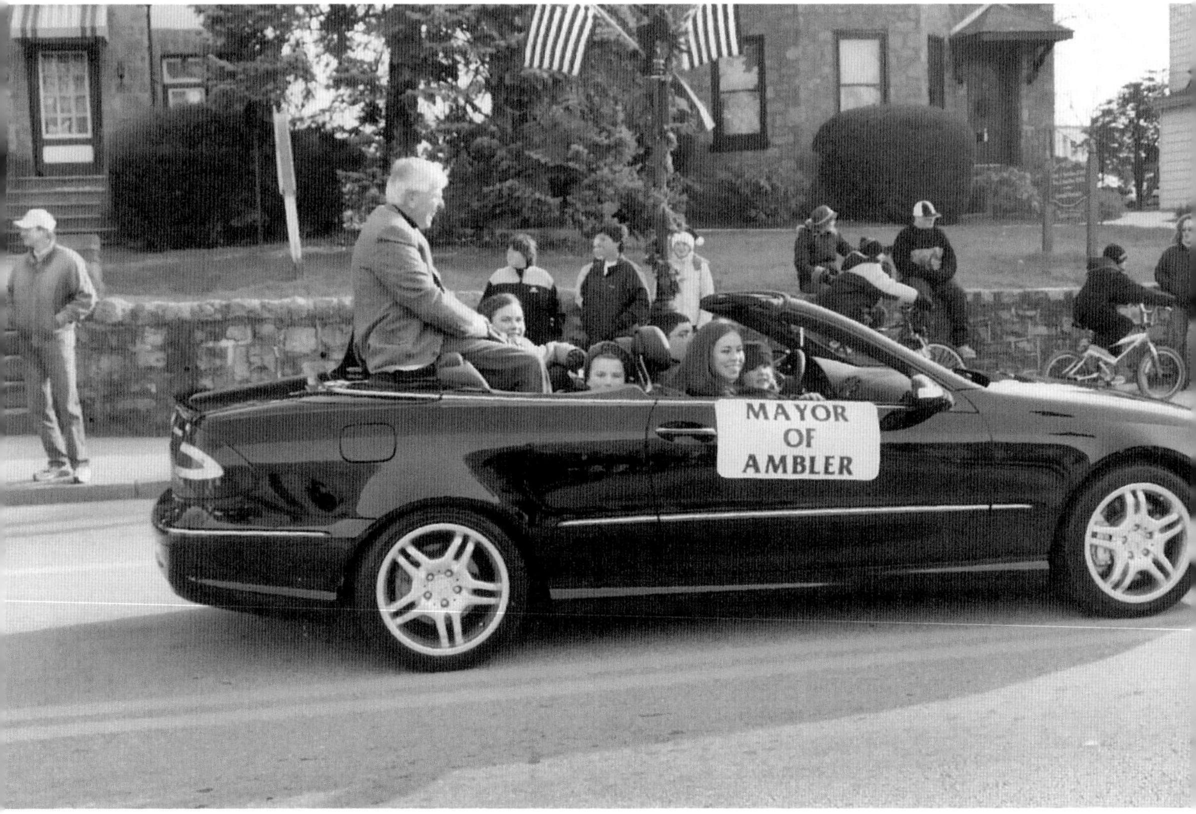

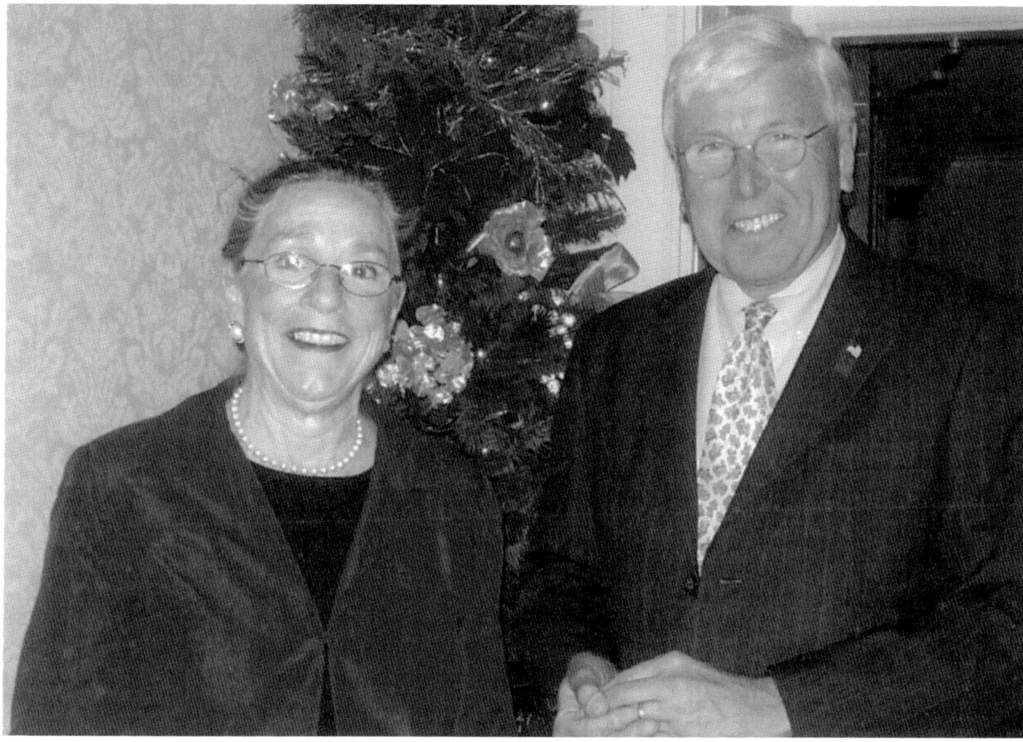

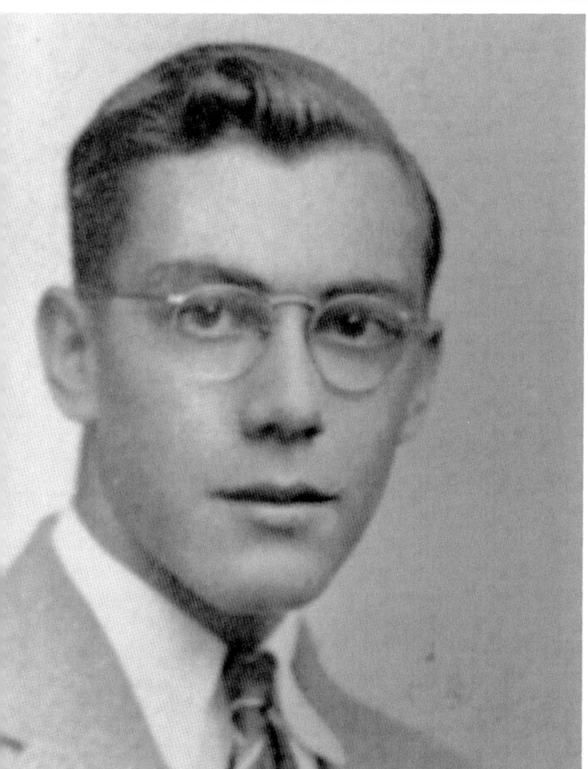

Honorable Citizens

Mary Jane Wahl has also been active in community affairs, from running the Senior Adult Activities Center for 12 years to volunteering for hospice to working in the human relations department of the breastfeeding support group La Leche League International. She even found time to study at Montgomery County Community College in her 50s and earned her college degree in mental health at Hahnemann University at the age of 57.

A Bronze Star World War II veteran and faithful leader of the Ambler Rotary, William T. Weir (Ambler High School class of 1939) served as a civil engineer for municipalities including Ambler, Upper Dublin, Upper Gwynedd, and Upper Merion. Amazingly, he had the ability to hold detailed blueprints in his head. For his contributions to his field and his community, he was honored by the Pennsylvania House of Representatives. (Above, courtesy of the Wahl family; left, courtesy of Wissahickon High School.)

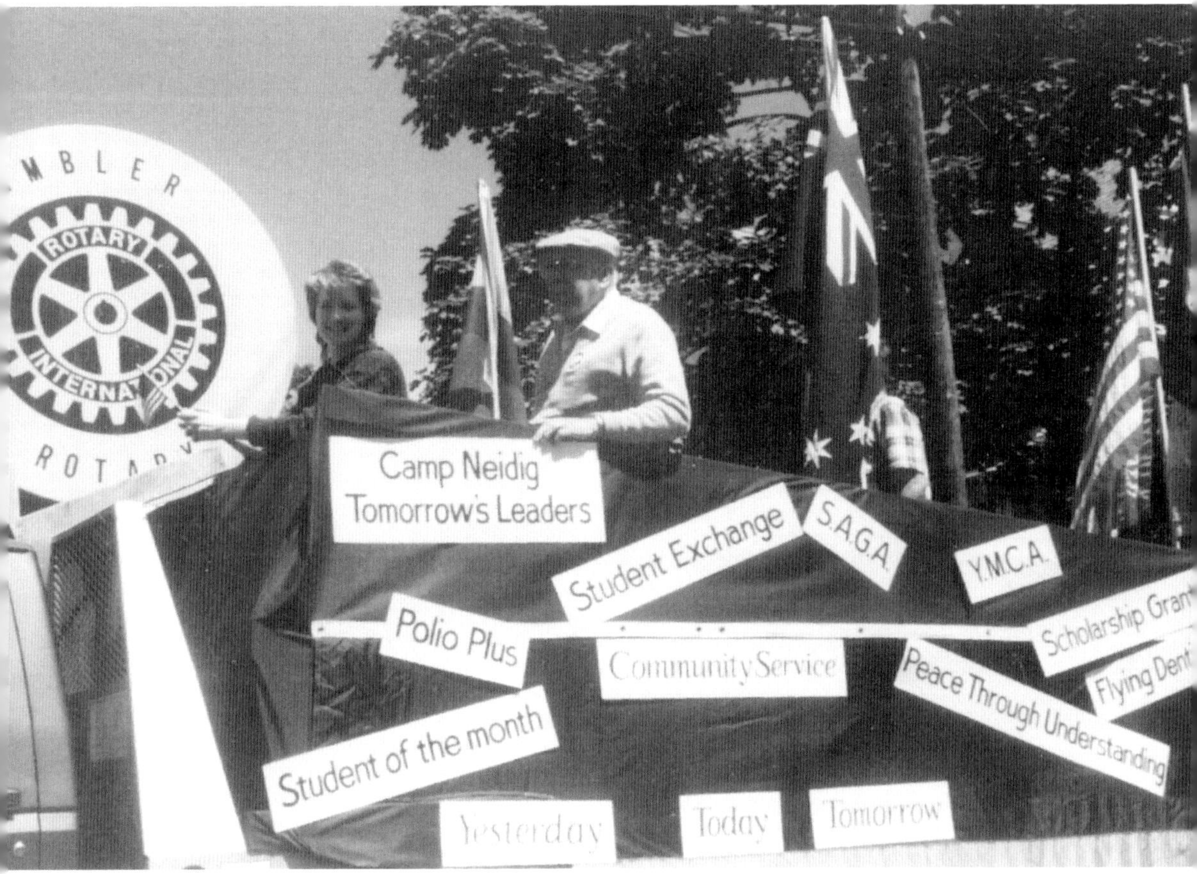

Ambler Rotary Float

Ambler loves a good parade. And its two annual parades, held on the Fourth of July and just before Christmas, have enough fireworks (well, at least during the summer celebration), food, floats, and fun to satisfy any taste. Seen here is the Ambler Rotary float at one of Ambler's recent Fourth of July parades. A major force for positive change and growth in the borough, the Amber Rotary has contributed to everything from securing a new home for the Mattie N. Dixon Community Cupboard to financially supporting the construction of a footbridge over the Wissahickon Creek to allow not only Wissahickon Valley Watershed–guided walks across the creek but also to allow local residents to enjoy the beauty of the creek during the changing of the seasons. (Courtesy of William E. Strasburg.)

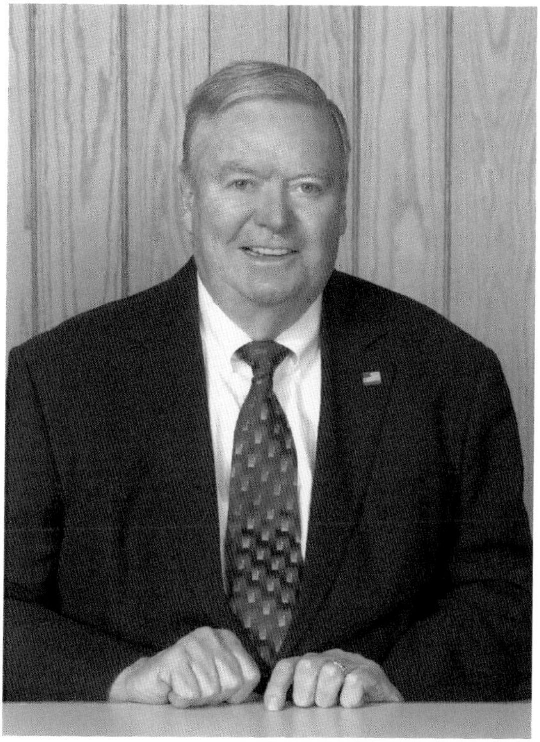

Mr. Lower Gwynedd

Known as "Mr. Lower Gwynedd" for his years of visionary, dedicated service to the residents of Lower Gwynedd Township when he was a leader on the board of supervisors, Ed Brandt also made his mark in neighboring Ambler, where he chaired the Jaycees' annual Christmas Parade for 25 years and then launched the Kiwanis Club of Ambler's annual Fourth of July carnival and fireworks display, which he ran for three decades. (Courtesy of Lower Gwynedd Township.)

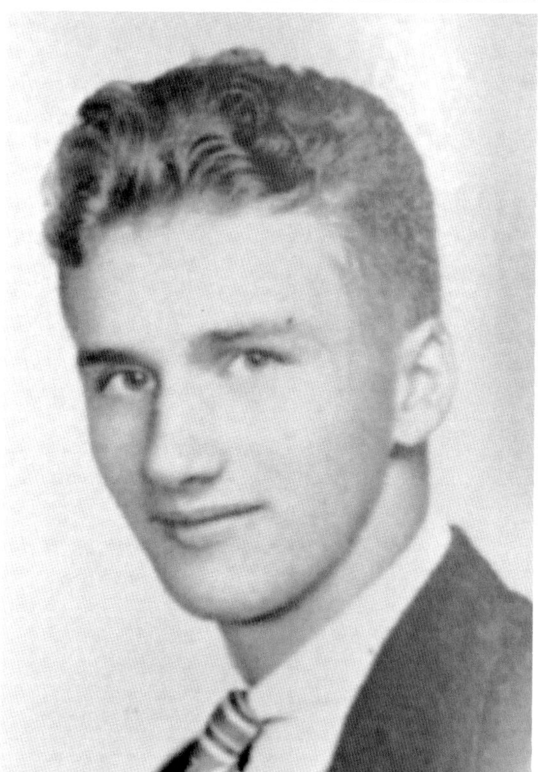

Fire Power

A great sportsman at Ambler High School (class of 1939), George Macort was a longtime steelworker who is probably best remembered for his leadership in the Wissahickon Fire Company. He joined the company in 1945, serving, among many other roles, as fire chief from 1955 to 1959 and from 1963 to 1964. He also served on the Ambler Borough Recreation Board and was a member of the Wissahickon Athletic Club. (Courtesy of Wissahickon High School.)

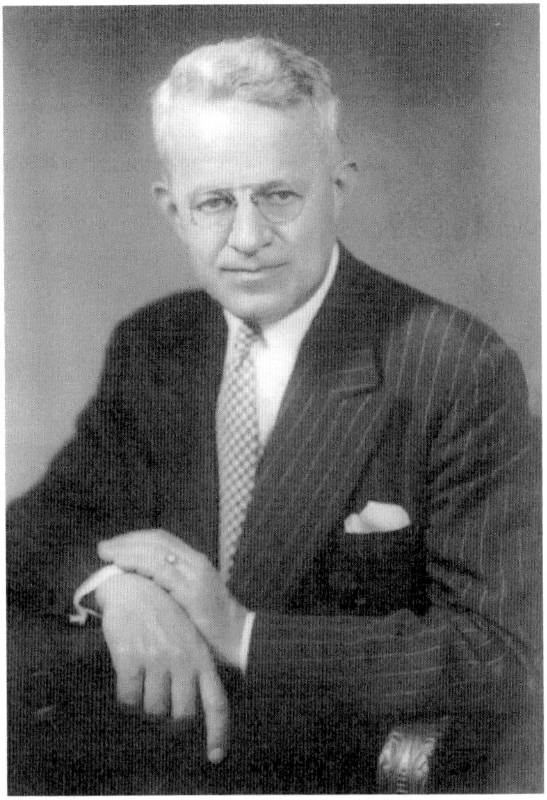

Voice of the Navy
Ambler's own J. William Ditter was not only a respected teacher and attorney, but he was also elected to the House of Representatives, where he served with distinction before he was killed in a plane crash near Lancaster, Pennsylvania, on November 21, 1943. During World War II, Ditter, a fierce advocate for the Navy, was the ranking minority member of the Naval Affairs Subcommittee of the House Appropriations Committee, where he argued successfully for the creation of a two-ocean navy. (Courtesy of the Ditter family.)

USS *Ditter*
Shortly after his death, the Navy honored him by naming a chapel at the Willow Grove Naval Air Station after him, as well as the destroyer USS *J. William Ditter* (DM-31), the only ship ever named after an Ambler resident. It saw action in the Pacific theater, sustaining massive damage after being struck by two kamikazes off the shores of Okinawa in 1945. (Courtesy of the Ditter family.)

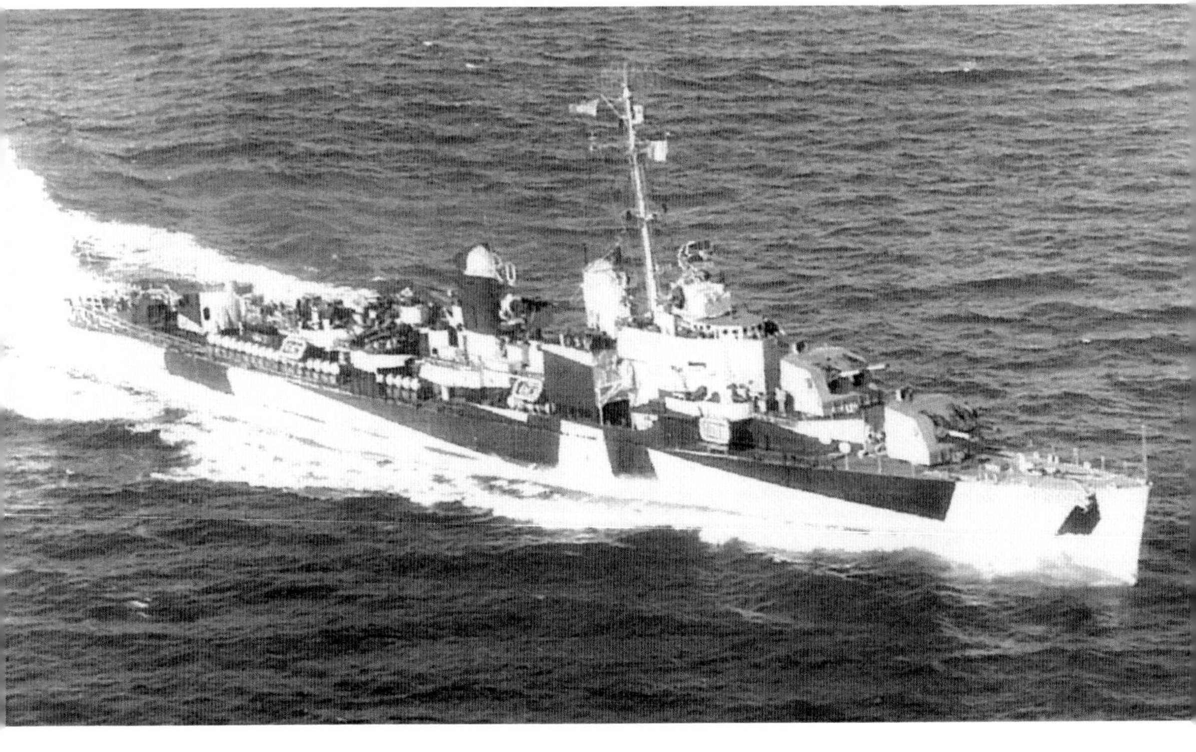

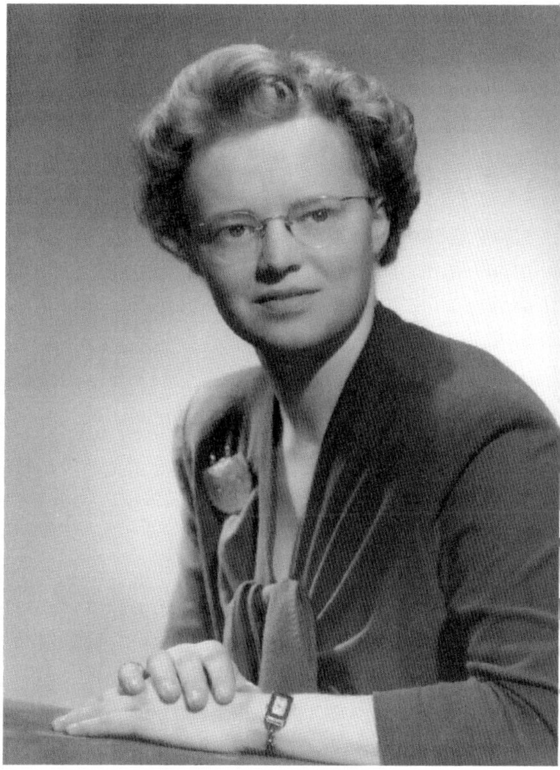

Regal Legals

Her brother, federal judge J. William Ditter, describes Mabel Ditter Sellers as "a feisty, five-foot, four-inch tiger of a lawyer." When he calls his sister "a trailblazer for women in the legal profession," he is not exaggerating, as she became Montgomery County's first female assistant district attorney. The second woman to be admitted to the bar in her county, she was known as a fierce but intensely empathetic advocate. Sellers was also active in her church, in the Visiting Nurses Association, the public library, the Young Women's Christian Association (YWCA), and the Girl Scouts. Her nephew George B. Ditter (below) said, "My grandfather [J. William Ditter Sr.] was a congressman; my father is a federal judge; so it is only natural that I become an attorney too." Besides practicing law in Ambler and North Wales, Ditter is also part-time solicitor at the Montgomery County Office of Children and Youth. (Both, courtesy of the Ditter family.)

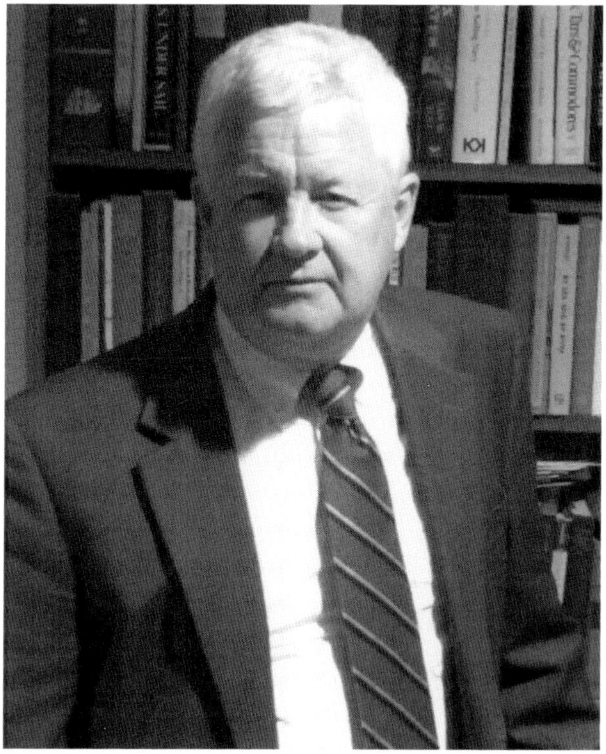

Ambler's Solomon

Nationally acclaimed artist and sculptor Garth C. Herrick painted this magnificent portrait of the Hon. J. William Ditter Jr. in 2007. At the time, Judge Ditter had already been serving on the federal bench for 37 years, ever since Pres. Richard M. Nixon nominated him for a new seat on the US District Court for the Eastern District of Pennsylvania on September 28, 1970. Presently, in 2014, Ditter is a senior district judge of the Third Court of Appeals. The son of Congressman J. William Ditter Sr., a passionate advocate for a two-ocean navy who served in the House of Representatives from 1932 to 1943, Judge Ditter also served in the military. A member of the US Naval Reserve in 1942, he was called to active duty in the Philippines during the war and also served his country in the Korean War. He retired from the service in 1968, having attained the rank of captain in the Supply Corps.

He received his law degree from the University of Pennsylvania in 1948, became a law clerk for the Court of Common Pleas of Montgomery County, and served, like his sister, Mabel Ditter Sellers, as an assistant district attorney of Montgomery County. In addition to serving for years on the Board of Consultors for the Villanova School of Law, he also helped incorporate the Historical Society of the United States District Court for the Eastern District of Pennsylvania, where he serves on its board of directors. Proud of his early education at Wissahickon High School, where he was active on the newspaper, yearbook, and honor society, Judge Ditter (according to his son George B. Ditter) is still active on the Ambler/Wissahickon High School Reunion Committee, having partially directed the class of 1939's 75th Reunion in October 2014. He has been honored by his high school, the Montgomery County Bar Association, and various civic organizations. Also active in his church, he has been a Sunday school teacher and chairman of many church committees. Among the judge's hobbies are beekeeping, photography, gardening, genealogy, softball, and skiing. (Courtesy of the Hon. J. William Ditter Jr.)

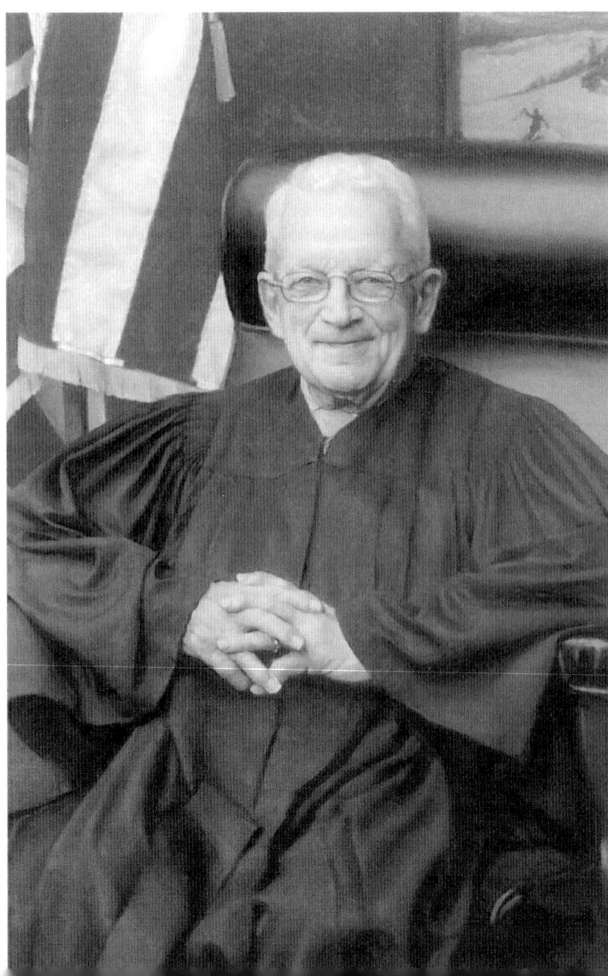

CHAPTER TWO

Educators and Religious Leaders

For some reason, photographs of the religious leaders and educators of Ambler are harder to come by than most others. But the borough has seen more than its share of excellence and leadership. Wissahickon High School, formerly known as Ambler High School, has maintained high standards throughout its history, but in the past few years, its reputation as one of the finest secondary schools in the commonwealth is well documented.

In the 2014 *US News & World Report* survey, Wissahickon High School was ranked ninth in the state and stood at number 607 in the entire nation—a tribute to the school's incredible 13-to-1 teacher-to-student ratio as well its commitment to securing and maintaining some of the best teachers in the country. The hall-of-fame wall at the high school is filled with success stories—from journalists Fred D. Behringer and Ronald Miller to Judge J. William Ditter Jr., from field hockey superstar Katie O'Donnell to celebrated actress/director Melanie Mayron. And no one who was blessed to have her for a teacher could forget the redoubtable Frances Behringer, Fred D. Behringer's mother, whose exceptional work with the Wissahickon Valley Public Library led to its naming one of the rooms in its Ambler branch after her.

Church leaders include Rev. Benjamin Kittinger, the first paid minister in the history of Ambler's Church of the Brethren, a sign of stability in the years following incorporation (1888); Rev. Henry Stommel, former pastor of Our Lady of Mount Carmel in Doylestown and builder of Catholic churches in Lansdale, Quakertown, and Sellersville, who founded St. Anthony of Padua Church in Ambler, arguably the most notable church in the region's history; St. Anthony's beloved Msgr. Eugene Sullivan and Msgr. Stephen McHenry, honored by the Wissahickon Faith Community Association for his work in bringing together the religious leaders in the region to support the Inter-Faith Housing Alliance.

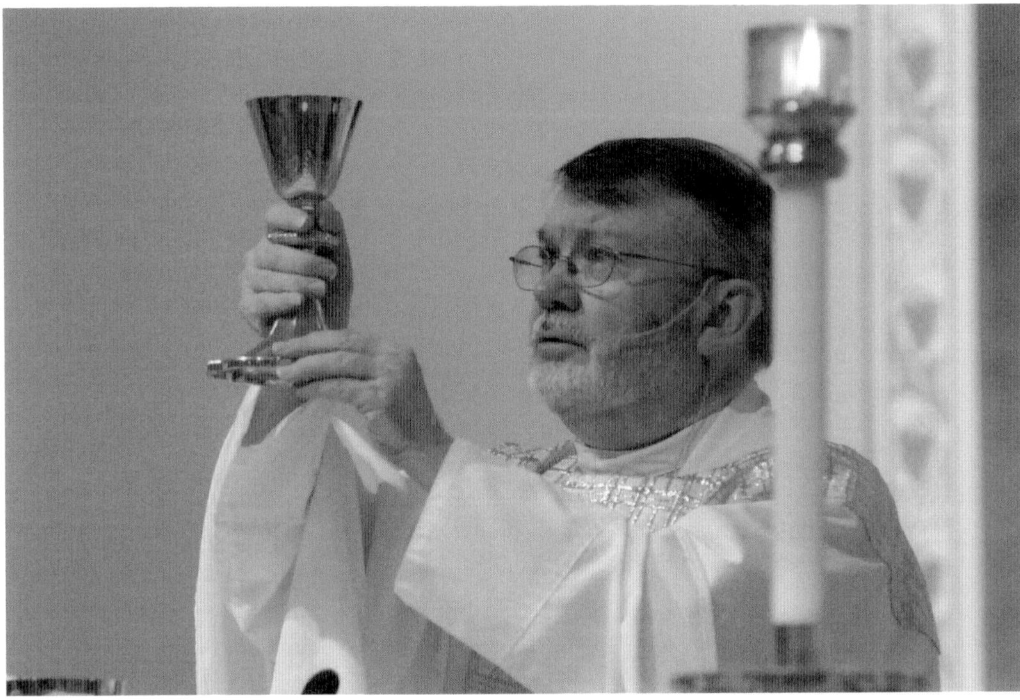

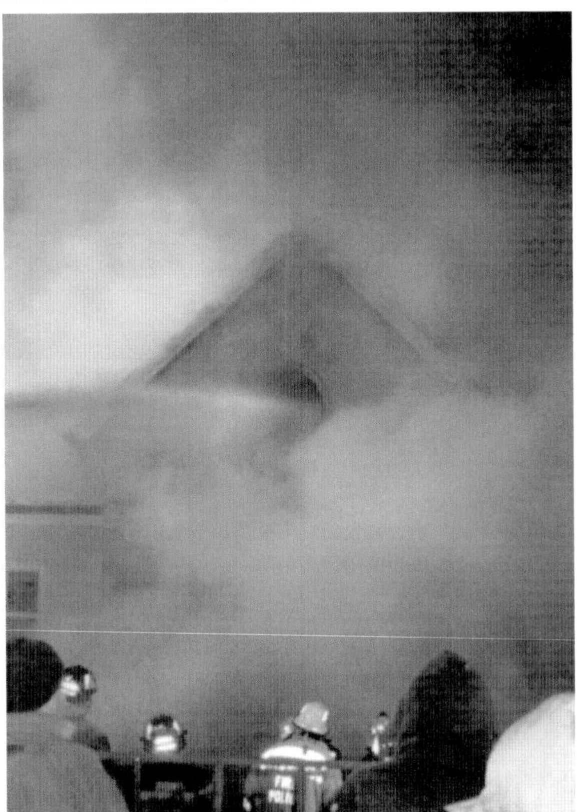

Resurrection

When the venerable church of St. Anthony of Padua (built in 1886) was gutted by a predawn fire on Christmas Eve 2000, more than 1,500 devoted parishioners inhaled deeply. But their resolve and spirit could not be broken. Under the inspired leadership of longtime pastor Msgr. Stephen McHenry, they quickly set about to rebuild, hopefully at the same location. McHenry, who presently serves as chairperson of the Philadelphia Archdiocese's Council of Priests, said that when Pastor Charles Quann of Bethlehem Baptist came to him, at a Christmas service nearby, with an unsolicited check for $2,000, and when CNN picked up the story, he knew his beloved church would rise again, which it did on April 28, 2000. Active in archdiocesan and community affairs, McHenry is pleased that St. Anthony's has become such good friends with the ministers and rabbis of the area. He is pictured above celebrating Mass. At left, firemen battle the disastrous church fire in 2000. (Courtesy of St. Anthony of Padua Church.)

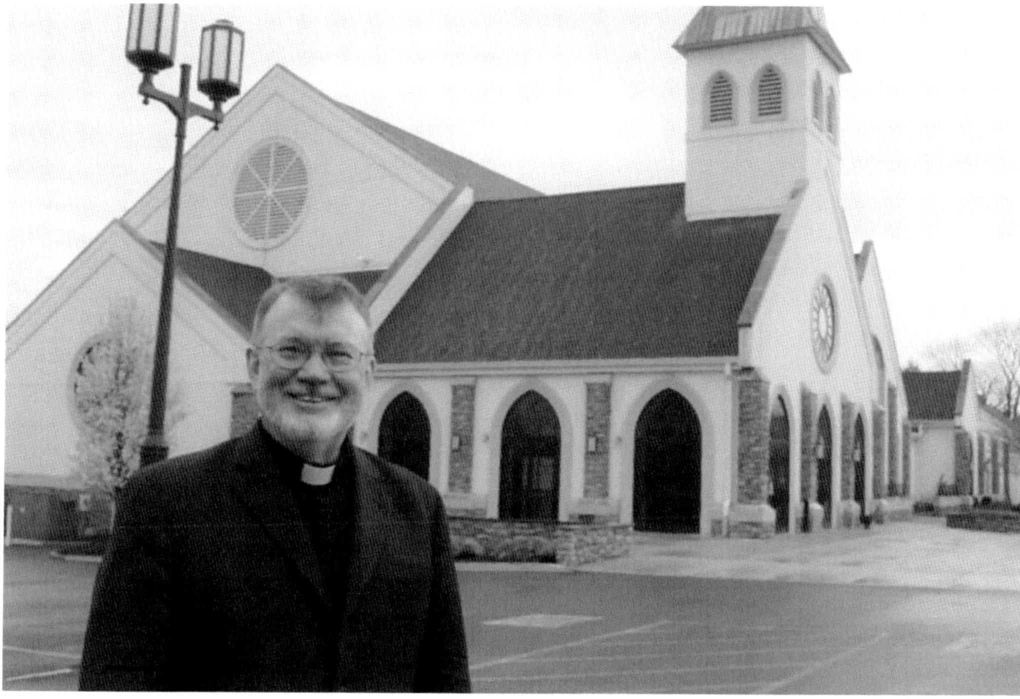

Celebrating 125 Years

Standing outside St. Anthony of Padua Church in Ambler on April 21, 2011, Msgr. Stephen McHenry smiles gratefully for the church's good fortune. The parish was about to begin a yearlong celebration of its 125th anniversary. Founded by Fr. Henry Stommel in 1886 to serve 30 families, the parish had grown to more than 1,500 families when a Christmas Eve fire in 2000 leveled the church. In the nearly quarter of a century that McHenry has been serving his congregation (more than 10 as its pastor), he had built up so much good will in the community that, even without asking, the parish had received $230,000 from various sources within four months of the fire. In the photograph at right, one of the church bells is removed shortly after the fire. (Above photograph by Bob Raines, courtesy of Montgomery Media; right, courtesy of St. Anthony of Padua Church.)

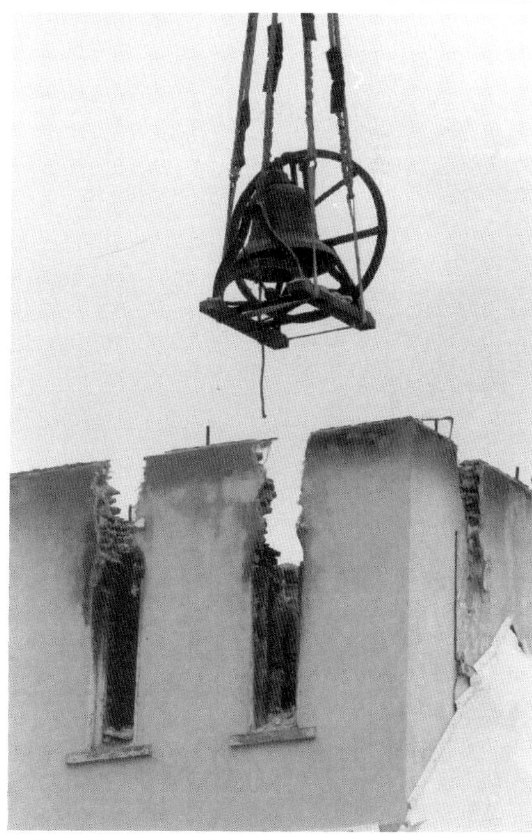

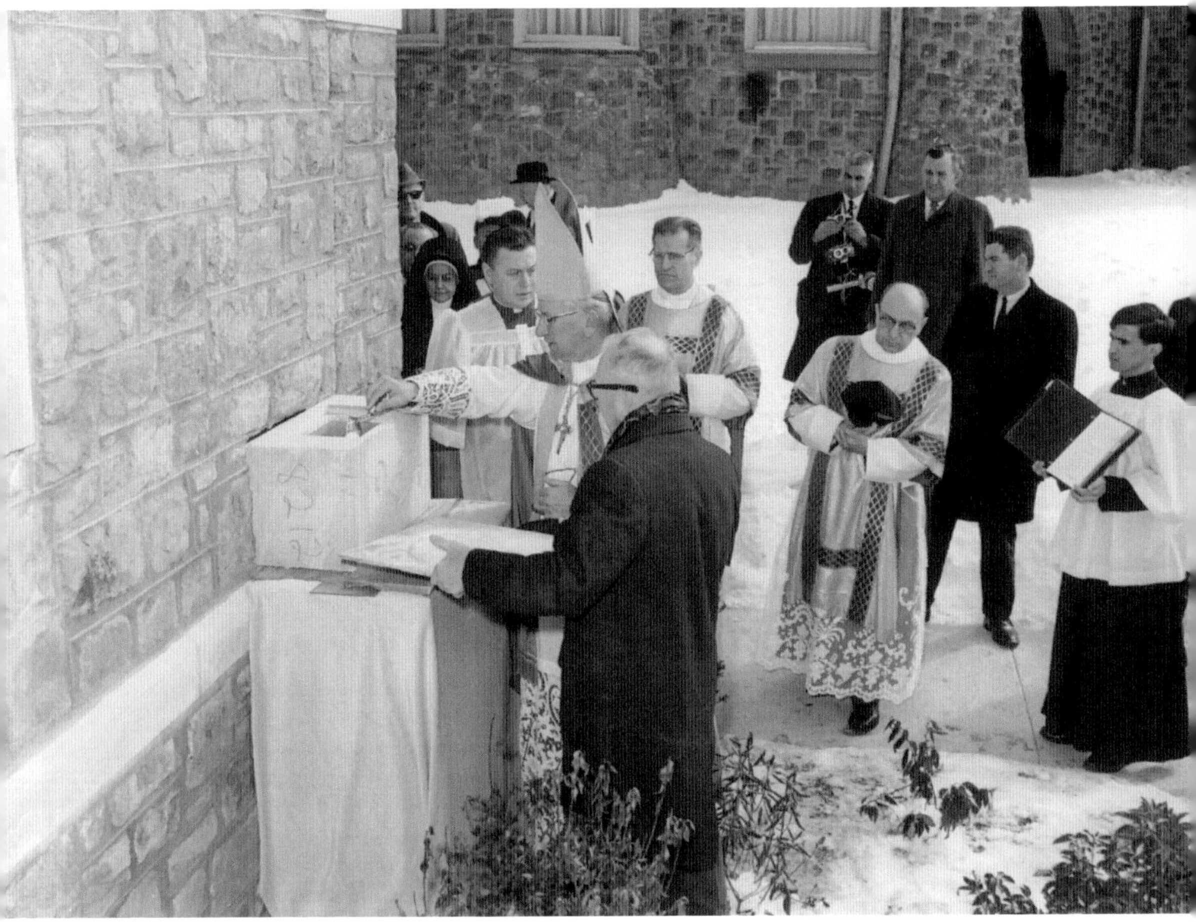

Laying the Cornerstone

The Sisters of the Holy Family of Nazareth emigrated from Poland to America in 1911 to found an orphanage for boys in Conshohocken. In 1936, they moved to Lindenwold, the former estate of Richard V. Mattison in Ambler, renaming it St. Mary's Villa, which continues its work through 2014. Seen here on February 6, 1966, blessing the cornerstone of the new chapel at St. Mary's, is Philadelphia's powerful archbishop, John Cardinal Krol (whose surname means "king" in Polish), the man who would soon become a friend to four US presidents (Lyndon B. Johnson, Richard M. Nixon, Gerald Ford, and Ronald Reagan) and Philadelphia mayor Frank Rizzo. It is also rumored that Krol was instrumental in laying the groundwork for the election of his good friend Karol Cardinal Wojtyla, a fellow Pole, as Pope John Paul II, on October 16, 1978. Canonized as a saint in 2014, Pope John Paul II was the first pope from behind the Iron Curtain and the first non-Italian to be elected to the Chair of St. Peter in 455 years. As long as Cardinal Krol served as the Archbishop of Philadelphia, he remained a good and faithful friend of St. Mary's Villa. (Photograph by Robert S. Halvey; courtesy of The Villa.)

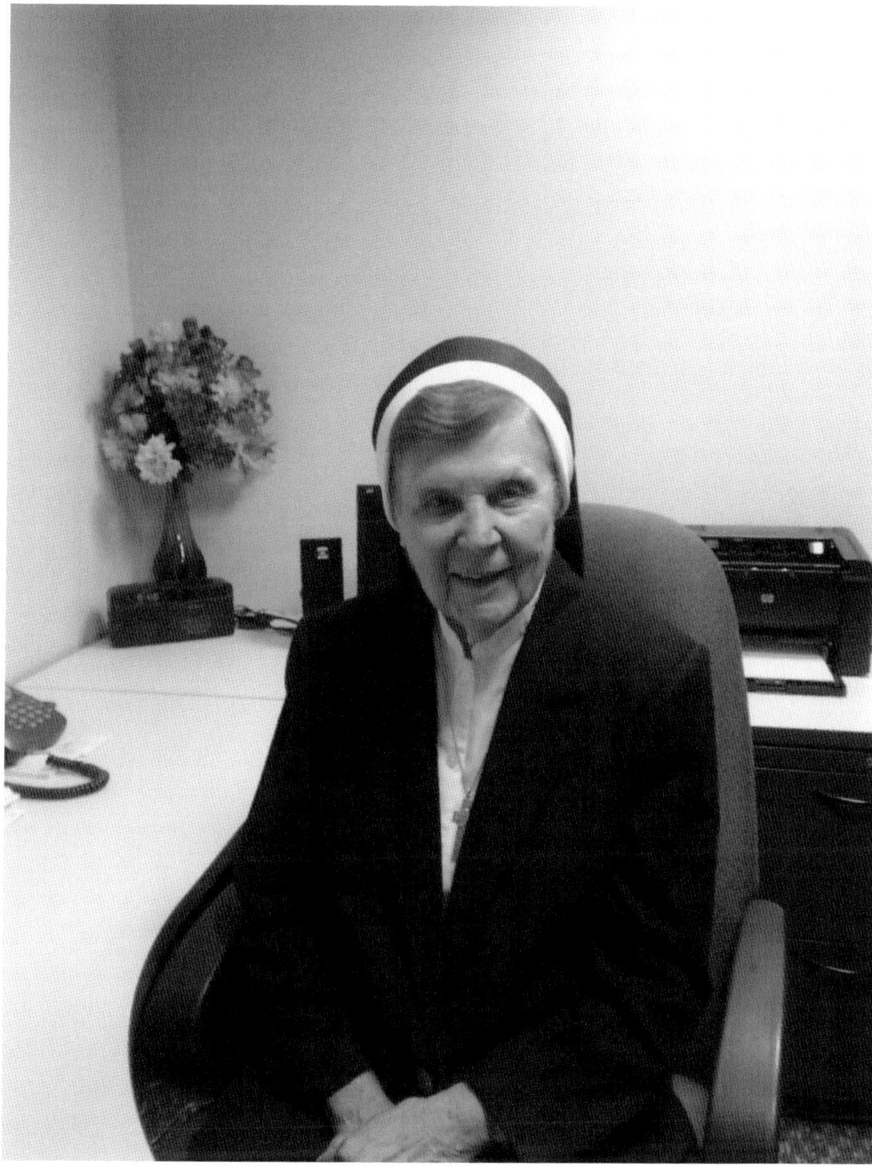

Sister Social Worker

Teacher, social worker, and educational reformer Sr. Eunice Leszczyska transformed St. Mary's from an institutional orphanage into a family culture for children ages 4 to 12 during her administration (1968–1977). St. Mary's was the first institution of its kind to take boys and girls. She turned large dormitories into four-bedroom apartments with two children living in each), closed the campus school and mainstreamed the children into local schools, involved the community by inviting them to take in the children during the holidays, introduced in-service training for her staff, as well as family therapy, counseling, child psychiatric therapy, and recreational therapy for the children, and created activities and vacations for the children beyond the Villa, at sites as near as Ocean City, New Jersey, and as distant as Quebec, Canada. Now teaching parenting at Holy Family University, Sister Eunice credits Cardinal Krol (through Catholic Charities) for his support and is "grateful that God permitted these wonderful things to happen." (Photograph by Eve M. Quattrone.)

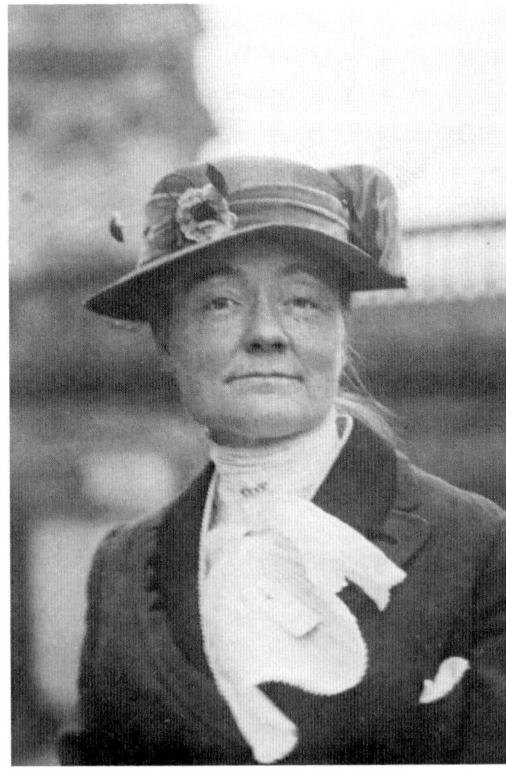

Pioneering Horticulturalists
Jane Bownes Haines, a Bryn Mawr College alumna who was passionate about horticulture, was so impressed by the colleges of gardening she visited in Europe that she determined to introduce one in the states. So in 1910, she purchased the 71-acre McAlonan farm in Ambler, where she founded the Pennsylvania School of Horticulture for Women, then the only school of its kind in America. With her hands-on approach, Haines offered classes in orchard care; farm tool use; care of lawn, shrubbery, and livestock; vegetable and kitchen gardening; beekeeping; poultry raising, botany; chemistry; and agricultural bookkeeping, laying the foundation for education for women as well as the Ambler campus of Temple University it became in 1958. In the photograph below are Louise Carter Bush-Brown, under whose direction the school would truly thrive between 1924 and 1952, and her fellow graduates in 1914. (Both, courtesy of Temple University Ambler Campus.)

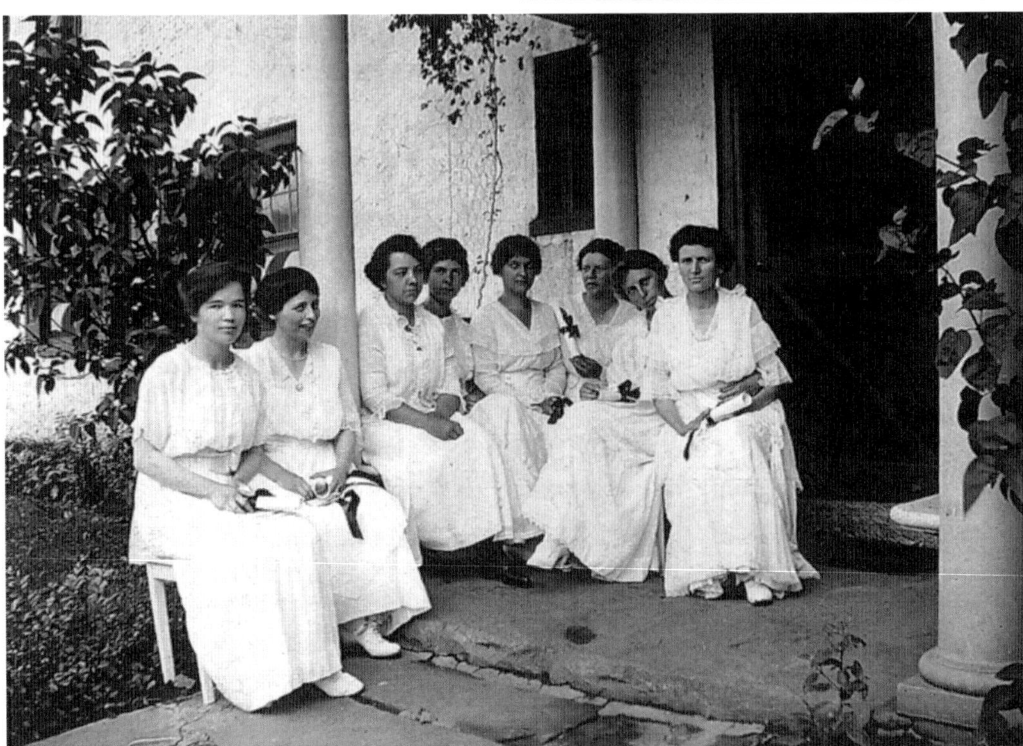

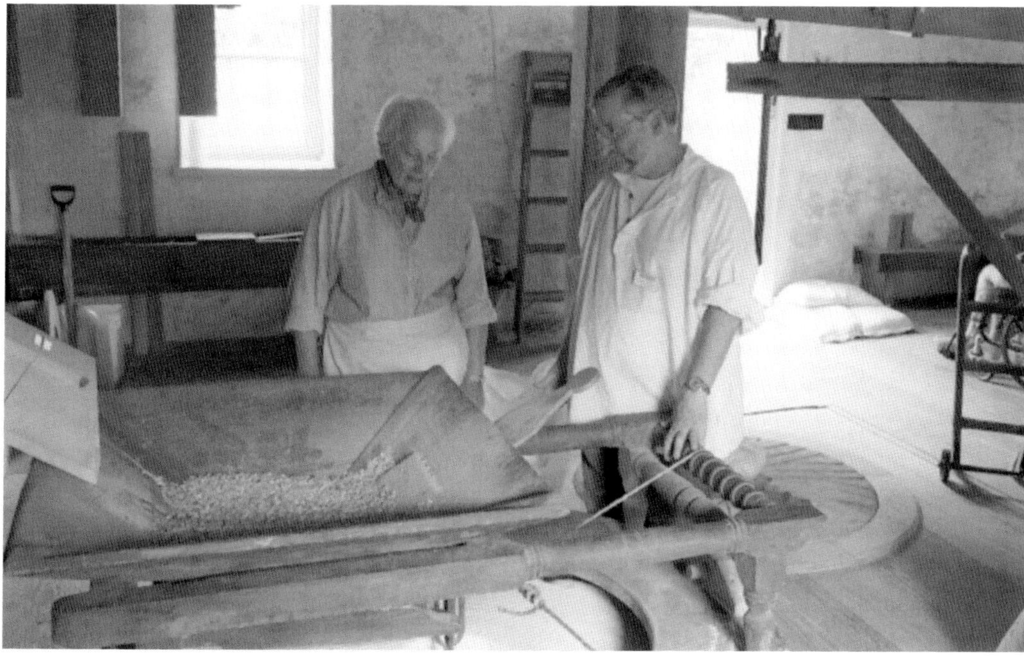

Wissahickon Watershed

At Evans-Mumbower Mill, head miller David Froehlich explains to Kate Pike how to prepare corn to be ground. The mill, located on Wissahickon Creek at Swedesboro Road and dating back to the early 1800s, is being painstakingly restored by the Wissahickon Valley Watershed Association (WVWA), whose headquarters are in Ambler. Froehlich, a city planner and environmentalist, served as WVWA's executive director from 1976 to 2006. During that time, he "built bridges" to government and regulatory bodies to enact ordinances to protect the creek, preserve valuable open space, monitor the creek's water quality and aquatic life, and educate the public about its rich natural environment. Below, Froehlich leads hikers on a 21-mile walk from Parkside Place in North Wales to the Canoe Club in Manayunk in a typical WVWA educational-awareness program called "Walk on the Wildside." (Photographs by Jamie Stewart, courtesy of Wissahickon Valley Watershed Association.)

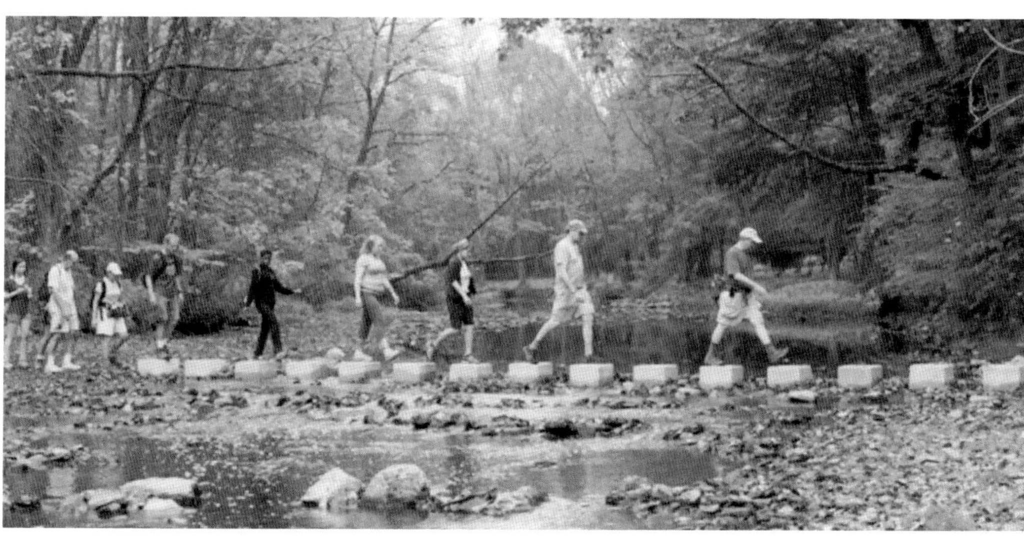

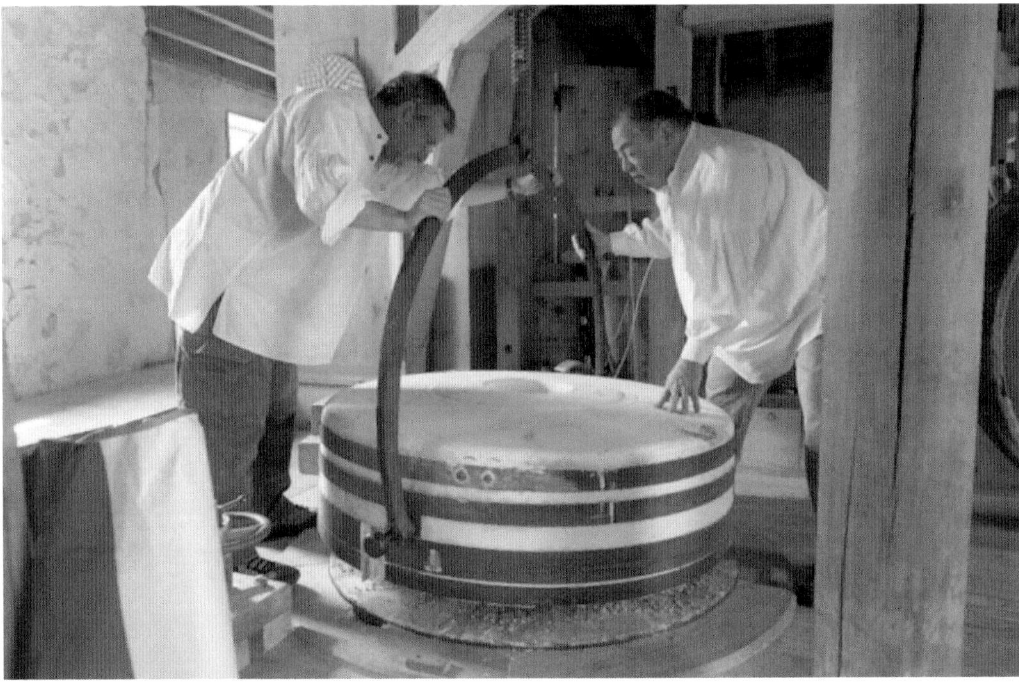

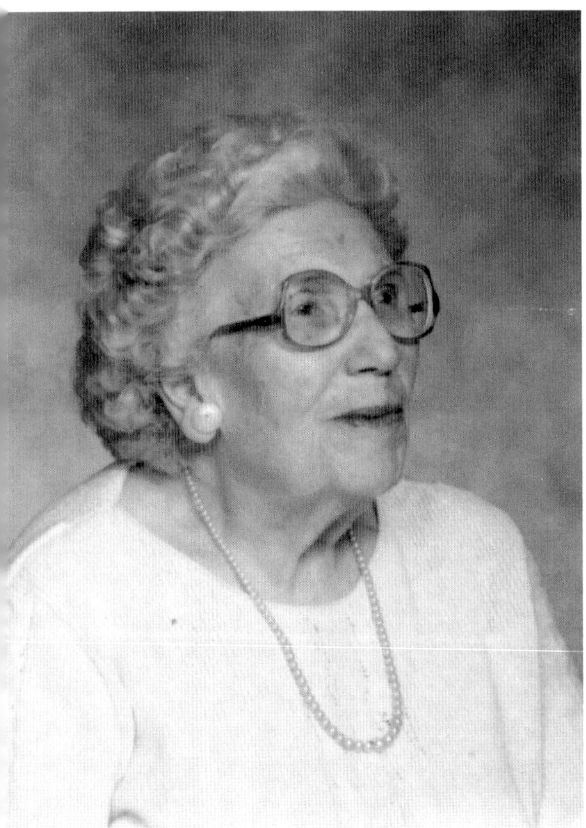

Modern-Day Miller

On Old Fashioned Mill Day in 2013, head miller David Froehlich (left) prepares to do a demonstration with Mark Prince at the Evans-Mumbower Mill. Froehlich is also president of the Wissahickon Waterfowl Preserve, a spinoff from the WVWA. The new organization has purchased a 15-acre reservoir in Ambler that is polluted by asbestos waste. As the reservoir attracts waterfowl, the group hopes to clean up the asbestos to make the area safe for waterfowl and community use. (Photograph by Jamie Stewart; courtesy of Wissahickon Valley Watershed Association.)

Beloved Teacher

Mary Frances Behringer loved children and loved books. For more than 40 years, she taught (primarily kindergarten) and told stories at Mattison Avenue Elementary School. She also assisted guests and served on the board of the Wissahickon Valley Public Library and devoted hours to senior citizens at the Colony Club. An avid sports fan, she adored Ambler High School football, the Philadelphia A's, and the Philadelphia Flyers. (Courtesy of Fred D. Behringer.)

CHAPTER THREE

Community-Minded Individuals

It almost seems redundant to name a chapter "Community-Minded Individuals" when virtually everyone in this book could easily be described as such. This chapter highlights the achievements of the borough's first female physician, Dr. Mary Hough, who gave local women more than hope; publishers and journalists like William E. Strasburg, Fred D. Behringer, and Mike Morsch, who strived mightily to keep their readers informed and involved as they reflected upon the key issues of the day. It also features great bankers like Martin Brown, whose common touch as well as banking acumen made him one of Ambler's most acclaimed citizens; Ambler horticulturalist and tireless, devoted citizen Phillip R. Albright, who serves on the board of directors of Temple University's Ambler Campus (among countless other boards); and attorneys like Berne Siergiej, whose work with Act II Playhouse and Ambler Main Street has helped rejuvenate the once tired borough. Also profiled here are Bernadette Dougherty, arguably Ambler's biggest booster and spark plug through decades of service to the community; historians like Newton M. Howard and William F. "Buck" Amey, who, like Ross Gordon Gerhart III, helped document the borough's rich history; and those who work quietly behind the scenes, like Dolores Loftus, a nurse who served the Community Ambulance Association of Ambler as well as St. Alphonus Catholic Church in various capacities. And then there are "families" like Ambler's legendary "Over the Hill Gang," who give their all to each other and their friends in Ambler's African American community; and the Zauzmers, a family whose community outreach begins in the Ambler area and extends to Harvard University, the state of Mississippi, the nation of Israel, and beyond; and, of course, the borough's namesake and "Angel of Mercy," Mary Ambler.

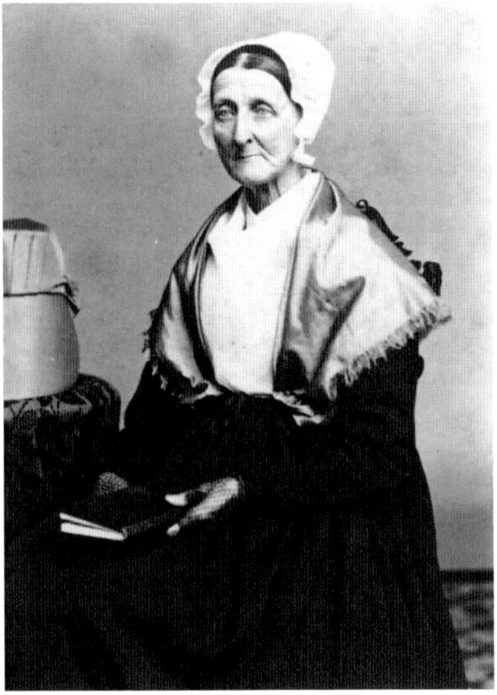

Angel of Mercy

Although the railroad brought commerce and thence prosperity to the humble milling town of Wissahickon, it also brought the potential for disaster. Local businesses began to grow, and the countryside started to attract folks from Philadelphia. So it was on July 2, 1856, when a "picnic special" heading northbound from the big city collided head-on with the southbound train between the Fort Washington and Camp Hill stations. The crash could be heard for miles around. The postcard painting below by artist Ted Knighton depicts Ambler's most famous and beloved citizen, Mary Johnson Ambler. Following the violent train wreck, at the time the greatest railroad disaster in the nation's history (59 killed with nearly 100 more injured), the kindly Quaker woman and miller Mary Ambler assisted and calmed the victims. When the town once known as Wissahickon was incorporated in 1888, the borough chose her name in gratitude. (Right, courtesy of Buck Amey; below, courtesy of George E. Saurman.)

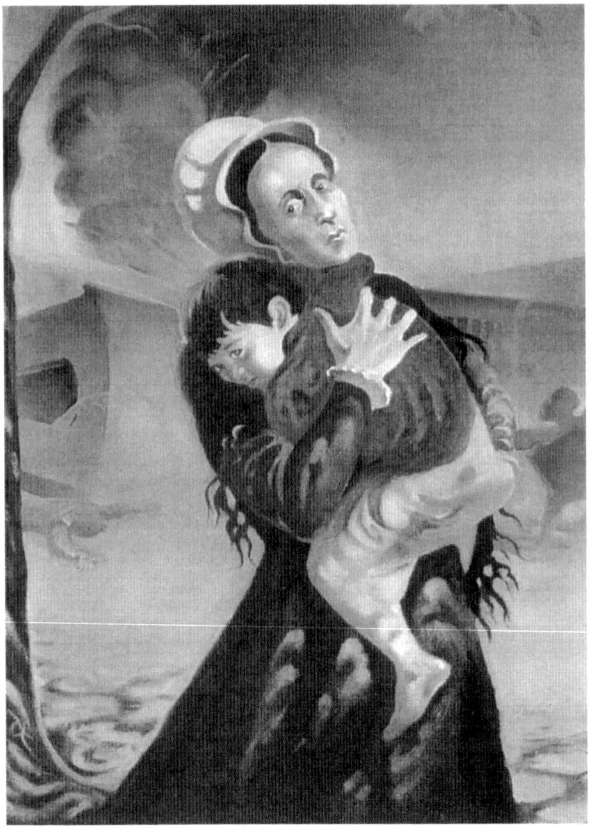

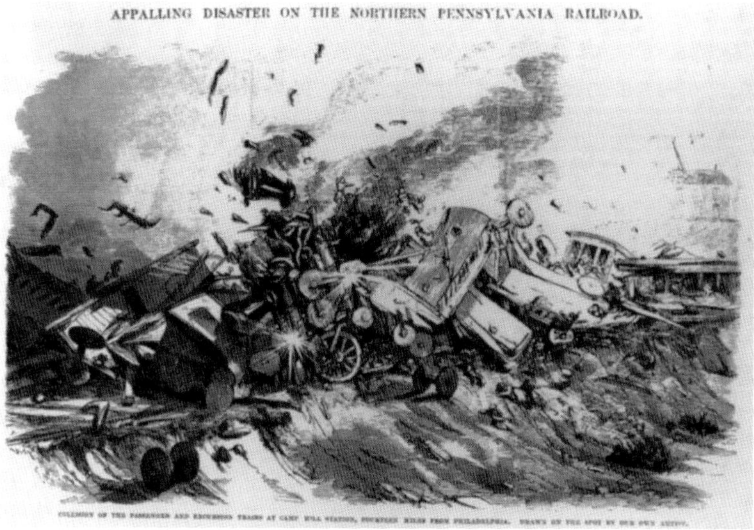

The Great Train Wreck

Years before the founding of the *Ambler Gazette*, a local paper ran this rendering of what was then (July 2, 1856) the greatest railroad accident in history. The headline reads, "Appalling disaster on the Northern Pennsylvania Railroad." The caption reads as follows: "Collision of the passenger and excursion trains at Camp Hill Station, fourteen miles from Philadelphia. Drawn on the spot by our own [unnamed] artist." The accompanying drawing, presumably in the same newspaper, states, "Scene of the disaster immediately after the collision. Drawn on the spot by our own [unnamed] artist." (Photographs from Newt Howard Collection, courtesy of Buck Amey.)

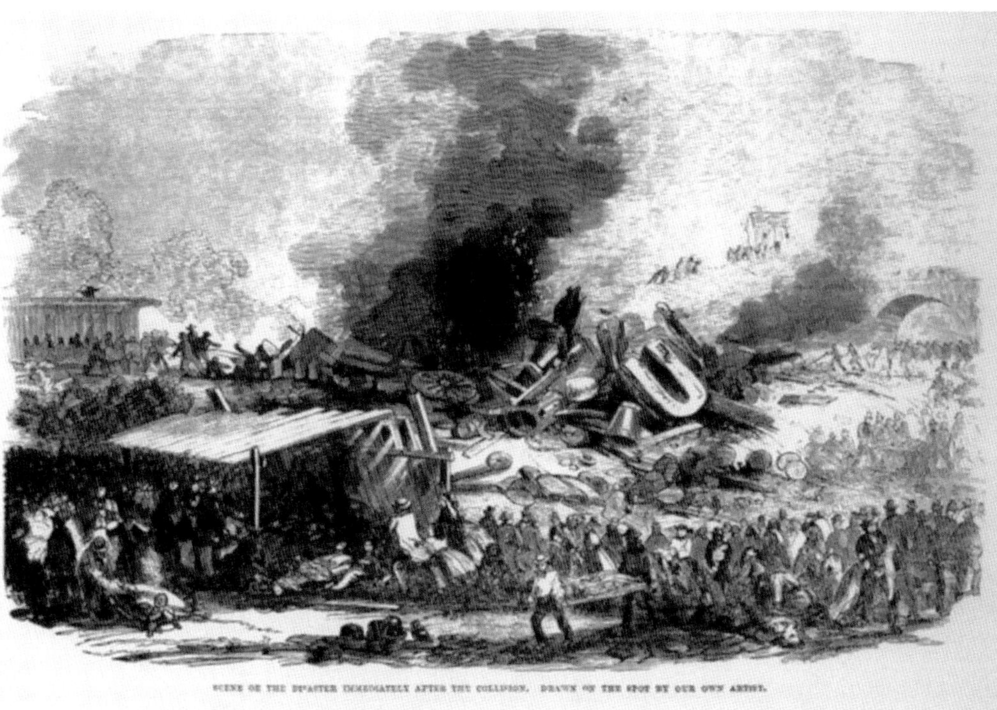

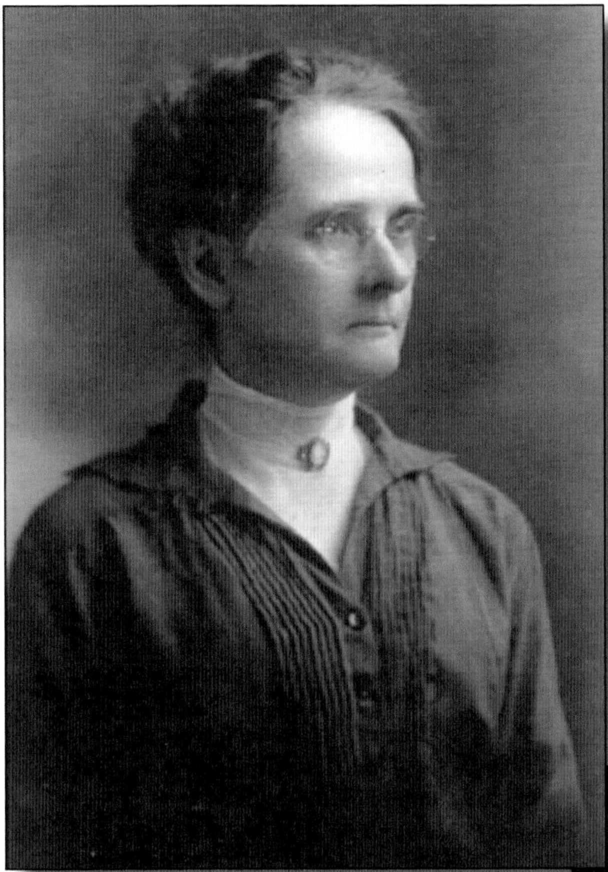

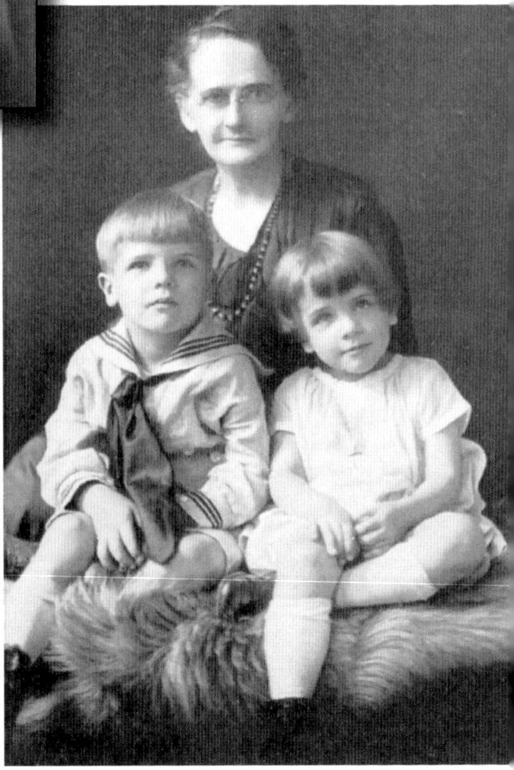

First Female Physician
After spending the night tending to a feverish boy, Dr. Mary Hallowell Hough rode away at dawn in her small, canopied horse-drawn carriage. One might wonder what her payment was for her night's work—it was a sack of potatoes. This form of payment was not unusual in 1887, when Hough opened her practice at the home she shared with her husband, Dr. Charles B. Hough, who was also a respected physician. What is remarkable is that this former farm-raised girl from Horsham became the first female physician in Ambler's history. Educated at the Women's Medical College of Philadelphia, Hough was a blessing to the women of Ambler, who were often too embarrassed by so-called "women troubles" to seek a male doctor's care. She also wrote an early history of Ambler and had a weekly column in the *Ambler Gazette*. She is seen here with two of her grandchildren, Jesse Taylor Brownback and Mary Hallowell Brownback. (Photographs from the Newt Howard Collection, courtesy of Buck Amey.)

Community Spirit

Putting his energy where his thoughts are, renowned newspaper publisher William E. Strasburg has brought his enlightened approach to journalism to countless community organizations and projects. A native Ohioan, Strasburg received his bachelor's degree from Ohio Wesleyan and his master's degree in international law from American University before serving in the Atlantic fleet during World War II. Once he had settled in Ambler, his community spirit was boundless. As a 60-year member of the Ambler Rotary, Strasburg—working with state legislators like George E. Saurman and Stewart J. Greenleaf (seen here on the left)—was instrumental in bringing badly needed parking to downtown Ambler, creating a new space for the Mattie N. Dixon Community Cupboard, and supporting the building of a new library and fire station on Race Street. A former associate director of the US Information Agency and executive vice president of the *Philadelphia Bulletin* during two leaves of absence from Montgomery Newspapers, Strasburg also helped found Montgomery County Community College in Blue Bell in 1964 and the Meadowood retirement community in Worcester (where he now lives with his wife, Sylvia Strasburg), among many other contributions and achievements. (Courtesy of William E. Strasburg.)

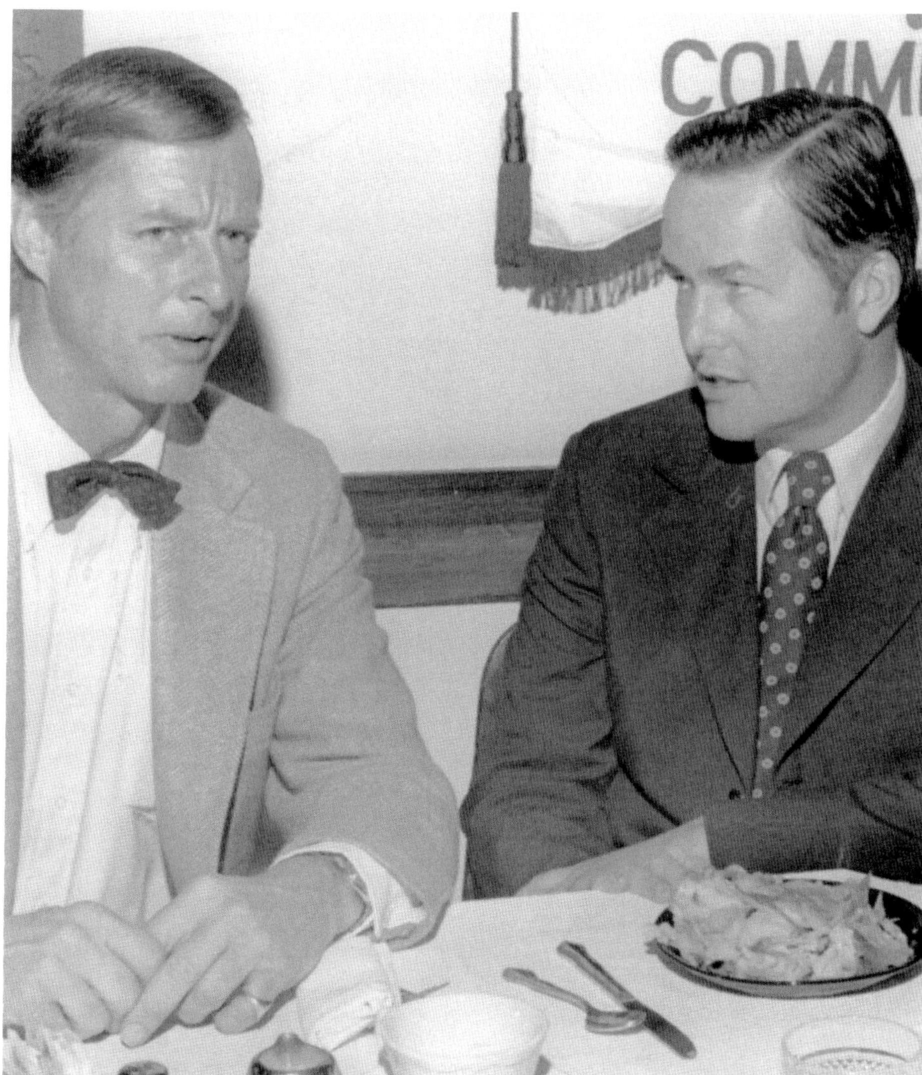

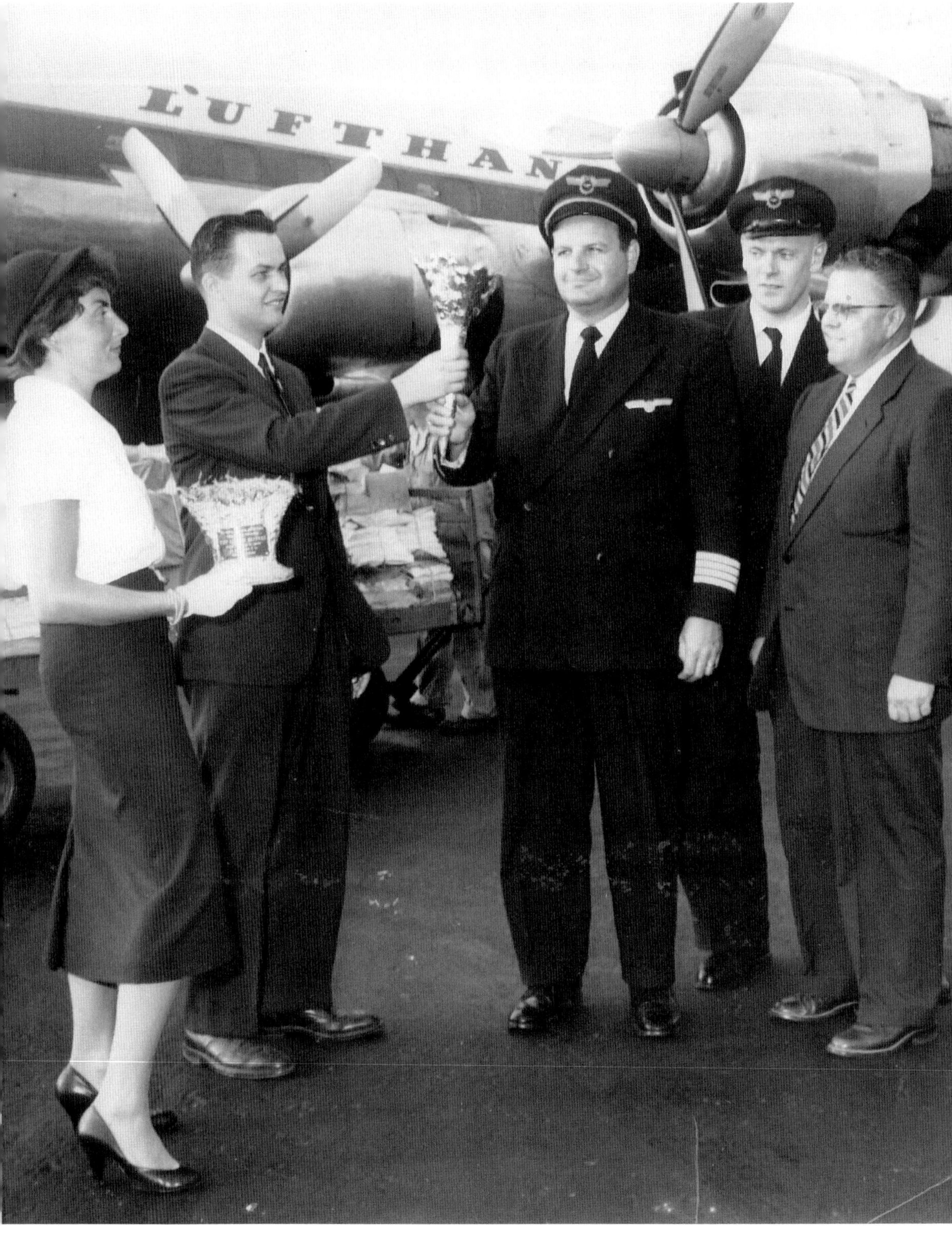
LUFTHAN

Carrying the Torch

Pictured in 1956, just four years after he purchased the *Ambler Gazette* to launch what would soon become Montgomery Newspapers, publisher William E. Strasburg (second from left) is extending the reach of his suburban newspaper group. Along with copies of the special Freedom Edition of the *Ambler Gazette*, Strasburg holds the torch of freedom—a salute to the citizens of Coburg, in Bavaria, Germany, from the people of Ambler. With Strasburg are the *Gazette*'s vice president for advertising, Carl Groth, and three unidentified Lufthansa crew members. Rubbing shoulders with powerful world leaders (including Chiang Kai-shek, Jawaharlal Nehru, and Jordan's King Hussein) and trips abroad were not unusual for the visionary publisher. On March 30, 1962, with other respected members of the Pennsylvania Newspaper Association, Strasburg was invited to a White House luncheon to exchange views on state, regional, and national issues with Pres. John F. Kennedy. And in 1968, he was twice a witness to history when he joined other Pennsylvania newspaper publishers in Europe to attend briefings on the Vietnam peace talks in Paris, where they met Ambassador W. Averell Harriman and North Vietnamese diplomats, and happened to be in Prague just as Soviet tanks and troops were invading Czechoslovakia. As always, Strasburg brought back great stories to the *Gazette*, the voice of Ambler's citizens since 1883, five years before the borough was incorporated. As a journalist, he had covered the Pentagon during the Korean War and the polarizing Army-McCarthy hearings. But he insists that his heart has always been with communities, where everyday people learn to live and work together in relative harmony. His mission for the *Gazette* and its dozen or so sister papers was this: To tell the truth, with clear and accurate reporting, in cooperation with community residents and with no interference by special interests. For his contributions to his profession and community, which include helping to create the Suburban Newspapers of America, Strasburg was awarded the Pennsylvania Newspaper Association's Lifetime Achievement Award in 1999. (Courtesy of William E. Strasburg.)

Committed Couple

Some call William E. Strasburg "Mr. Ambler" because of his longtime commitment to the borough. But his reach extended far beyond the borough. When he purchased the *Ambler Gazette* in 1952, his mission as publisher was for the paper "to reflect and direct the new spirit of the community." But his wife, Sylvia, also played her part. Active as Calvary Methodist Church's mission chairman, she invited all the mission committees in the region to help support the older citizens of Ambler, which they did. With Sylvia Strasburg as its first president, they founded Senior Adults for Greater Achievement (SAGA), the community's first senior center, which still serves the community as SAAC (Senior Adult Activities Center), bringing Meals on Wheels to Ambler as well as other programs to involve, enrich, and empower Ambler citizens 50 years old and over. (Courtesy of William E. and Sylvia Strasburg.)

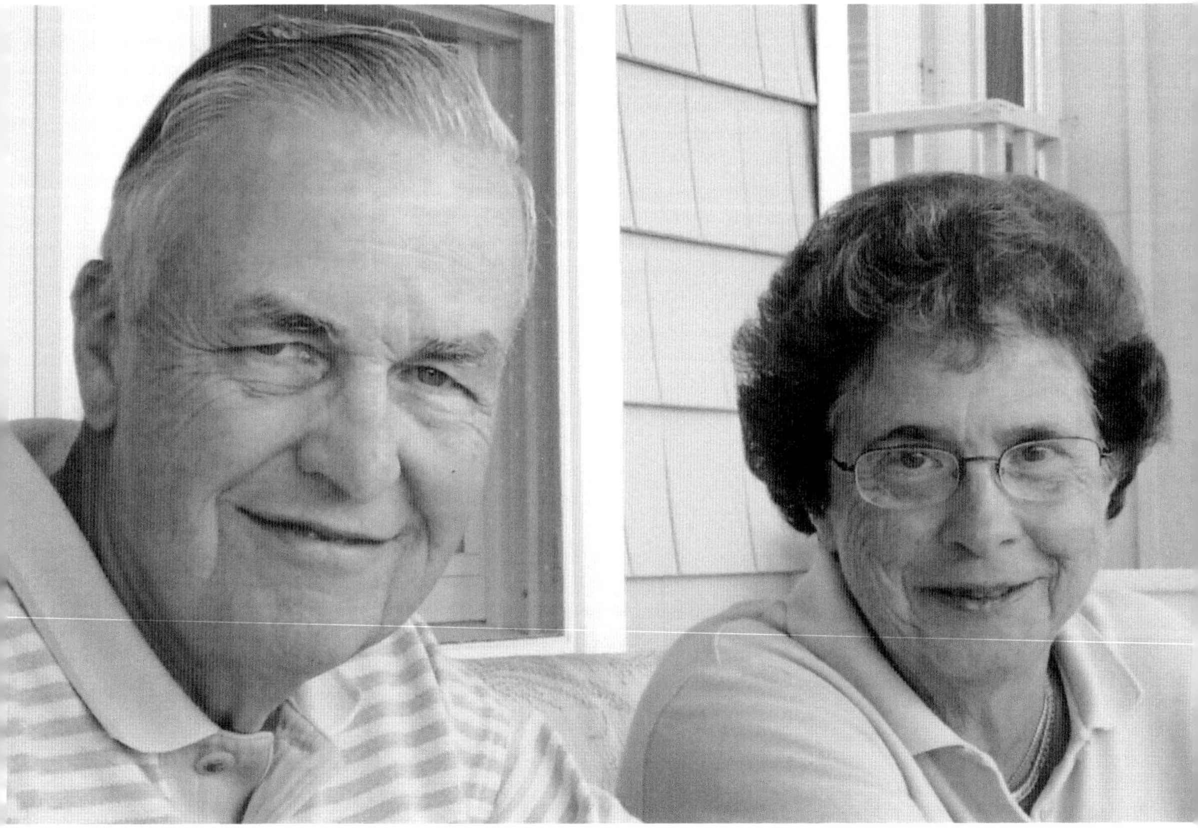

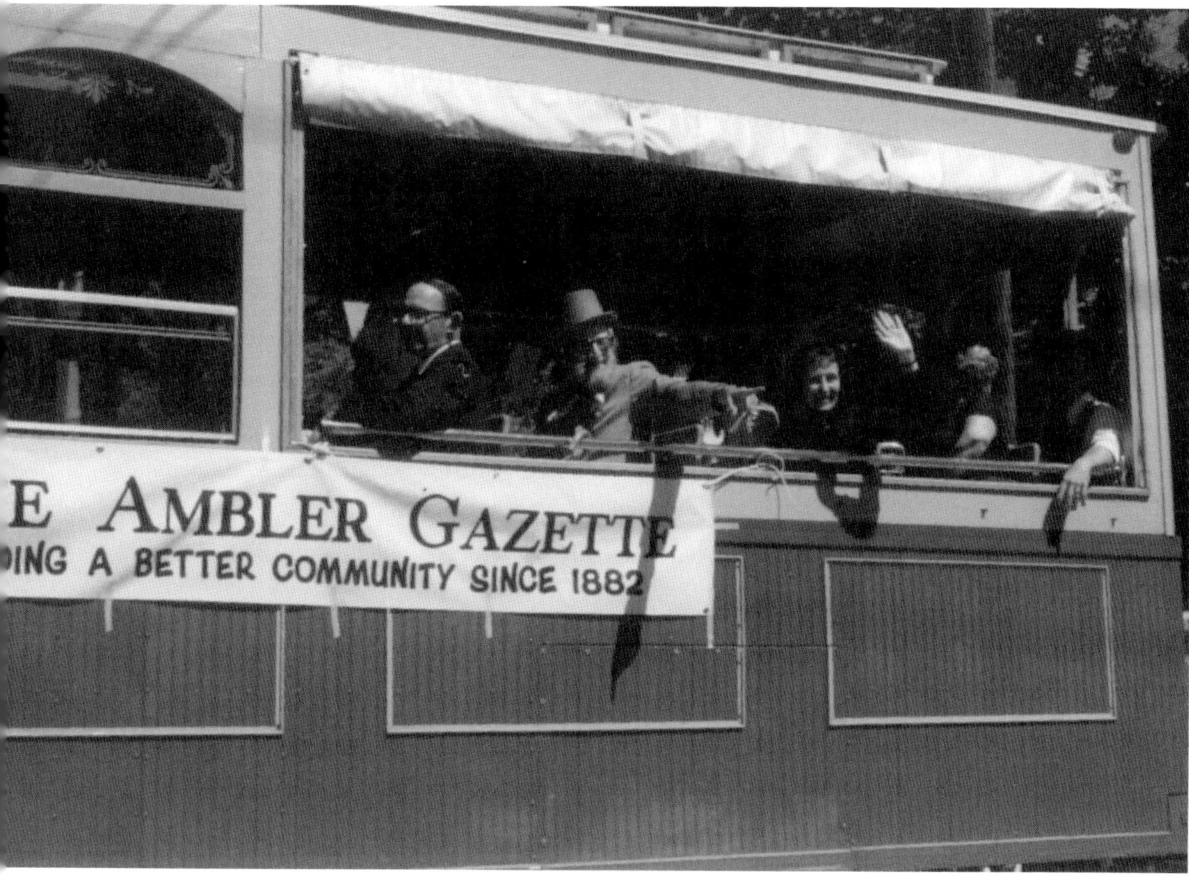

Gazette Float

Pictured here is an *Ambler Gazette* float at the annual Fourth of July parade (1988), a tradition relished by Amblerites for more than four decades. The first issue of the *Gazette* produced by Strasburg and his original staff of eight, laid out in the basement of its headquarters at 149 East Butler Avenue, was published on June 26, 1952. Strasburg said that those first editions of the paper—unlike today's pages, with their large and clever headlines, eye-catching photographs and attractive layouts, and limited featured stories—might include as many as 29 different items on the front page alone. Eventually, Montgomery Newspapers relocated to 290 Commerce Drive on a converted swampland in the Fort Washington Industrial Park complex, where it remained until a significantly reduced staff was moved to the site of the *Reporter* of Lansdale, one of four daily newspapers owned by the rechristened Montgomery Media in 2014. (Courtesy of William E. Strasburg.)

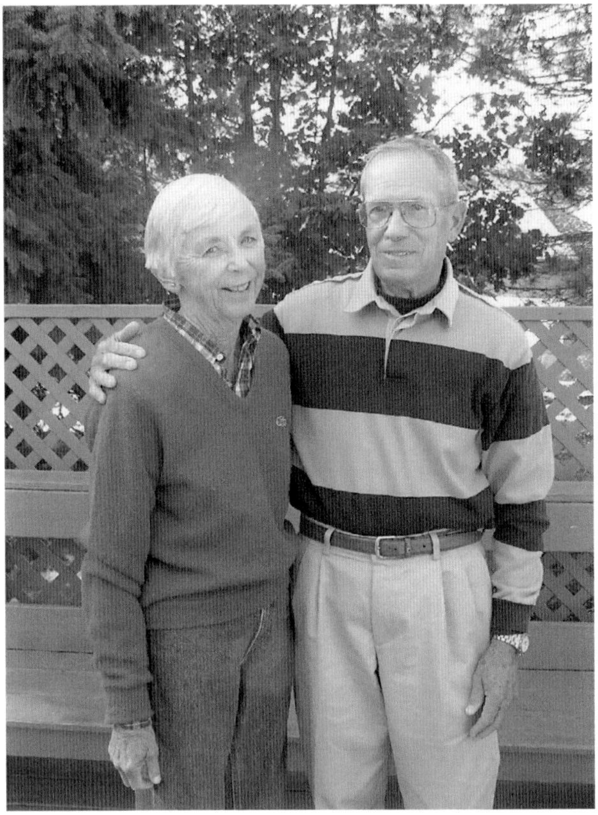

Pens and Tees

From his rousing beginning as a sportswriter for the *Ambler Gazette* (while he was still a high school sophomore), Fred D. Behringer quickly rose to prominence in the journalistic world. He became the *Ambler Gazette*'s sports editor before graduating from high school. An avid golfer, Behringer soon became executive editor of Montgomery Newspapers and vice president of Montgomery Publishing, where he founded *Philadelphia Golfer* magazine and *New Jersey Golf News*. He later edited the magazine of the Golf Association of Philadelphia. A beloved mentor to many journalists, Behringer still plays golf frequently and edits a golf publication in South Jersey. Behringer, seen here with his late wife, Joanne, was also a president of the Ambler Library so beloved by his mother, and served as president of the Greater Philadelphia Chapter of the Society of Professional Journalists. Behringer is pictured at home with his dog, Dix. (Both, courtesy of Fred D. Behringer.)

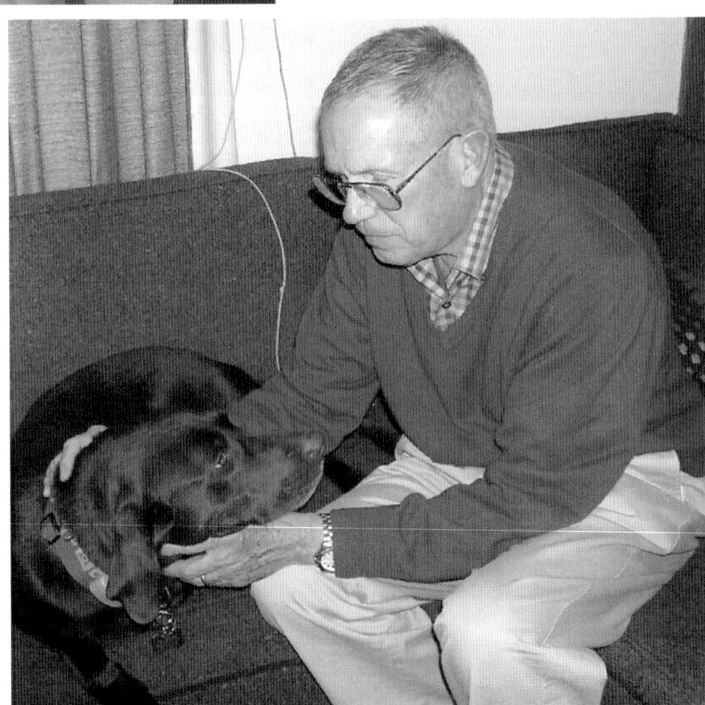

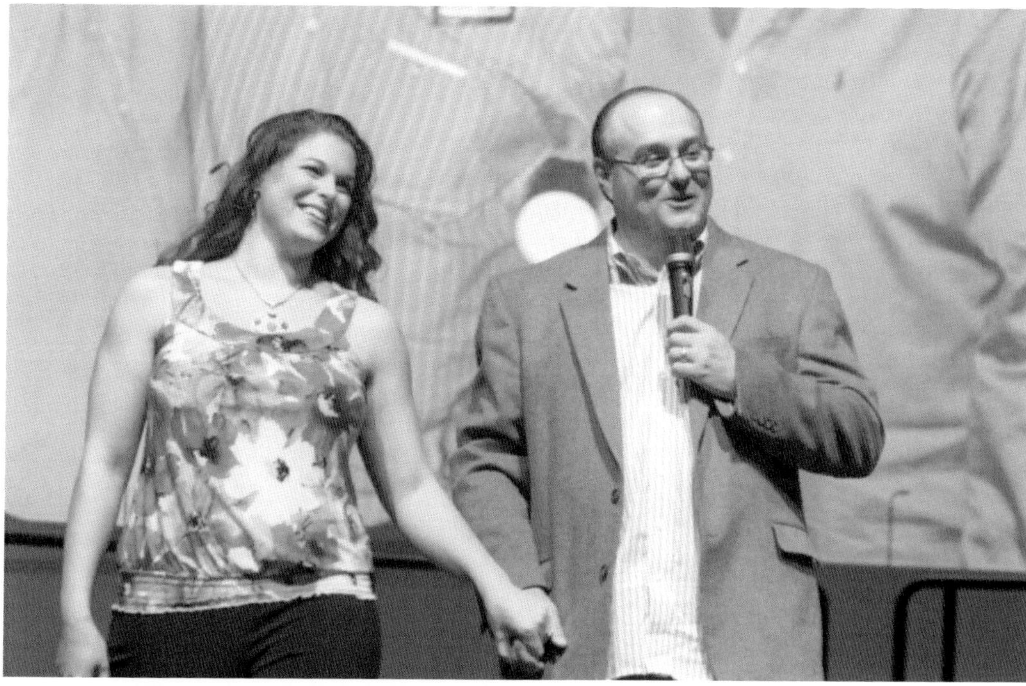

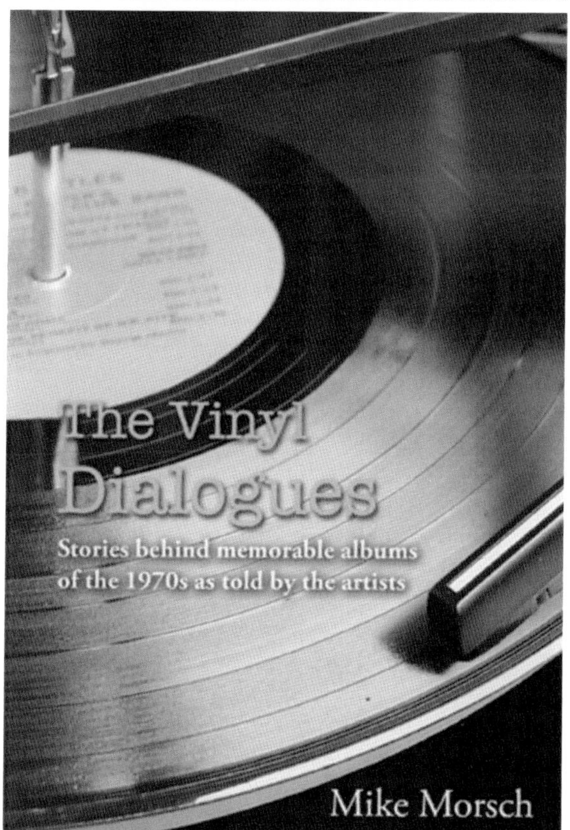

Media and Music

For a full decade, Mike Morsch served Montgomery County well as executive editor of Montgomery Media, where the *Ambler Gazette* sailed through calm and choppy seas as its flagship news and online paper. A 30-year veteran in his field, the tall Midwestern transplant maintained the highest professional standards for himself and his diminishing staff. During his tenure at Montgomery, Morsch was a constant presence in the community, teaching journalism in local schools, meeting regularly with civic institutions, chairing the Educator of the Year Committee for Upper Dublin School District, and volunteering as a judge at Ambler's annual summer dog parade. Presently, when he is not serving as editor/digital news director of Packet Media Group, he interviews musical artists for his blog and his books—the memoir *Dancing in My Underwear* and the recently published *The Vinyl Dialogues* (see cover at left). He is pictured above with his daughter Kiley at a book signing. (Both, courtesy of Mike Morsch.)

Banking on Commitment

After serving Ambler Savings Bank for 41 years—most notably as chief executive officer and president since 1998—Martin Brown retired in 2014. Under his leadership and with his acumen, the bank's assets grew from $25 million in 1973 (the year he arrived) to $315 million upon his retirement. Although he left the bank in excellent condition, there is no doubt that he will be missed. According to Dan Ritter, chairman of the bank's board of directors, Brown was respected for his kind and supportive management style that won "loyal support and created high morale throughout the organization. His emphasis on personal attention and service has elevated the bank to a position of being the only bank remaining with an office in the borough of Ambler." Brown was equally respected by the industry itself. In appreciation, in 2014, he was elected to the Pennsylvania Association of Community Bankers' Hall of Fame. His community involvement extended to the Kiwanis Club of Ambler, Community Ambulance Association of Ambler, Ambler Main Street, Greater Ambler Parking Corporation, Ambler Junior Baseball, Ambler Supporting Housing Association, Ambler Young Men's Christian Association (YMCA), American Legion Post No. 0125, Whitpain Recreational League, Act II Playhouse, Wissahickon Football Parents, and more. Among the civic causes he has championed are the Ambler Music and Arts Festival. Active in the Christ Evangelical Church in Zieglerville since 1971, he has been president of the church's board and a trustee. A man of integrity, Brown tries to avoid the spotlight. Nonetheless, he has been honored by the *Ambler Gazette* as Citizen of the Week, was named the Borough of Ambler's Citizen of the Year in 1997, received the Downs-Amey American Legion Post No. 0125 Citizen Award in 2008, and was a grand marshal of the Christmas Parade, and he still finds time to volunteer at the Annual Kiwanis Carnival and at the fireworks display held at Wissahickon High School at the borough's annual Fourth of July celebration. (Photograph by Eric Kovac; courtesy of Pennsylvania Association of Community Bankers.)

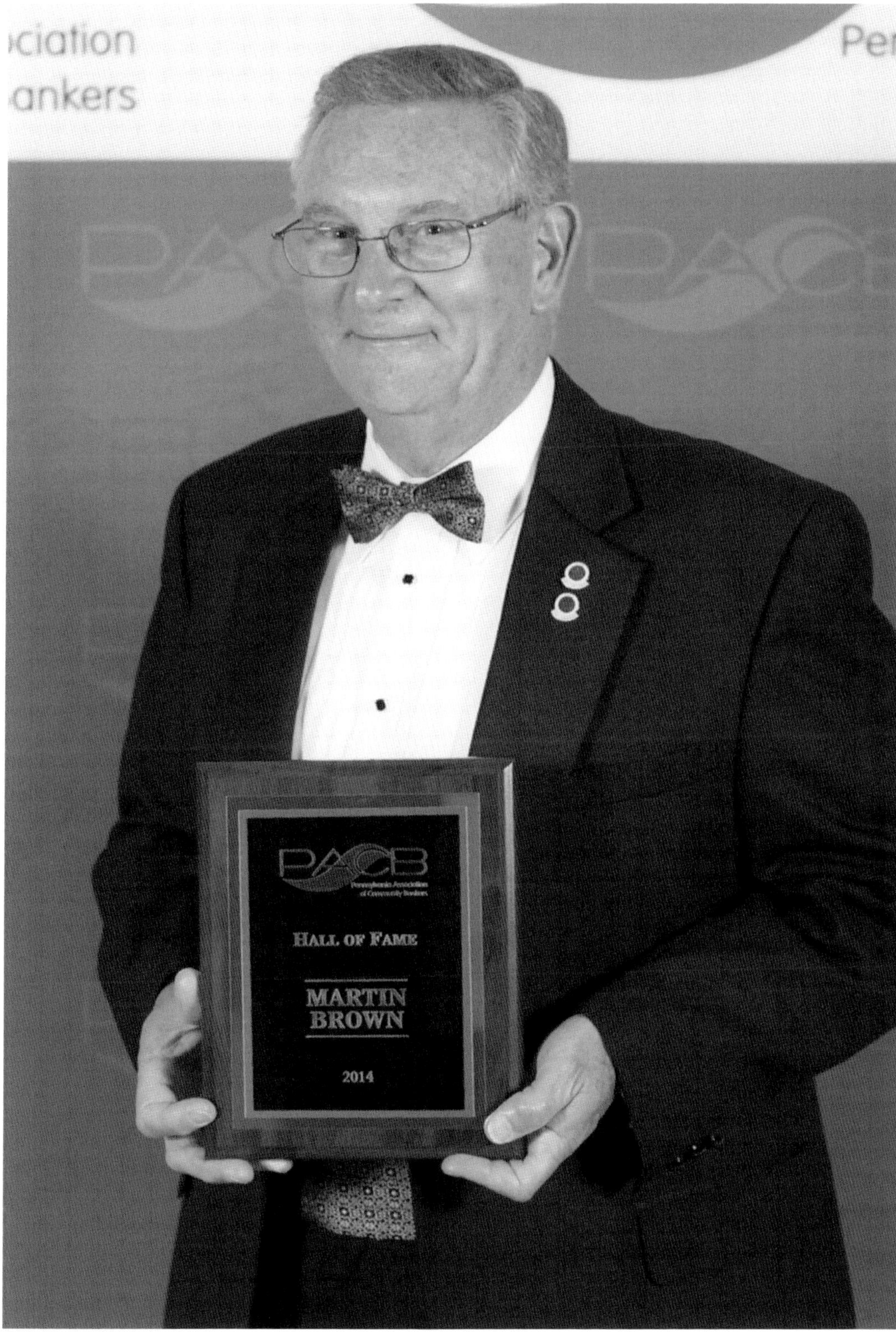
ciation
ankers
PACB
HALL OF FAME
MARTIN
BROWN
2014

Standing Tall

A retired civil engineer, insurance executive, and US Army veteran, Philip R. Albright is pictured opposite with his wife of 60 years, Barbara, at one of their favorite sites, the lush 180-acre arboretum at the Ambler Campus of Temple University, where he earned an associate degree in horticulture and landscape design. An avid gardener who has always been passionate about community service, Albright serves or has served on the boards of the Ambler Arboretum at Temple University, Wissahickon Valley Public Library, Gwynedd Mercy University, Ambler Theater, Act II Playhouse, Mattie N. Dixon Community Cupboard, Wissahickon Valley Watershed Association, Rotary Club of Ambler, Ambler Area YMCA, and Kelly Anne Dolan Memorial Fund, among others. Albright was instrumental in the purchase of the parking lot behind Act II Playhouse, which he considers "the center of Ambler." (Both, courtesy of Philip R. and Barbara Albright.)

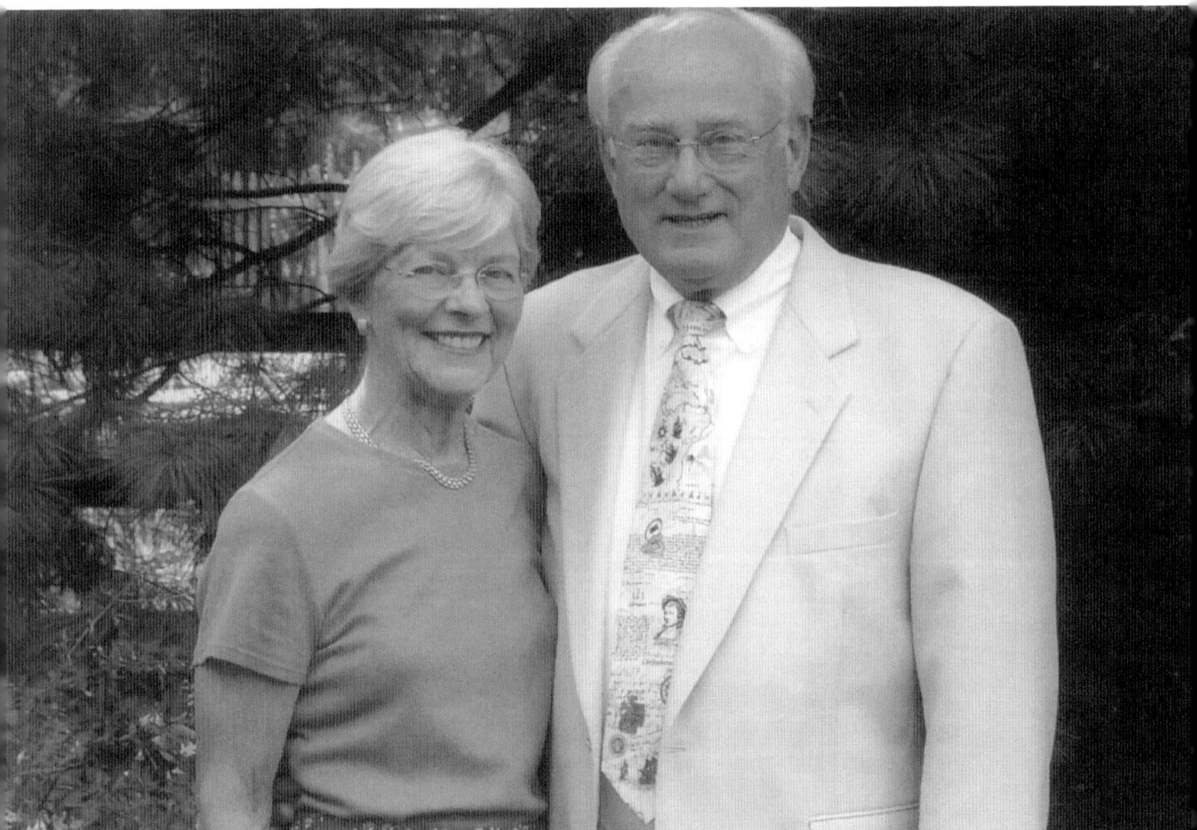

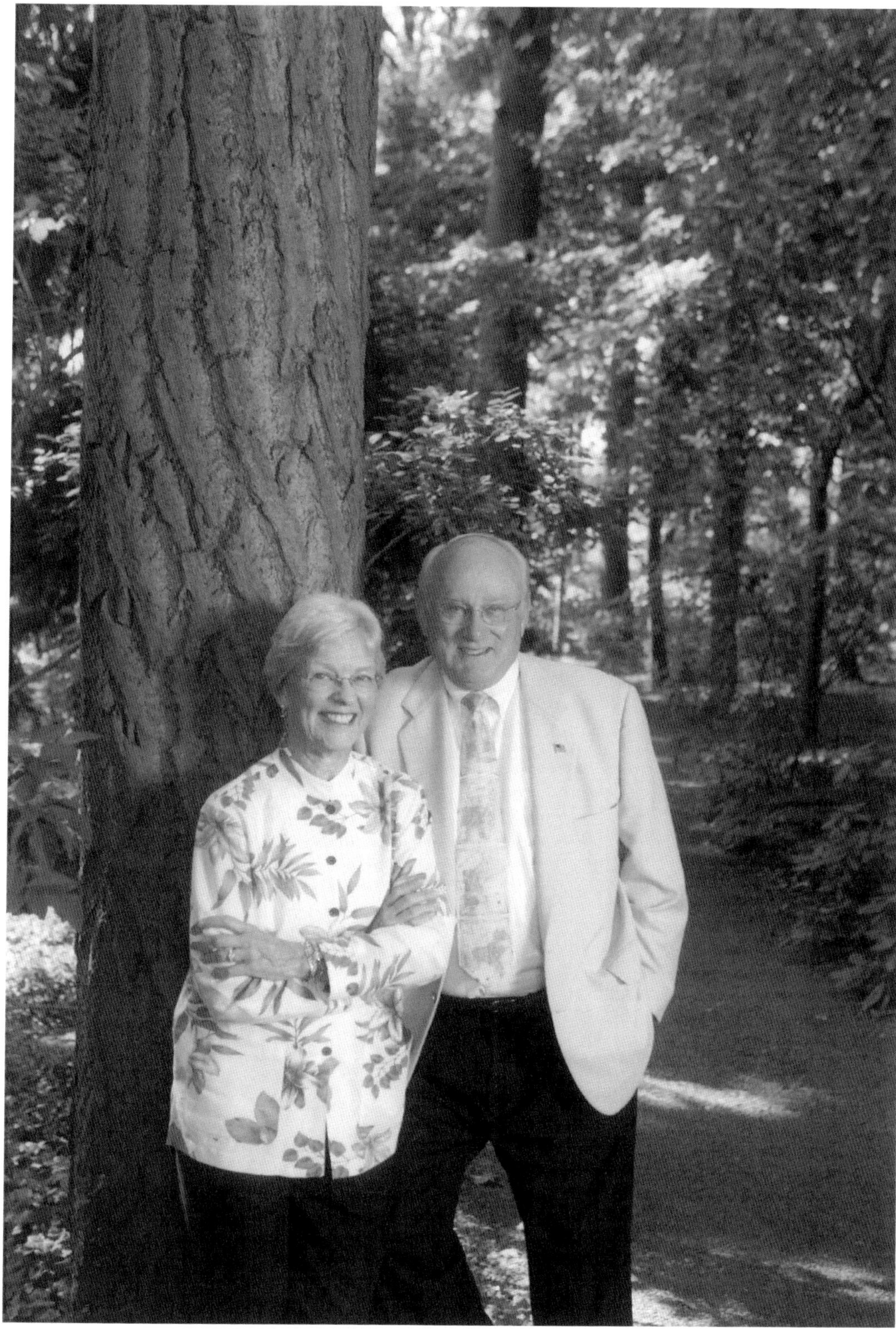

Renaissance Couple

Ambler attorney Berne Siergiej and his wife, Anne Dunnington, have served the community in countless ways. Presently co-vice president of Ambler Main Street and president and board member of Act II Playhouse, Siergiej has also, with his wife, produced two plays at Philadelphia's Kimmel Center, *The Big Bang* and *The Philly Fan*. Since his undergraduate days at Villanova University and his studies at Temple University School of Law, Siergiej has loved the written word and has been his homeowners' association's admittedly "quirky" recording secretary while he has served on its board for 23 years. He was also a member of the Ambler Jaycees and chamber of commerce. He has been practicing law in Ambler, concentrating on estates, wills, trusts, and income tax returns, since 1967. Dunnington, who once owned a title insurance company, has been a member of the Ambler Rotary and Wissahickon Valley Chamber of Commerce. Avid travelers, Siergiej and Dunnington have visited exotic sites throughout the world, from Caribbean islands to the infinitely varied countries of Europe, and remain avid supporters of the arts, particularly theater. (Courtesy of Berne Siergiej, Esq.)

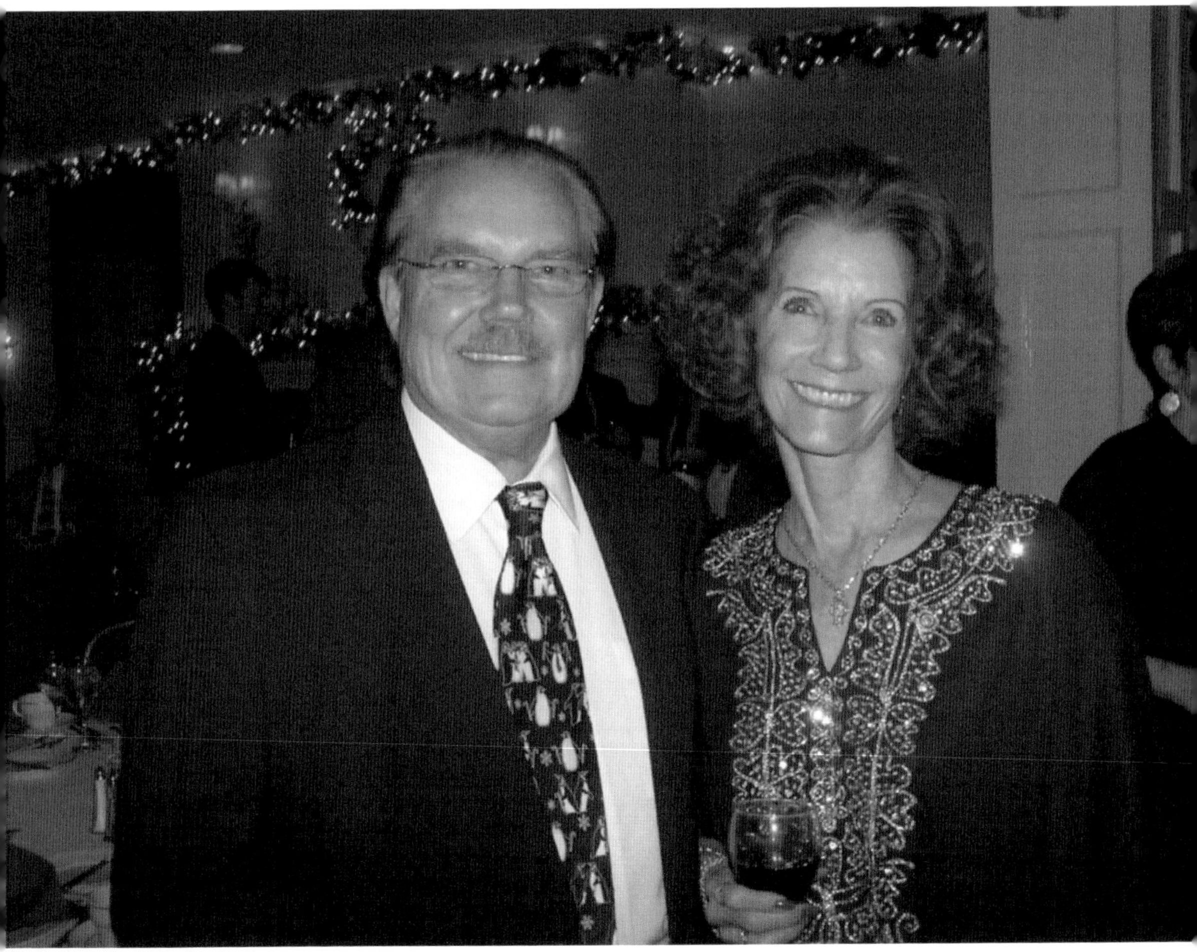

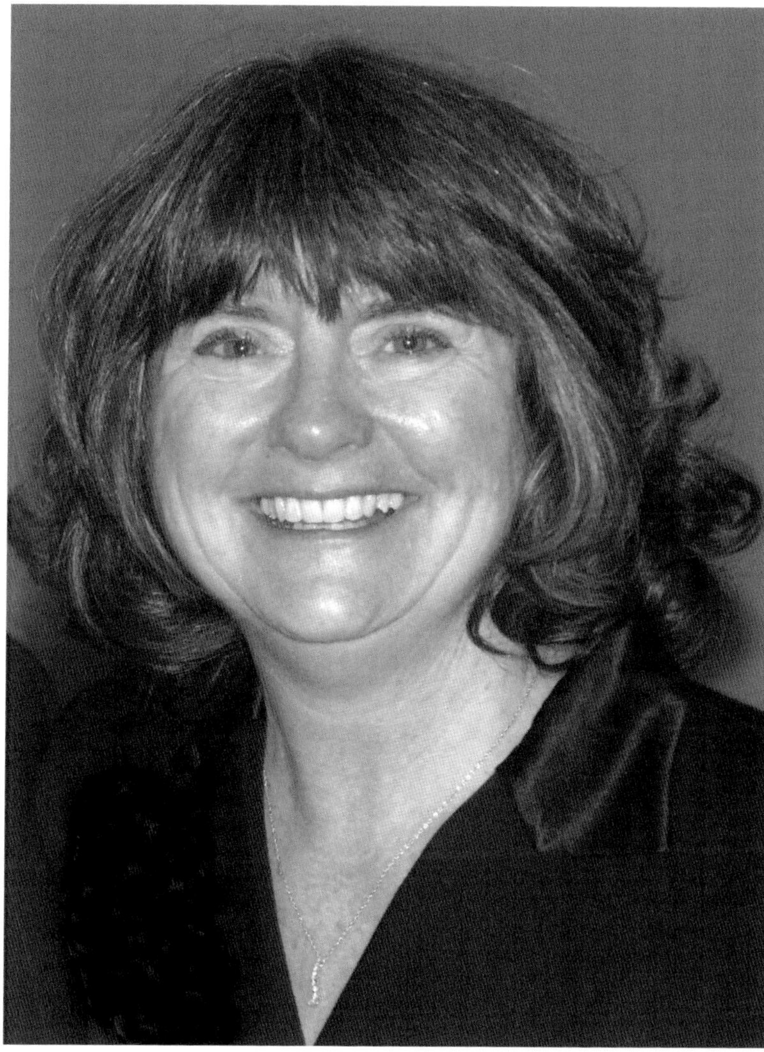

Miss Persistence

Around town she is known as "Miss Persistence." Without her poking, prodding, and knack for creating coalitions, modern-day Ambler would simply not be the attractive destination it has become in the last two decades. Bernadette Dougherty, a fixture at borough council meetings since her arrival from Abington in 1975, founded and drove Ambler Main Street as its first manager, from 1996 to 2007, working feverishly on projects to beautify Butler Avenue (Plant Ambler), encouraging and lauding local businesses (creating the Merchant of the Month Award), assisting in leasing or purchasing significant properties in danger of falling fallow (the Trax Restaurant site at the Southeastern Pennsylvania Transportation Authority [SEPTA] station and Ambler Theater), and generally serving as the borough's unofficial sounding board and spark plug. Dougherty has owned and operated countless Ambler businesses, including a children's toy shop (Choo-Choo), children's birthday parties (Celebrations), and a chocolate shop. She has also been active with the Wissahickon Valley Historical Society and the American Cancer Society and has served on various boards (including the Kelly Anne Dolan Memorial Fund, Act II Playhouse, and the Highlands), and presently serves as the borough's tax collector. She also wrote the chapter on Ambler in the updated 1983 edition of Theodore W. Beane's massive tome, *Montgomery County: The Second Hundred Years*. (Courtesy of Bernadette Dougherty.)

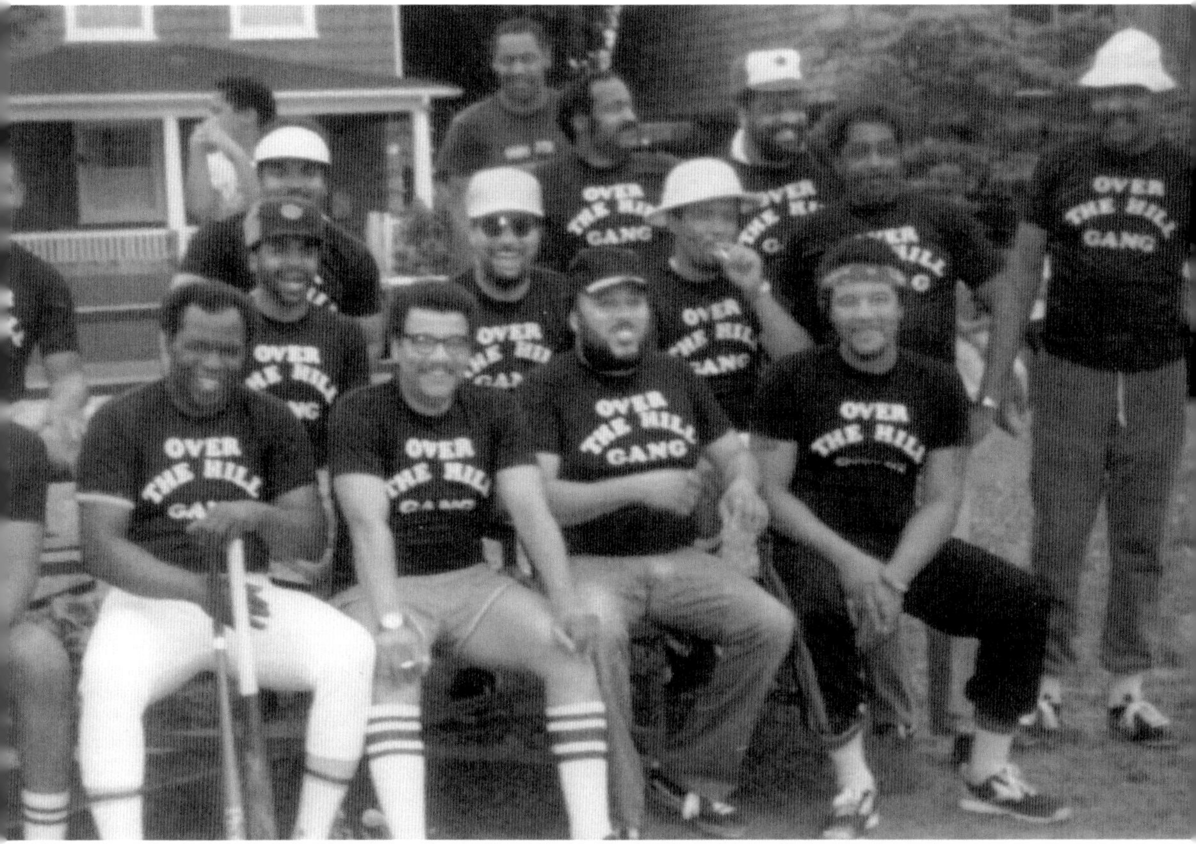

"Over the Hill Gang"
This is the colorful name chosen by Ambler's youthful old buddies who have stuck together for years to help each other out during times of crisis and joy. They are, from left to right, (first row) Buddy Lofton, Edward "Eagle" Johnson, Sterling Flowers, Steve Richardson, and Kevin Flowers; (second row) Eddie Curtis (to right of "Eagle"), Darryl Joel, Jimmy Flowers, Poochie Tate, and (standing) Al Gaskins; (third row) John Blaylark, Eddie Quenan, Bill Newman, and Avon Wilson; (fourth row) unidentified boy and (standing) John Carter. They are seen here around 1990 just before taking the field for a unity baseball game during the American Legion's annual Unity Day. Post commander Eddie Curtis, despite his impressive resume as a security officer, policeman, and presently serving his second term on the Ambler Borough Council (he is the chairperson for public safety), says that the Over the Hill Gang is "the highlight of my life. We really take care of each other." Curtis says that he has always adhered to a key principle that his late father taught him: "You'll do things in life correctly and stand by them. The hardest thing is to stand firm. And always come back to your roots." That principle seems to apply amply to the Over the Hill Gang, the American Legion post, and a majority of Ambler's committed citizenry. (Courtesy of Eddie Curtis.)

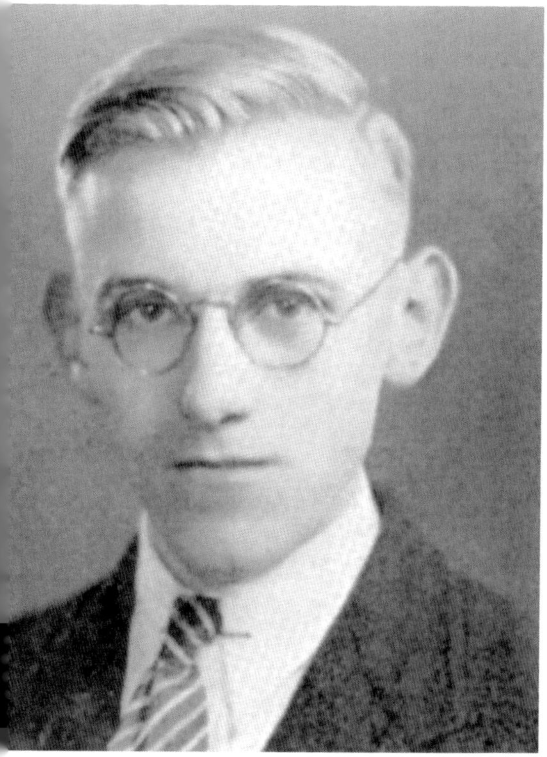

Hooked on History

Using his camera shop in the heart of Butler Avenue as his home base, Newton M. Howard was a tireless chronicler of the daily life and history of Ambler. Before he died, he willed his entire collection of articles and photographs, many of which were published in local community papers, to the Historical Society of Montgomery County. His disciple and friend William F. "Buck" Amey is writing a book on Howard's work. A regular customer at Howard's camera shop, Amey became hooked on local historical research and writing when he discovered what turned out to be his paternal grandfather's tombstone at the Union Cemetery in Whitemarsh—bearing Amey's own name! Since then, he has authored Images of America: *Fort Washington*. Active in the Boys Scouts for more than 50 years, Amey has also been involved with the fire company, ambulance corps, and Red Cross. (Both, courtesy of Buck Amey.)

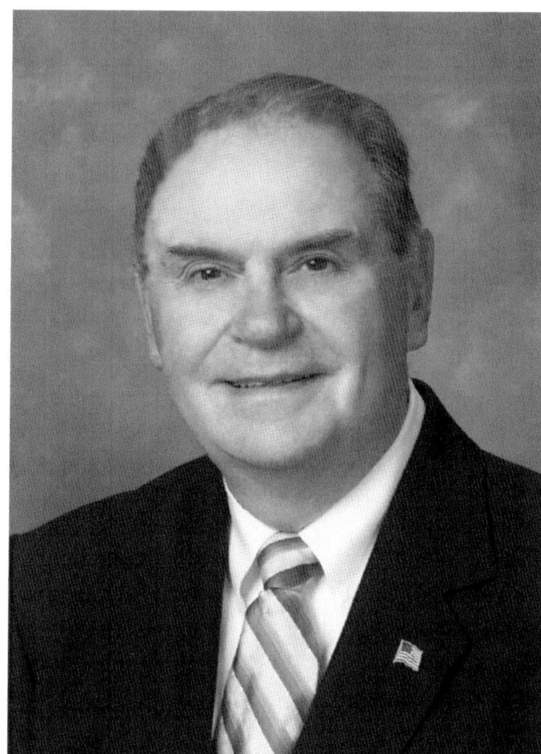

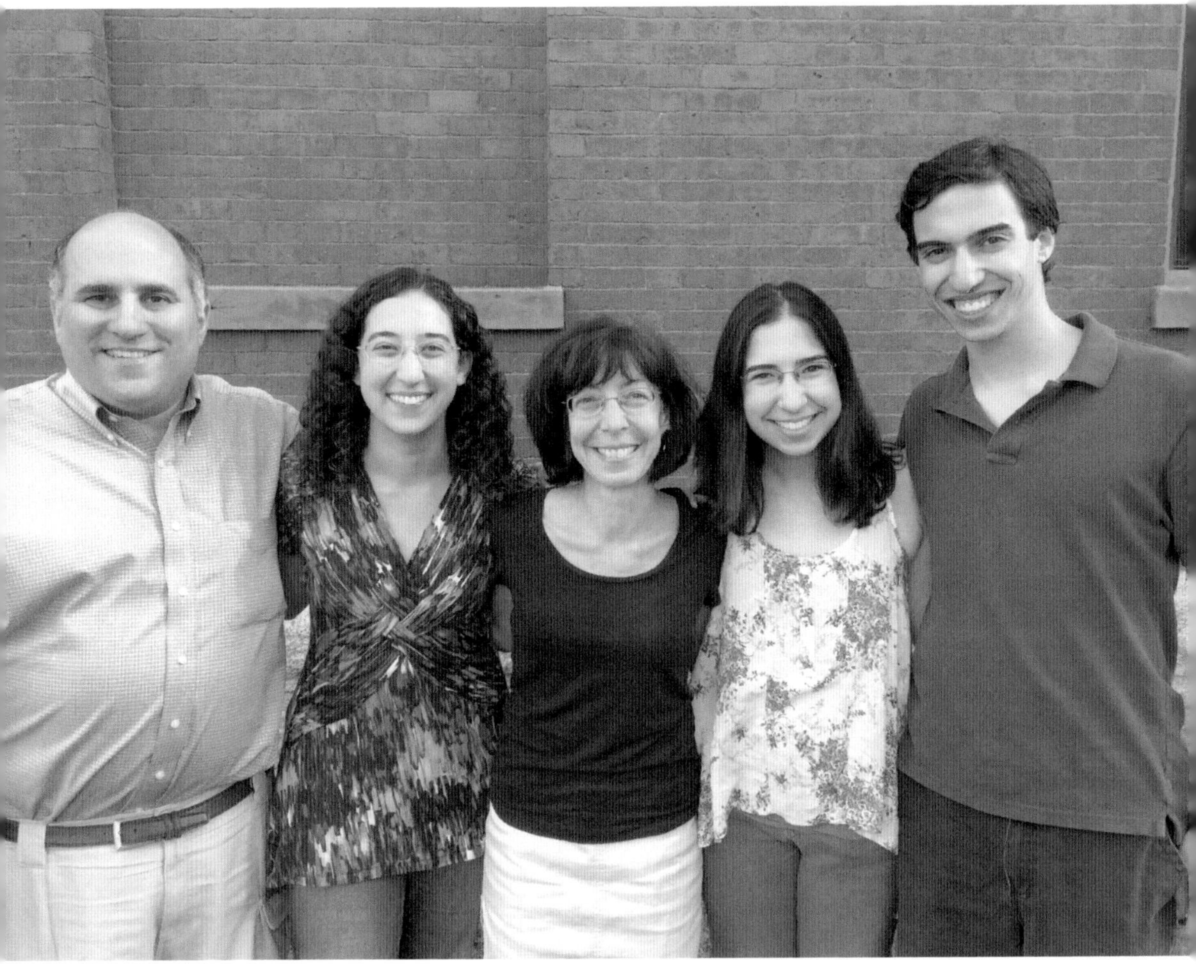

Dynamic Family

Ambler-area residents Robert and Jan Zauzmer (left and center) say that their three Harvard-educated children—Julie (second from left), Ben (right), and Emily (second from right)—are "each other's best friends and seek out each other's company." It's hard to imagine their having much time to do so these days, as their activities span the Eastern seaboard. It is even harder to conceive of a more civic-minded family, as the parents have instilled a shared belief in public service and charity. Fired up by the Watergate scandal, Robert soon turned to law as his profession. As a federal prosecutor in the US Attorney's Office for the Eastern District of Pennsylvania since 1990, he has been the lead prosecutor in countless corruption and fraud cases, including the 2005 Philadelphia City Hall corruption case, the prosecution of former state senator Vincent Fumo, and the prosecution of former US congressman Michael Mezvinsky. Jan, who met Robert at Stanford Law School, assumed numerous lay positions, including president of Congregation Beth Or, the preeminent Reform synagogue in the Philadelphia area, for more than two decades. Among her initiatives were webcasts of services and the charitable "Corner of the Land" community garden. At Beth Or, through their children's bar and bat mitzvah projects, the Zauzmers inspired their children's community involvement. Julie, also a professional balloon artist, started a book drive for schools in Israel and established a library in a town in northern Israel. While still the managing editor of the *Harvard Crimson*, Julie authored the book *Conning Harvard* (Globe Pequot Press), freelanced for the *Philadelphia Inquirer*, and, shortly after delivering the valedictory address at Harvard, became a staff reporter for the *Washington Post*. Ben, whose self-produced CD *Mitzvah Music* has already raised thousands of dollars for disabled children in Mississippi, is an applied mathematics wizard at Harvard, has captained an eastern Pennsylvania team in the American Regions Mathematics League to three national championships, and has created an Oscar-prediction model that earned him a column in 2014 at the *Hollywood Reporter*. Emily, like her siblings an exceptional writer, has written *Once Upon a Masterpiece*, a children's art history book, and wrote the winning play at the Philadelphia Young Playwrights' contest in 2013. The founder of two food allergy charities, www.EZgreetings.org and www.EZeatings.org, Emily also spoke at National Arts Advocacy Day in Washington, DC, as the winner of the Educational Theatre Association's national essay contest. (Courtesy of the Zauzmer family.)

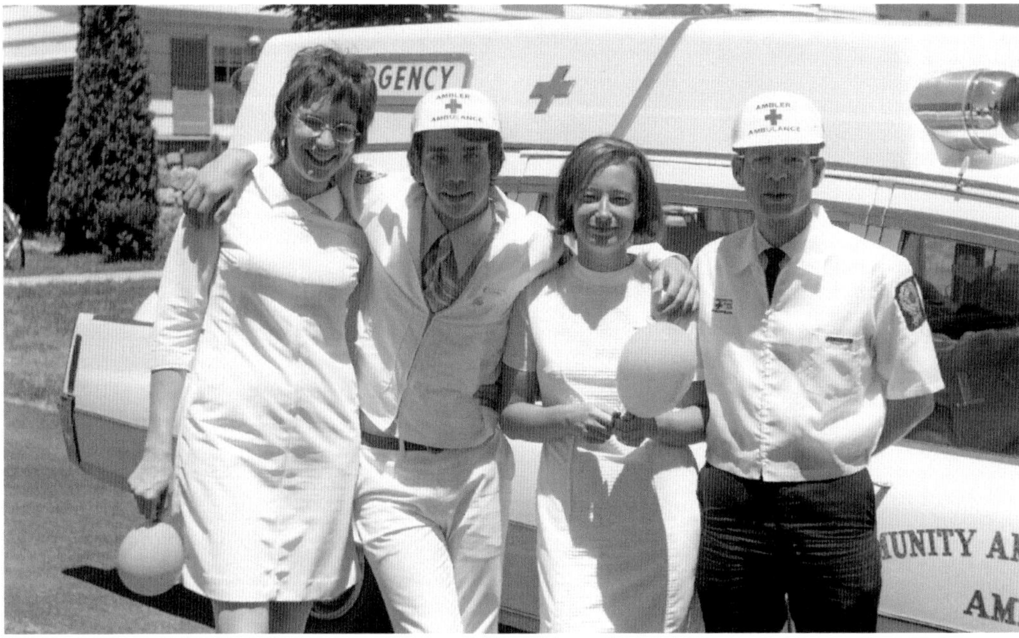

Humble Servant

Like so many of Ambler's unsung heroes, Dolores Loftus, a devoted wife, mother, and grandmother, preferred a life of service well behind the scenes. A registered nurse, Loftus served the sick at ACTS (Adult Communities Total Service) Retirement-Life Communities in Spring House and at Fort Washington Estates for more than 20 years. This energetic soul also relished being a Eucharistic minister with her "second family," at St. Alphonsus Catholic Church in Maple Glen, where she served as a magnet for the needy and sick, and where she chaired Aid for Friends for 25 years, organizing the collection and distribution of 60,000 meals to housebound seniors. Loftus (second from right) is seen here with Fran Amey, Dave Bail, and Woody Woodward, all volunteers for the Community Ambulance Association of Ambler. Another of her passions was making and repairing rosaries for children and the missions in Africa. And she loved her vacations at the shore. (Both, courtesy of the Loftus family.)

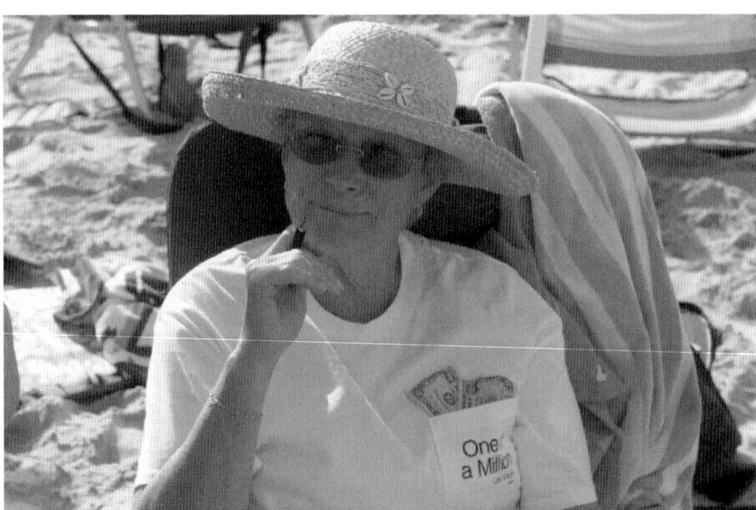

CHAPTER FOUR

Industrialists, Entrepreneurs, and Builders

Ambler's story would pale indeed without the larger-than-life figure of Richard V. "Doc" Mattison, strutting and fretting his hour upon the stage with all the fustian and bombast infusing a highly entertaining late-19th-century melodrama. He might glower and fuss, combing his beard with his long fingers and twirling his luxurious mustache before consigning his minions to their beds—without supper.

Yet there he is in the next scene, kindly as Santa, stroking his children's hair, setting his roses in their long vase, sipping his tea from an elegant English cup, welcoming the archbishop to his ornate drawing room, speaking in hushed, measured tones.

So will the real Doc Mattison please stand up?

A complex, polarizing figure, a towering scientist and industrialist of the first order, Mattison, even more than Mary Ambler, is the central figure in the borough's history. Love him or hate him, he brought the jobs. From the asbestos factories to the library and opera house, from the fire company to the elegant Trinity Memorial Episcopal Church and many of the homes still standing—he built the town.

All Amblerites seem to have some connection to the Baron. Deck's Hardware, dating back to 1908, still carries special nails and other supplies for Ambler's Mattison-built houses that the big box stores never seem to have. Artist Eddie Flotte has made a small living painting details from K&M's boiler plant and other architectural flourishes created by Mattison's Italian stonemasons. Real estate agent/writer Kelly Kroll, director of the Bonnie Kroll Melanoma Memorial Fund, recalls a story she heard about her pop-pop, Victor Romano Sr. Mattison's head gardener, the romantic Romano was once caught in the act of cutting and picking roses for his wife-to-be, Millie. Mattison told him, in a clearly threatening tone, "No more roses!"

But Ambler has been blessed, on a more modest scale, by the entrepreneurial spirit of immigrant families like the Costas, who gave the borough Costa's Delicatessen and Ambler Fireplace & Patio; roofing and siding whiz Dan Ritter; master electrician Bob King; acclaimed chemist David Mayron; and more. But the shadow of Doc Mattison still hovers over all.

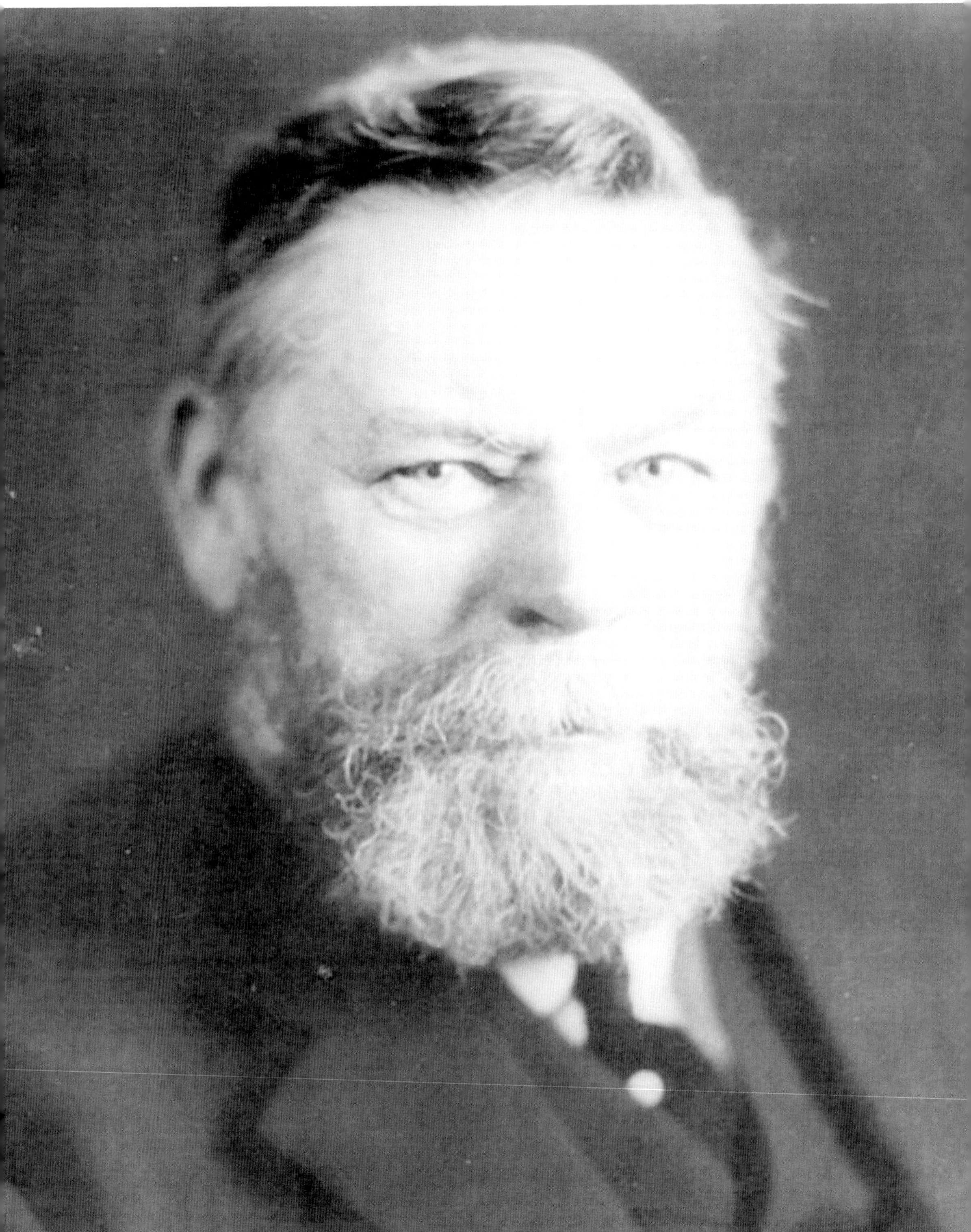

The Baron Builds Ambler

Perhaps the most seminal moment in Ambler's history came in 1881, when financier Henry G. Keasbey and brilliant chemist Richard V. "Doc" Mattison relocated their Keasbey & Mattison Company from Philadelphia to Ambler, just as the milling industry collapsed. Founded in 1873, the company amassed its first fortune creating patent medicines. But Mattison's 1886 discovery of the insulating properties of magnesium carbonate, an extract of dolomite in plentiful supply just outside the town, put Ambler on the map. Mattison soon perfected asbestos insulation. When World War I broke out in 1914, K&M had become the world's largest manufacturer and supplier of asbestos products. Keasbey ultimately became a silent partner, but Mattison's entrepreneurial vision and influence continued to prevail. By the turn of the 20th century, he had transformed Ambler into the quintessential company town. He hired laborers from France, Germany, Poland, Hungary, and Ireland, and many African Americans from Westmoreland County, West Virginia. Most significantly, he imported hundreds of Italian stonemasons and builders from Maida in Calabria and from Minturno, near Naples. By 1980, a third of Ambler's residents were of Italian descent, a figure that holds true today. Mattison built 400 homes in Ambler, more than 80 percent of which are still standing and lived in—an astounding figure, by any reckoning. He created, in effect, a caste system, erecting grand Victorian stone mansions for his company's top executives, sturdy stone twins for superintendents, and row houses for blue-collar workers. Mattison and his family resided in Lindenwold, his 24-room 50-acre estate resembling England's Windsor Castle. K&M thrived until the Great Depression forced Mattison to sell the company. In 1936, the year he died, he also sold Lindenwold to the Catholic Sisters of the Holy Family of Nazareth, who converted the mansion into St. Mary's Villa for Children. The ego-driven Mattison was also a civic-minded pioneer and community leader who helped inspire Ambler's incorporation in 1888. He paved the streets, improved the water supply, introduced electric streetlights, built the borough's first opera house and library, and, generally, took good care of his employees. Although he might have known about the potentially harmful effects of asbestos as early as 1900, no conclusive evidence has been found. In 1984, the Environmental Protection Agency (EPA) mandated that all 25 acres of asbestos waste located in south Ambler and in Upper Dublin Township (often manifested in brush fires burning on what the locals call "white mountains") had to be covered with dirt and fenced in. Asbestos, of course, has been discovered to be a carcinogen and is known to cause asbestosis, a lung disease similar to emphysema that afflicts many former employees of K&M. (Courtesy of Buck Amey.)

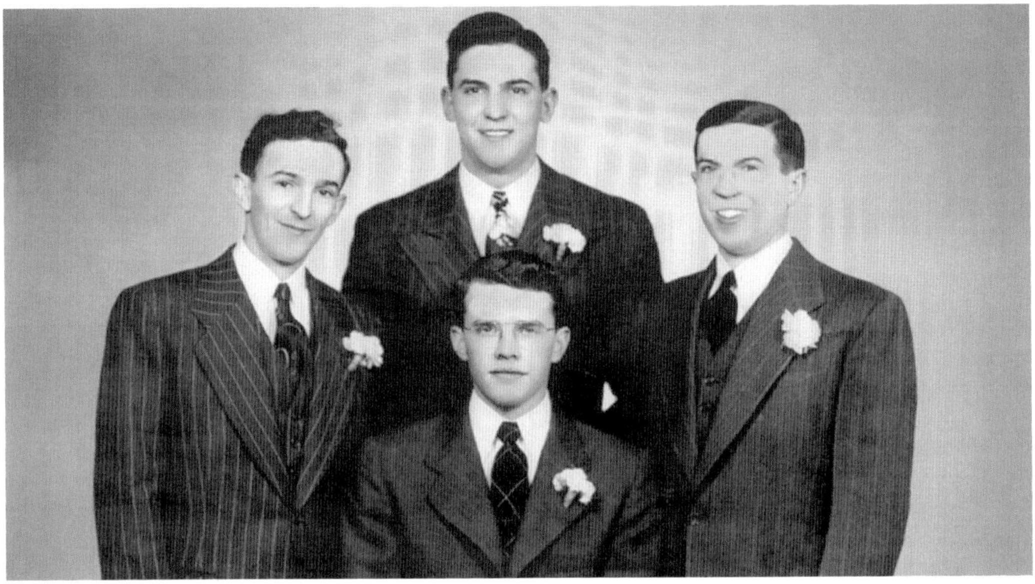

On Deck

Garnet G.M. Deck had a head for figures. His studies in accounting melded well with his knowledge of tools, paints, and gardening supplies, so when he purchased Reed's Hardware in 1908 and rechristened it Deck's Hardware, he launched a family business that thrives well into the 21st century. The second-generation of Decks (clockwise from left)—brothers Truxton "Tuck," Dawson "Tiny," Richard "Nel," and Gordon "Cliff"—even during the darkest days of the Great Depression, kept the family tradition alive. Today, everyone in Ambler patronizes Deck's. Tiny (center), the youngest and only surviving Deck brother, still comes to work every day to support his two sons, Tim (left) and Tyler. They thrive, despite the big box stores proliferating America's strip malls, by being service oriented, by keeping supplies in hand for the older houses built by Richard V. "Doc" Mattison at the turn of the 20th century, and by developing lasting relationships with their customers. (Above, photograph by Newt Howard, courtesy of Buck Amey; below, photograph by Frank D. Quattrone.)

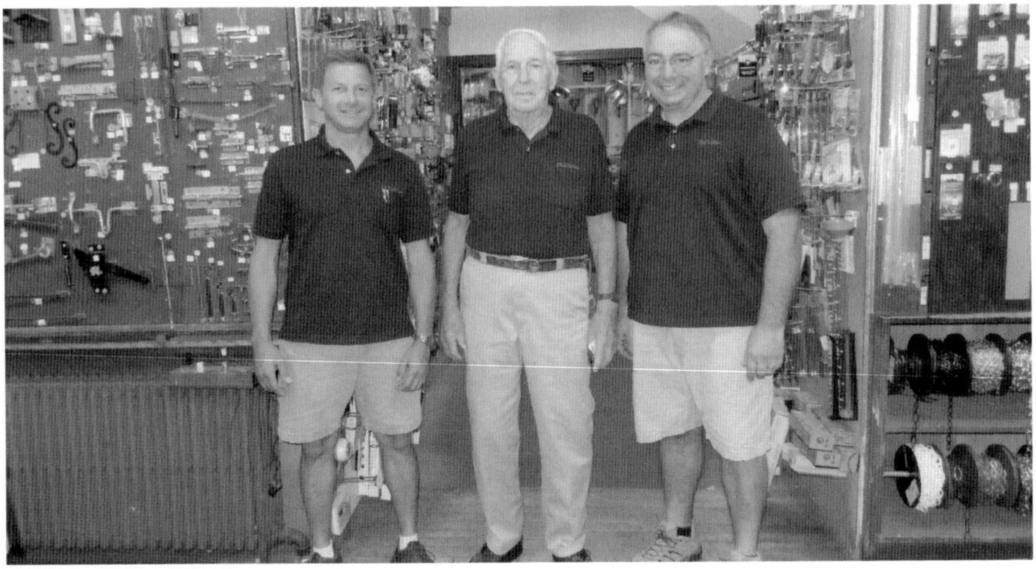

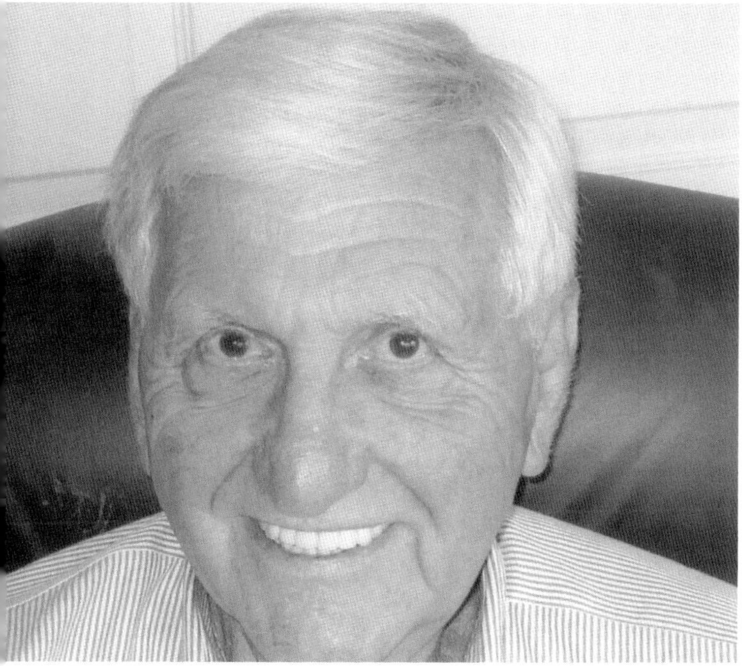

Mr. Everyman
Typical of the great-hearted spirit of Ambler's business leaders and property owners, Dan Ritter has been "Mr. Everyman" ever since he arrived in the borough more than 50 years ago. President and founder of BeautyGuard, a thriving roofing and siding business, Ritter is chairman of the Board of Ambler Savings Bank and an active member of the Ambler Rotary. He has also served on the boards of Gwynedd Mercy University, Ambler YMCA, and the chamber of commerce. (Courtesy of Dan Ritter.)

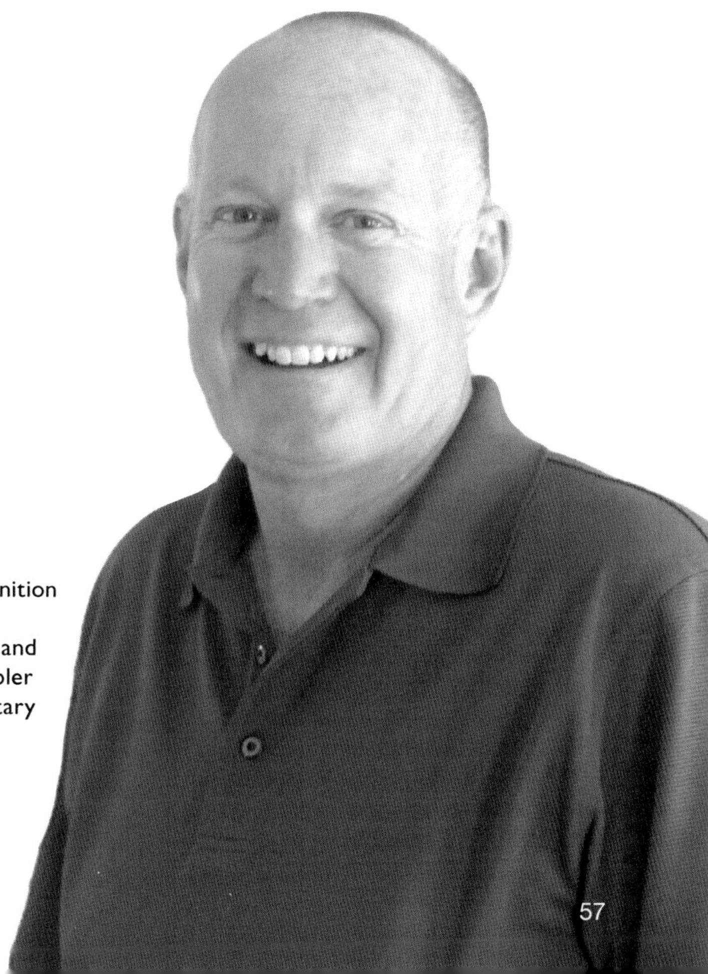

Electric King
Master electrician Bob King, president of Ambler Electric, likes to deflect any recognition for his part in the 2007 completion of a footbridge across the Wissahickon Creek and the launching of the successful annual Ambler Arts and Music Festival to the Ambler Rotary (he has been a member and, recently, its president, for 24 years) and to the great people of Ambler—typical of this selfless community servant. (Photograph by Eric Devlin; courtesy of Montgomery Media.)

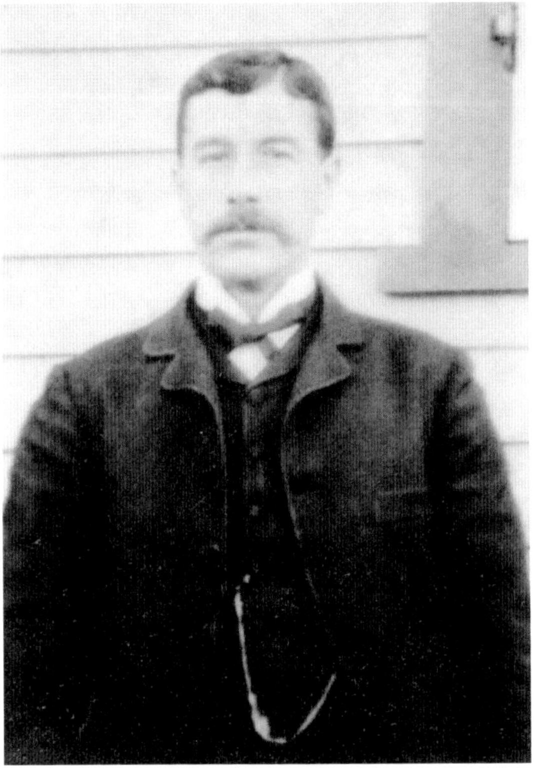

Antiques Family

Ross Gordon Gerhart III, local historian and genealogist, said that his great-great-grandfather Charles Weikel Gerhart Sr. (pictured here) started the family business in 1894, when this photograph was taken. That business, which began as a moving and storage operation, kept evolving over the next century or so. His son Ross Gordon Gerhart Sr. and his grandson Ross Gordon Gerhart II became the town locksmiths, conducted furniture and state appraisals, and repaired model trains until its final incarnation, Gerhart Antiques & Cabinet Shop, finally closed its doors in 2004. In the photograph below, helping to celebrate Ambler Borough's diamond jubilee during the Grand Float Parade in June 1963 are, from left to right, Ross Gordon Gerhart Sr., Ross Gordon Gerhart III, and Ross Gordon Gerhart II. (Both, courtesy of Ross Gordon Gerhart III.)

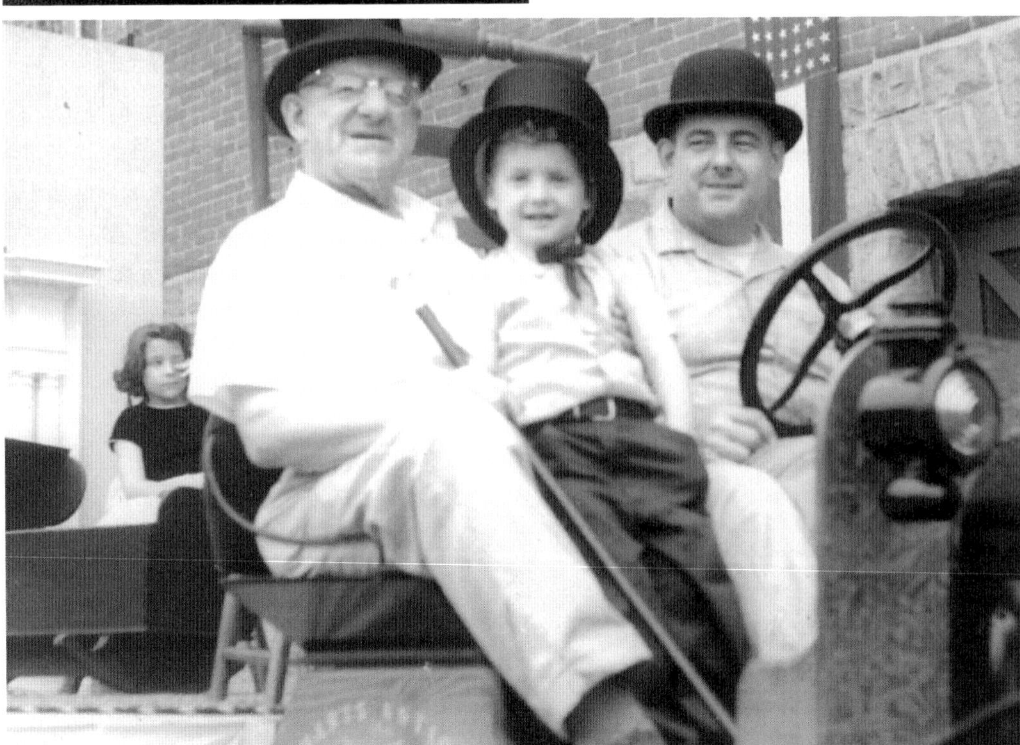

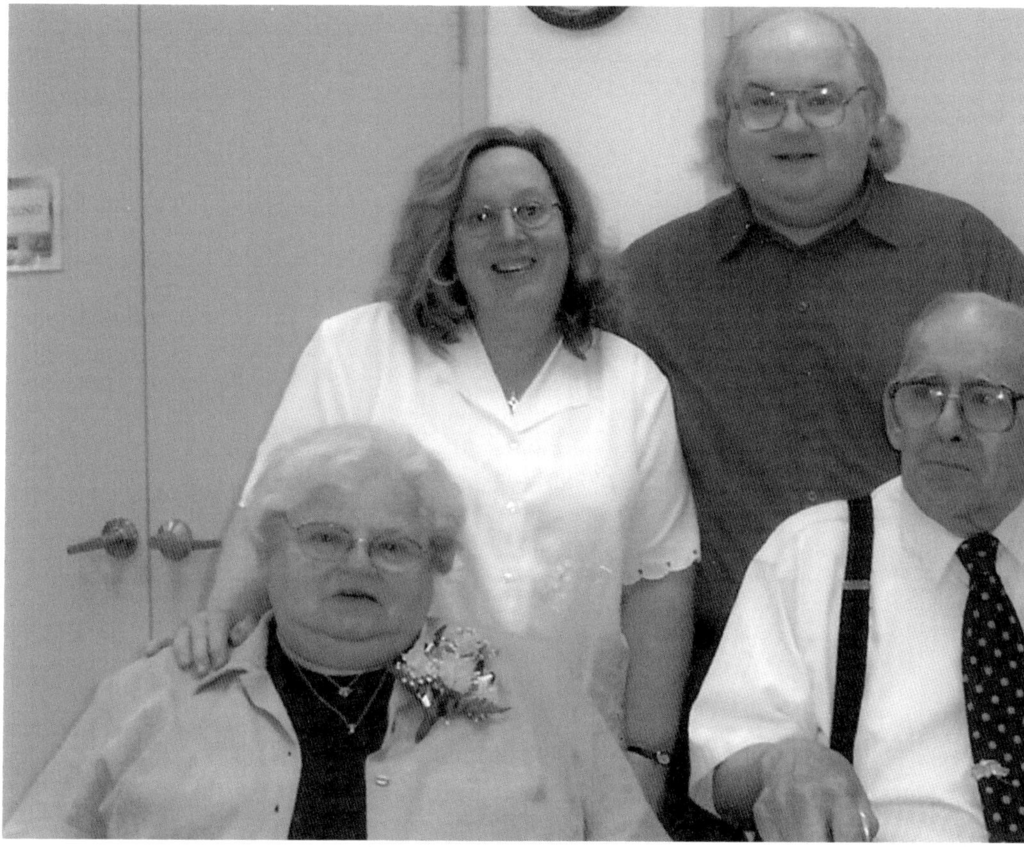

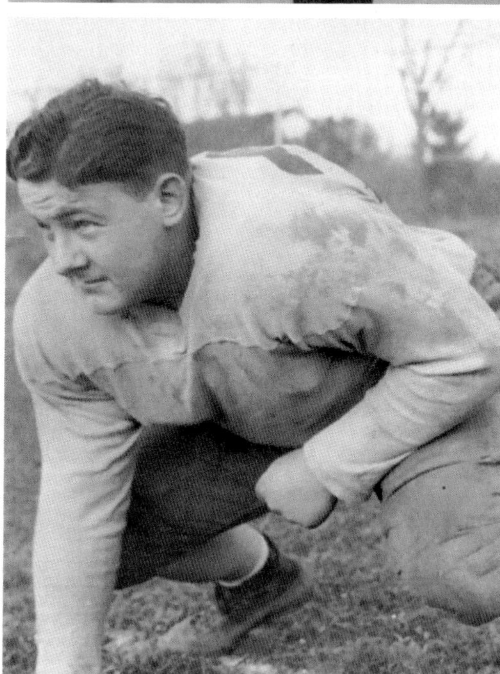

The Sun Rises

Always involved in the fabric of Ambler life are the Gerhart family, seen here at the 50th wedding anniversary of (seated) Ross Gordon Gerhart II and Florence Saul Gerhart. Behind the couple are their son Ross Gordon Gerhart III and his wife, Elaine Carol. The youngest Gerhart's passion for genealogy and local history has resulted in a drawing room brimming over with family and local photographs, articles, and artifacts dating back more than 100 years, plus his self-published *The Gerhart Book* (1990). When his American ancestors, Peter and Elizabeth Gerhart, emigrated from Germany in 1739, they settled along the rolling hills of what is now Franconia Township and established Gerhart's Tavern in 1752, still thriving today as the Rising Sun Inn. At left is Ross Gordon Gerhart II on the Ambler High School football team in the 1940s. (Both, courtesy of Ross Gordon Gerhart III.)

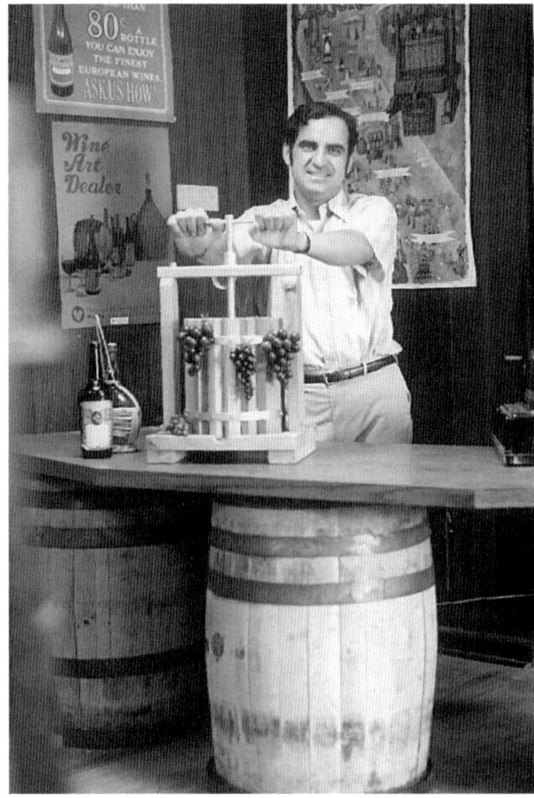

Wine Press Man

John Costa, before he turned his wine supply business into Ambler Fireplace & Patio, could often be found behind his barrel-based counter at his handmade grape press, made by his friend Paul Pearsal, of Perkasie. In addition to his business, Costa has been an avid sponsor of Ambler Junior Baseball and Softball and Whitpain Recreation Association soccer teams since 1994. (Courtesy of the Costa family.)

A Busy Corner

There has always been a tavern, grocery store, or delicatessen at the corner of Bethlehem Pike and Butler Avenue since 1770, when it was a public house (tavern). Andrew Gilkyson built the present stone building in 1803. In can be seen below, with Mr. Porter and Mr. Stout, during its tenure as Porter's Store, between 1931 and 1940. Rocco and Maria Costa took over the deli in 1950 and it has been thriving ever since. (Photograph by Al Whitcomb; courtesy of the Costa family.)

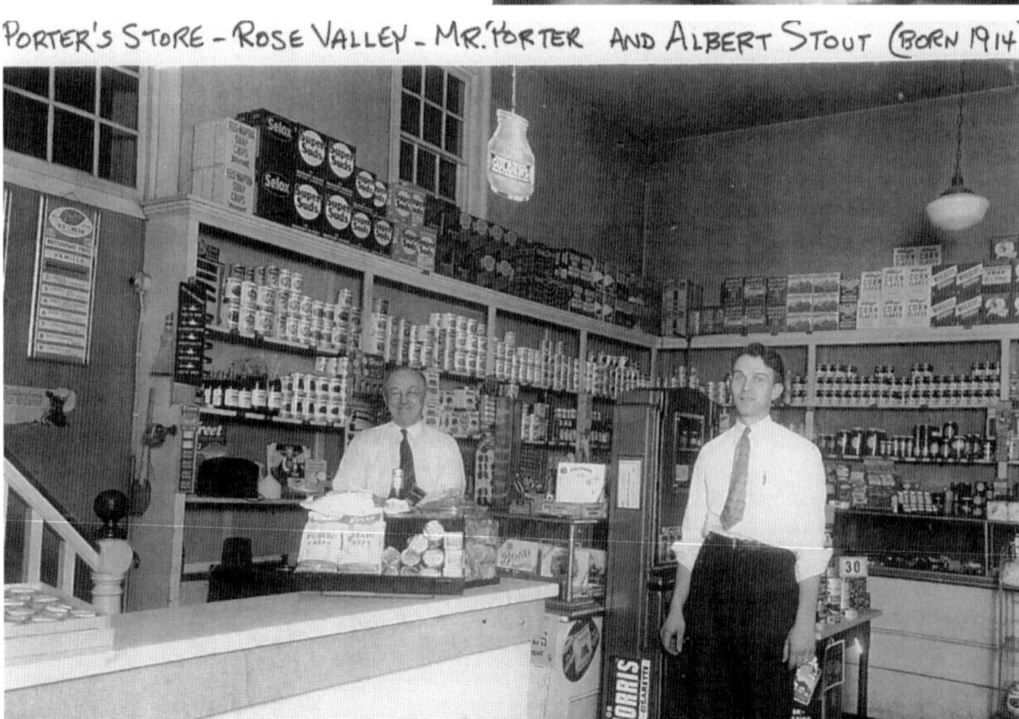

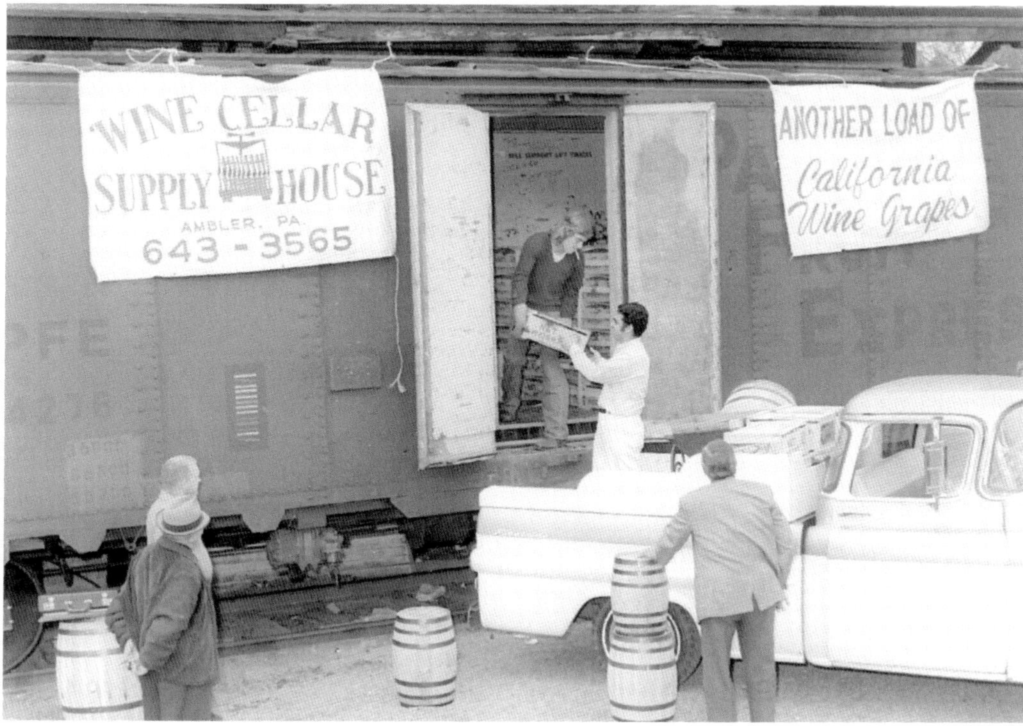

Wine Supplies & Wood Stoves

Typifying Ambler's entrepreneurial spirit is the Costa family, Italian immigrants who have dominated a busy corner where Bethlehem and Butler pikes meet, since 1950, when Rocco and Maria Costa purchased the corner deli. But in 1969, their son John opened the Wine Cellar Supply House next door to the deli to service the tastes of the large Italian population of Ambler. John can be seen (center, in white) unloading supplies at the Ambler Train Station. But the energy crisis of 1973 triggered John's entrepreneurial spirit, when he discovered the marvelous heating capabilities of wood stoves, relatively unknown at the time. To wine supplies he soon added wood stoves and fireplaces to his burgeoning business, which now includes a second location in nearby Colmar. John (right) is pictured below in 1987 with his sister Maryann Ryan (center) and a representative of Vermont Castings. The Costas remain active in community affairs. (Above, photograph by Franklin B. Blank; both courtesy of Costa family.)

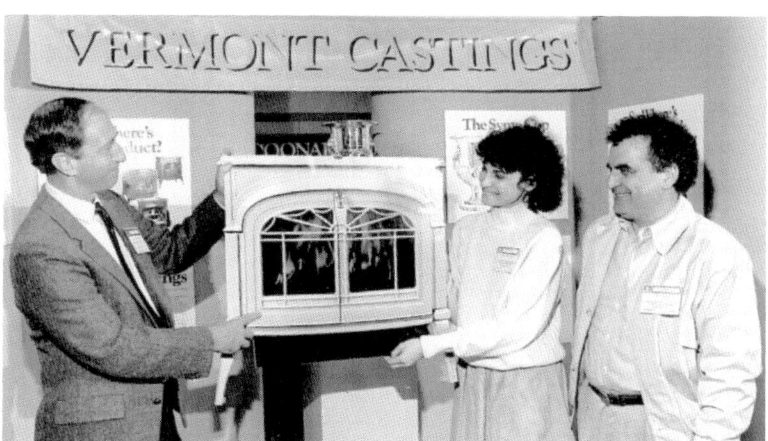

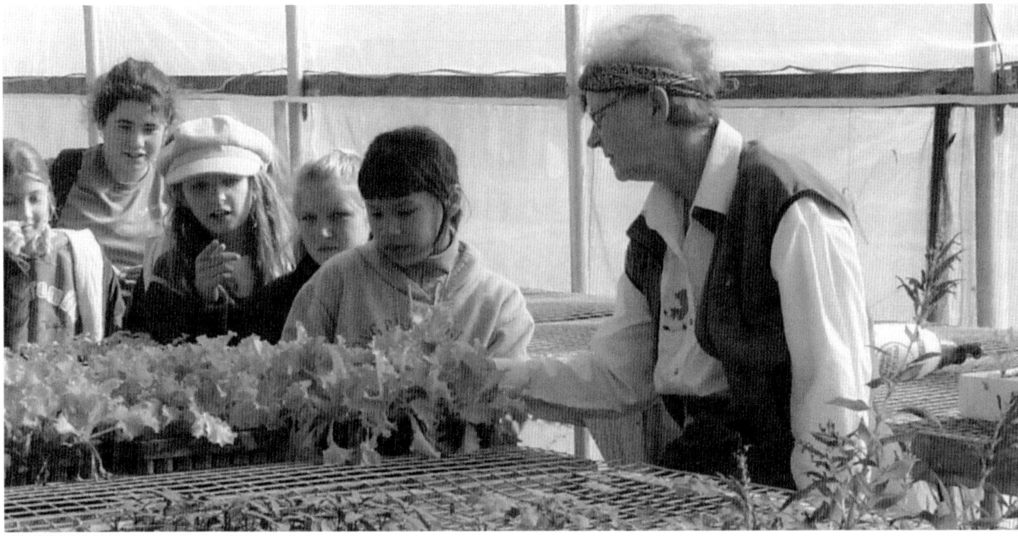

Environmental Activist

Susan Curry, who founded Pennypack Farm and Education Center, is seen above in 2005 in the farm's greenhouse with students from Germantown Academy. Since she founded the center in 2003, Curry has served as a board member, farm educator, developmental director, and medicinal herb garden and culinary herb garden manager. The success of this new farm inspired others to start the Ambler Food Co-op and Ambler Farmers Market. Curry, after successfully leading an effort to organize all nine of the Environmental Advisory Councils from municipalities in the Wissahickon Watershed, is seen below receiving the Clean Water Fund's Florence Nielsen Environmental Leadership Award from Pennsylvania state representative Rick Taylor in November 2009. She has also organized tree plantings and has been a sustainability advocate, farm educator, arborist, and landscaping consultant, all in the service of her community. (Both, courtesy of Susan Curry.)

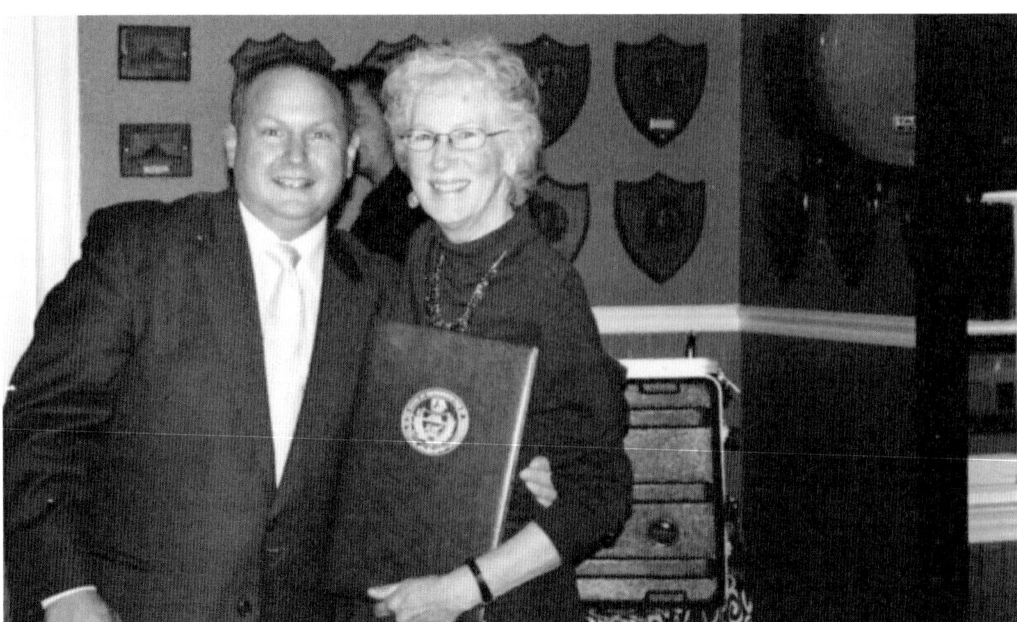

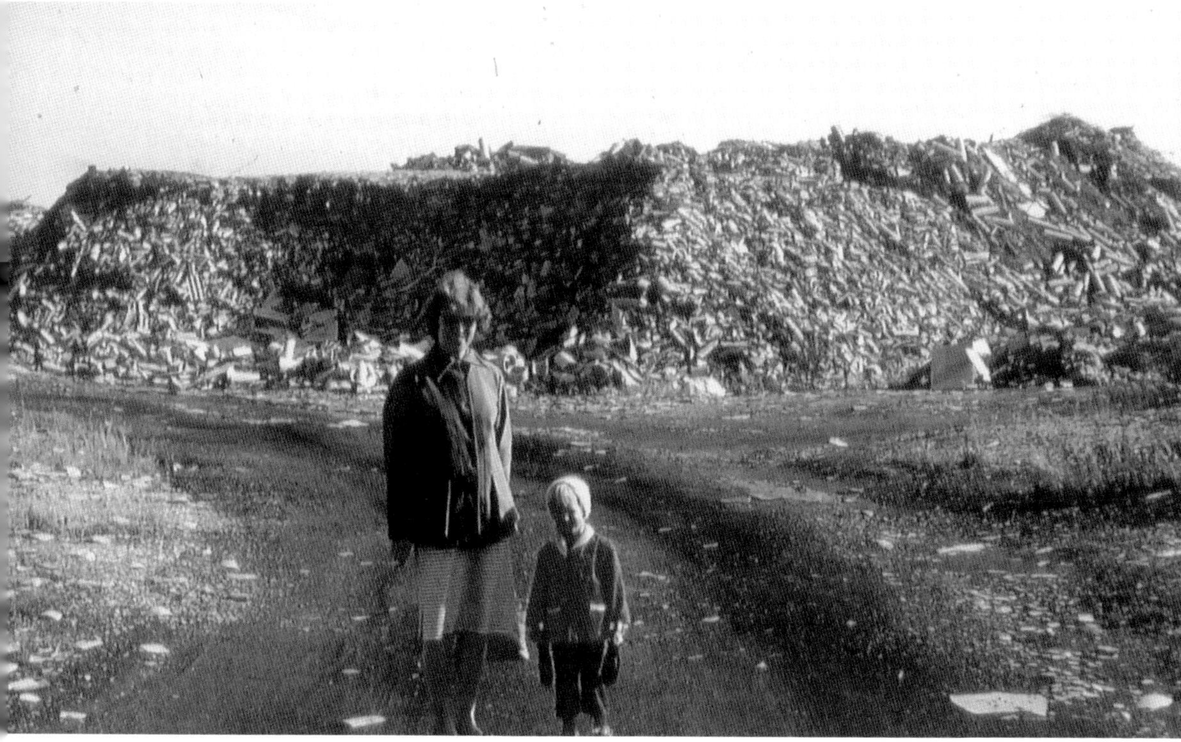

White Mountains

Two unidentified Ambler residents stand at the foot of the infamous "White Mountains," the drying beds from the water used to wash finished shingles produced at the Keasbey & Mattison Company, Ambler's leading manufacturer of asbestos and related products. Several studies discovered that the chalklike substance posed no threat unless someone was digging in the pile. The US Environmental Protection Agency chose to cover the piles with five feet of topsoil. (Photograph by Albert Degidio.)

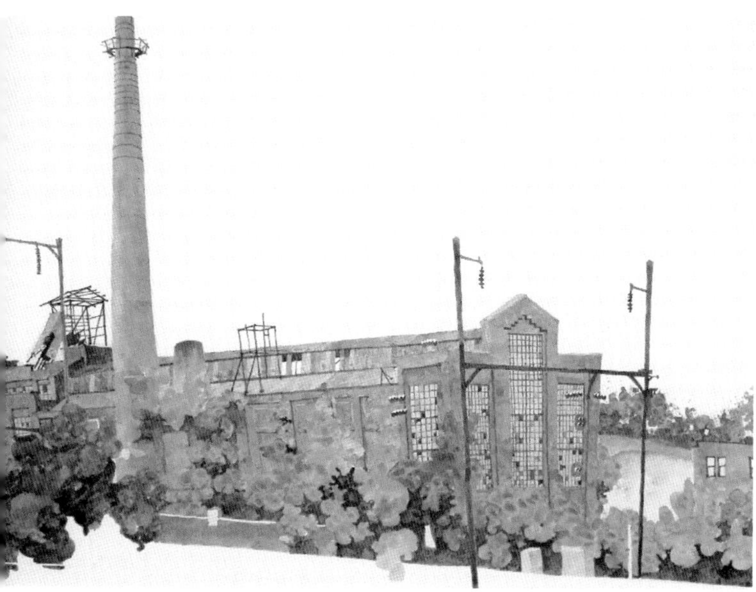

Boiler Plant

Ambler artist Eddie Flotte says that many of his old neighbors get emotional when they see paintings like this of the boiler plant belonging to the Keasbey & Mattison Company, one of the world's leading manufacturers of asbestos products. The dads of many Amblerites worked there and, later, died from breathing in asbestos flakes. (Courtesy of Eddie Flotte.)

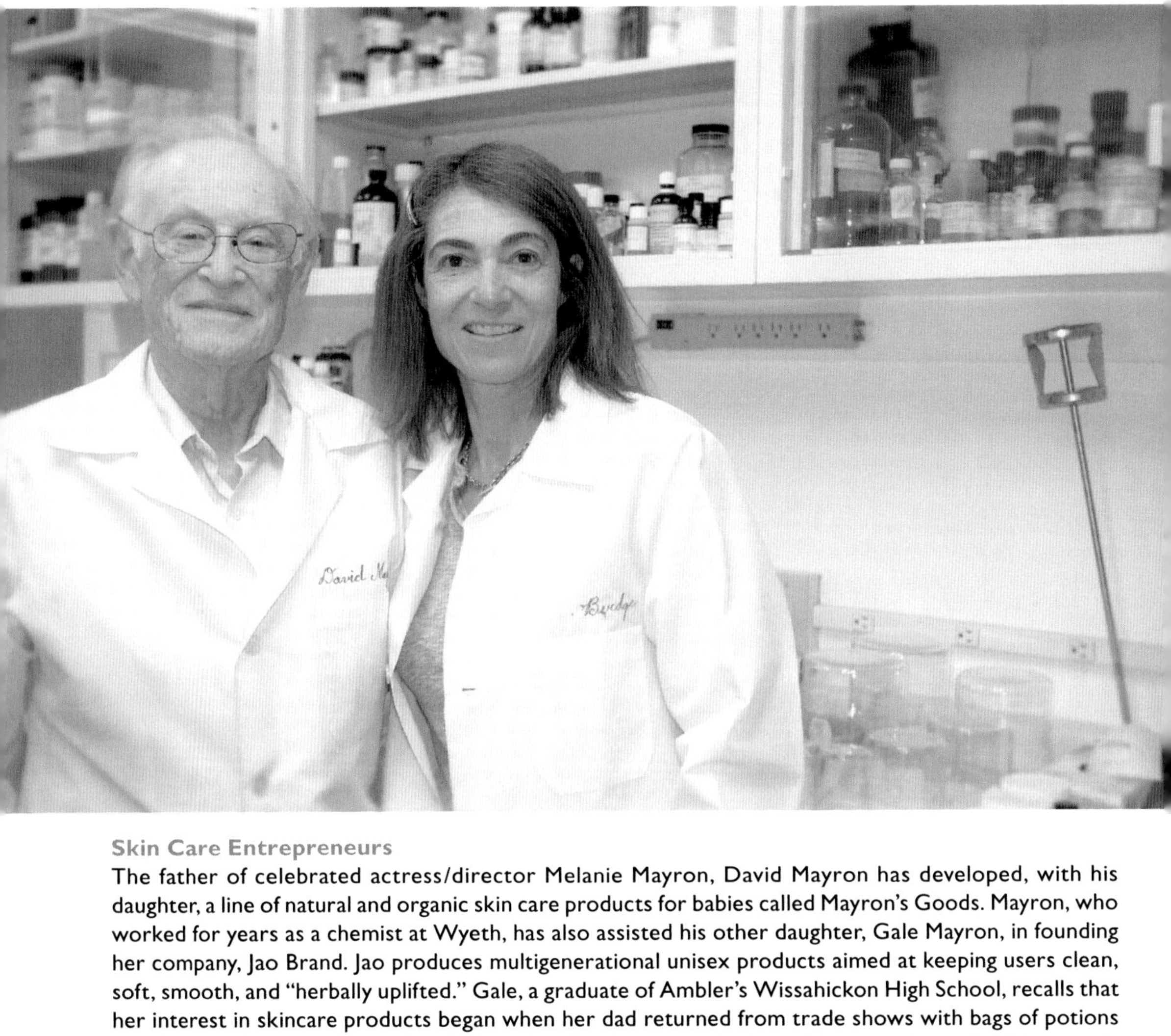

Skin Care Entrepreneurs

The father of celebrated actress/director Melanie Mayron, David Mayron has developed, with his daughter, a line of natural and organic skin care products for babies called Mayron's Goods. Mayron, who worked for years as a chemist at Wyeth, has also assisted his other daughter, Gale Mayron, in founding her company, Jao Brand. Jao produces multigenerational unisex products aimed at keeping users clean, soft, smooth, and "herbally uplifted." Gale, a graduate of Ambler's Wissahickon High School, recalls that her interest in skincare products began when her dad returned from trade shows with bags of potions that his daughters could smell and play with. "Jao" is a mystical word inscribed on a 2,000-year-old charm believed to prevent and cure disease. According to Jao Brand's website, its products, made from pure plants, fruits, and flowers, represent "the artful synthesis of ancient pharmacopoeia and modern science." Chemist David Mayron, who studied his chosen profession at Philadelphia College of Pharmacy & Science, has more than 35 years' experience in the pharmaceutical industry. In 1989, in Hatfield, Pennsylvania, he founded Mayron Research Laboratories, an independent contract laboratory specializing in the development of pharmaceuticals, cosmetics, and personal care products. Working closely with his daughters, Melanie and Gale, he developed the skin care products offered by their companies, Mayron's Goods and Jao Brand, respectively. (Courtesy of the Mayron family.)

CHAPTER FIVE

The Arts Come to Ambler

Rightfully so, Ambler's turn-of-the-century revitalization has been attributed largely to the opening of Act II Playhouse, Montgomery County's first professional theater, in 1999, as well as the grand reopening of the borough's Hollywood-style movie house, the Ambler Theater, in 2003 (not to mention the fruitful efforts of a coalition of committed Amblerites to bring parking to the borough). Truth be told, the success of the theater company, which produces a nifty mix of edgy revivals (like *Man of La Mancha* and Shakespeare's *The Tempest*) and rarely produced contemporary plays, and the cinema, which alternates four films on its three screens, the best in art-house fare, has contributed mightily to Ambler's viability and desirability as an entertainment destination.

But Act II, founded by Stephen D. Blumenthal and now under the artistic direction of comic genius Tony Braithwaite, one of the most popular and sought-after actors in the Philadelphia region, and the movie house are not producing in a vacuum. Ambler also boasts a symphony orchestra; a choral group; an innovative "Art in the Storefront" exhibition space; and some exceptional artists, including Maui-based Eddie Flotte, who has brilliantly captured so much of his borough on canvas, plus Karen Kieser and Mark Elliott, codirectors of Art in the Storefront; and a robust music scene, featuring an array of eclectic artists, including environmental rockers Rick Denzien and Debra Lee, Bill Bloom, John Conahan, David Morgan, and Irish troubadour Gerry Timlin, whose Irish pub, the Shanachie (now closed and replaced by the Lucky Well), brought exciting Celtic rhythms to the bustling borough.

There is also the cinema. Famed Hollywood leading lady Rosalind Russell filmed parts of *The Trouble with Angels* and its sequel at St. Mary's Villa (on the old Mattison estate), and Emmy Award–winning actress Melanie Mayron (*thirtysomething*), who has made her mark as an actress/director on the big and small screen, graduated from Wissahickon High School.

And there is a story that famous pop singer Johnny Mathis would come into town frequently, just to meet with world-class songwriter Linda Creed (she wrote "The Greatest Love of All"), because only this talented Ambler resident could write songs for him that would minimize his slight lisp.

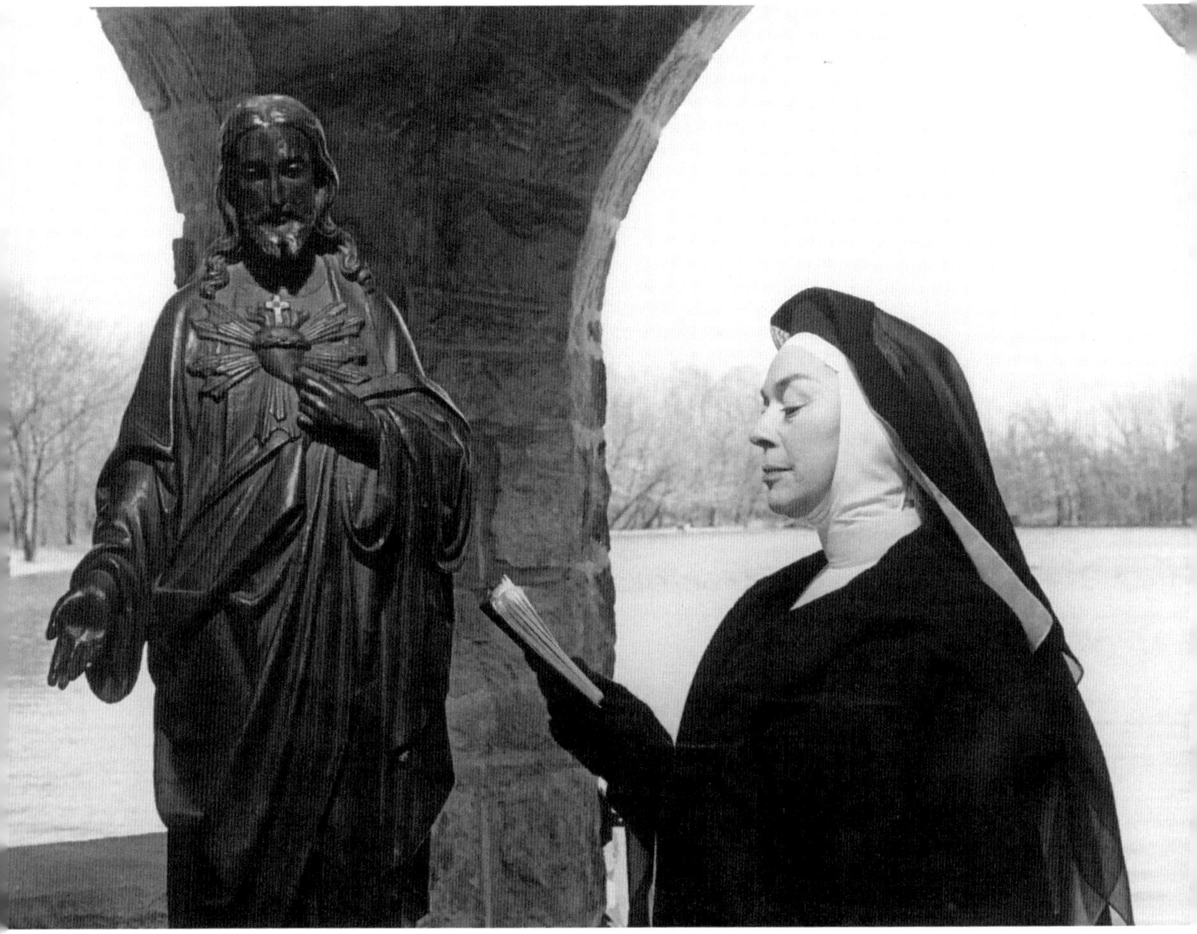

Mother Superior

Acclaimed actress Rosalind Russell spent several weeks on location in Ambler and environs. Often, she could be seen on the streets of Ambler in 1966, when she starred as Mother Superior in the comedy *The Trouble with Angels*, and in 1968, when she returned to shoot its sequel, *Where Angels Go, Trouble Follows*. She is seen here at St. Mary's Villa, a Catholic home for troubled and at-risk youth that was originally called Lindenwold, the castle home of industrialist Richard V. "Doc" Mattison and is now known as the Villa. The Ida Lupino-directed comedy *The Trouble with Angels* followed the adventures of two high-spirited young students, played by Hayley Mills and June Harding, at St. Francis Academy for Girls, who keep things lively for the challenged Mother Superior and her staff of bewildered nuns. The critical and box office success of the movie led, of course, to the sequel, which featured a cross-country journey to an interfaith youth rally taking place in California and conflict between the more conservative Mother Superior (Russell) and a glamorous, progressive young nun played by Stella Stevens. *Where Angels Go* also featured some pretty big stars, including Milton Berle, Arthur Godfrey, Robert Taylor, and Van Johnson. In the sequel, Susan Saint James and Barbara Hunter played the two rebellious, trouble-prone students. Although Russell was a huge draw during the shooting of her two movies in the Ambler area, the Villa was not the only site where filming took place. Other scenes (specifically for the sequel) were filmed at Germantown Academy, in neighboring Fort Washington; at Dorney Amusement Park, just north of the area in Allentown; at Independence National Historical Park in Philadelphia; along the Pennsylvania Turnpike; and, far from Ambler, at Eaves Movie Ranch in Santa Fe, New Mexico. (Courtesy of The Villa.)

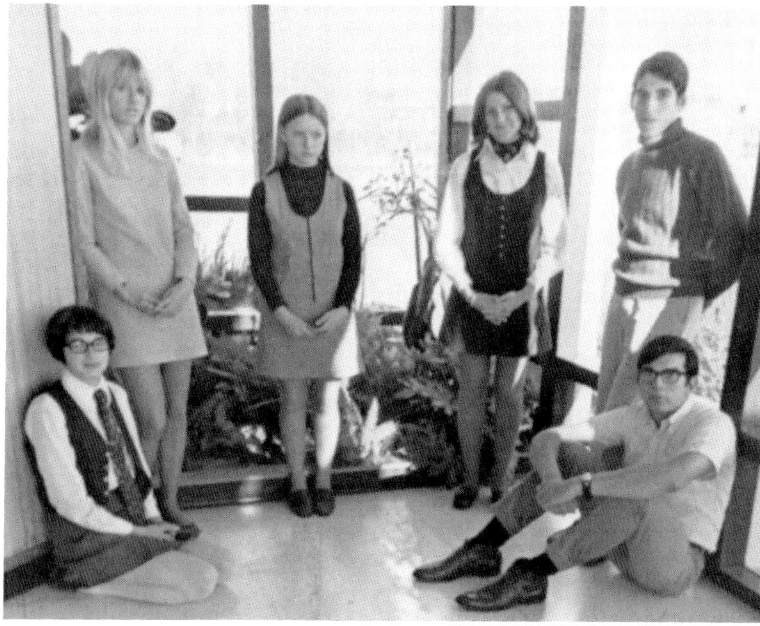

***thirtysomething*: Before & Beyond**

Wissahickon High School graduate Melanie Mayron (class of 1970) was a tireless, dedicated student. Not only did she participate in the band, choir, and the drama club, but she also played softball, managed the field hockey team, and was editor of the *Trojan Times*, the school newspaper, and *Aura*, the poetry magazine. In the above photograph, Mayron (far left) can be seen with the *Trojan Times* staff. Below (third row, fifth from left), she is with students from *Aura*. Mayron later gained fame as an Emmy Award–winning actress in the popular TV series *thirtysomething*. She also starred in the film *Harry and Tonto* and has become a movie and TV director and writer as well as a beauty entrepreneur, offering natural and organic skin care products formulated by her father, renowned chemist David Mayron. (Both, courtesy of Wissahickon High School.)

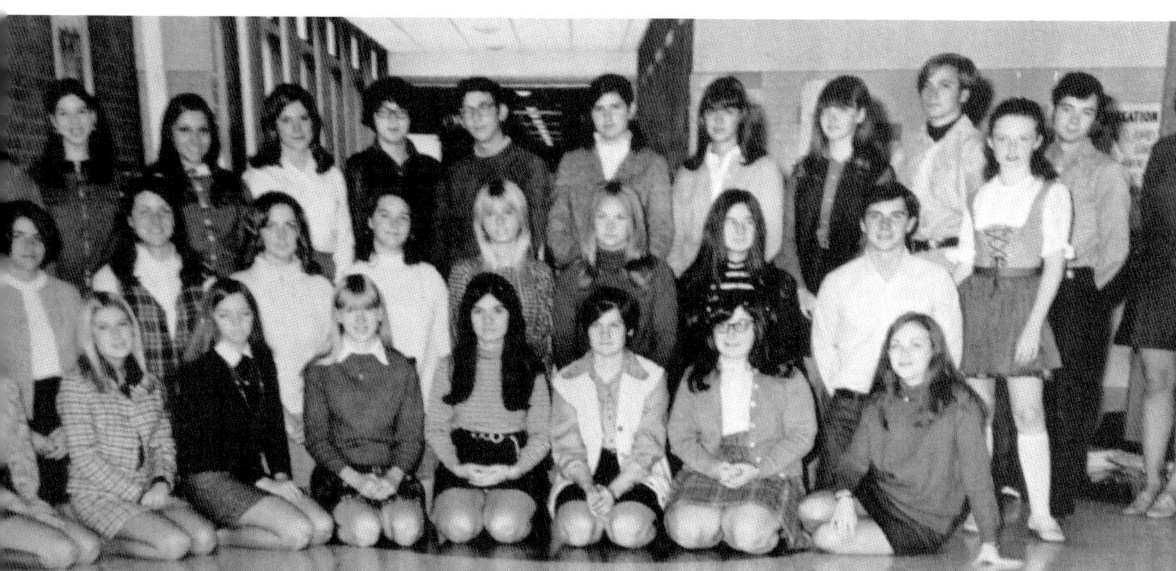

America's "Girlfriend"

Perusing Melanie Mayron's high school resume, one can easily trace the roots of her career trajectory. A triple-threat artist in the entertainment game, Mayron clearly gravitated toward the written word by assuming positions as editor of the newspaper and poetry magazine at Wissahickon High. She would later write the screenplays for two feature films—*Tribeca* and *Sticky Fingers*. Best-known as an actress, however, Mayron has scored leading and featured roles in nearly 50 TV series, TV movies, and full-length feature films. Her experience with her high school's drama club, choir, and band certainly did not hurt her aspiring career as an actress. Just four years after graduating from Wissahickon, Mayron landed one of her best roles, in the Oscar-nominated Art Carney film *Harry and Tonto* (1974). Within a year, she had appeared in her first TV movie, *Hustling*, and her first role in a TV series, *Medical Center*. Mayron would go on to star in Claudia Weill's *Girlfriends* (1978), for which she won the Best Actress Award at the Locarno Film Festival in Switzerland. For that film, she was also nominated for a British Academy Award for Best Newcomer. But the role for which she is most famous, and for which she won a prime-time Emmy in 1989, is for Best Supporting Actress in a Drama Series, *thirtysomething*.

Most recently, she has directed for and appeared on the TV series *Pretty Little Liars* (2012) and had a role in the TV movie *Breaking the Girls*. Mayron has also toured the country in musicals like *Godspell* and appeared on Broadway in Herb Gardner's *The Goodbye People* and Off Broadway in *Crossing Delancey*. But in recent years, Mayron has exercised much of her artistic talent behind the lens, directing more than 40 feature films (*The Babysitters Club* and *Slap Her She's French*), TV movies, episodes of TV and cable series (*Tell Me You Love Me*, *In Treatment*, *Switched at Birth*, and *The Fosters*), and documentaries. In 1998, she was nominated for a Directors Guild Award for Outstanding Directorial Achievement in Children's Programs for ABC's *Toothless*, starring Kirstie Alley and Lynn Redgrave.

In her spare time, the energetic actress/director and her father, David Mayron, have launched a new line of natural skin care products for babies and adults in their company Mayron's Goods. She writes weekly blogs on her website, mayronsgoods.com, and makes regular visits back to the Ambler area to see her family. (Courtesy of Melanie Mayron.)

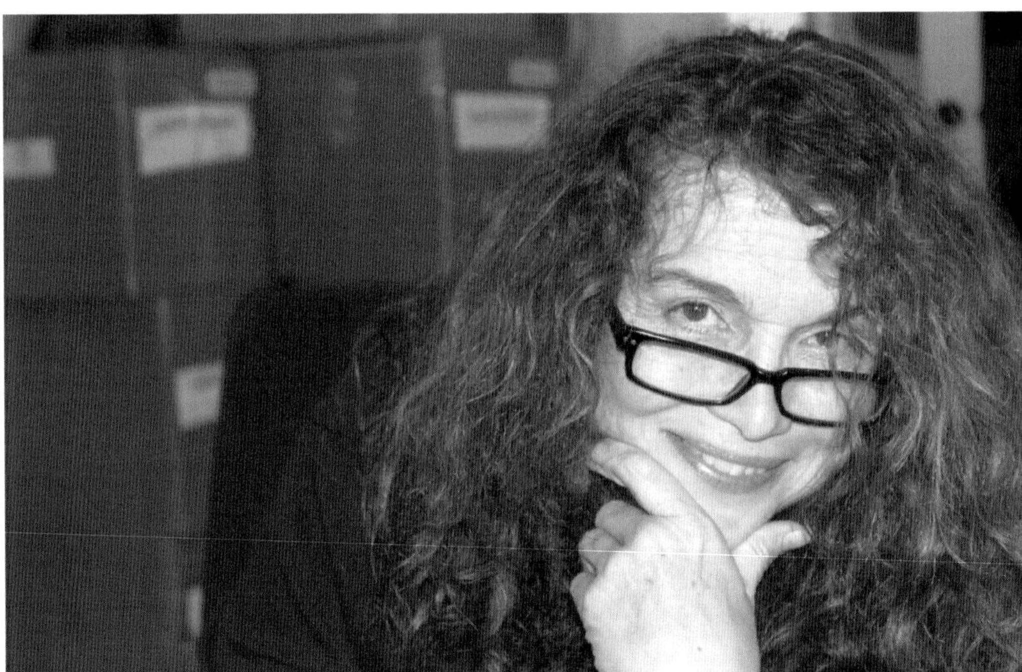

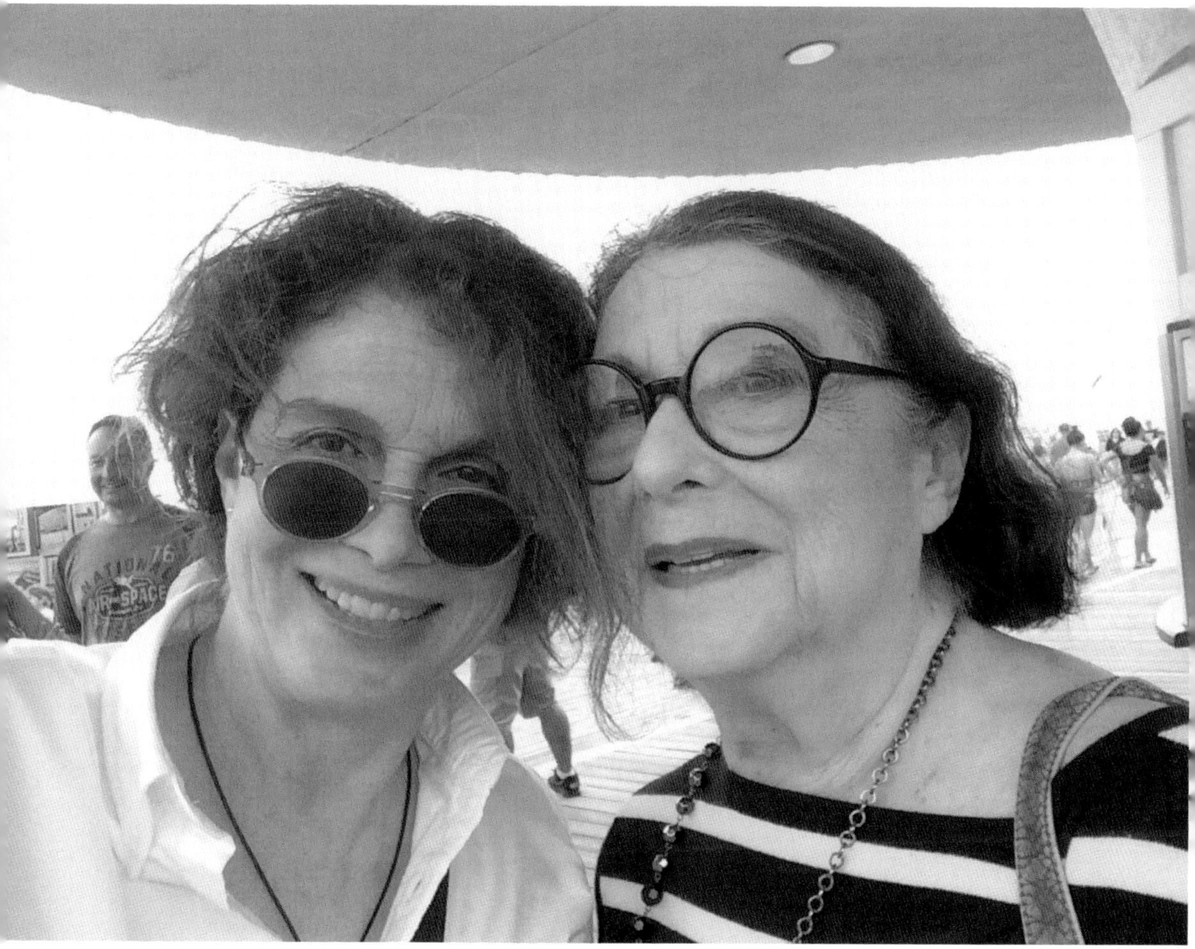

Melanie and Mom
During a visit with her family, Melanie Mayron and her mother, Norma Mayron, took a trip to the Jersey Shore. Melanie said that her mother always supported her children's career choices. Melanie's sister, Gale Mayron, owns a skin care company, and her brother, Sheldon Bruce Mayron, is an architectural renderer who owns Mayron Renderings in New York City. Norma's field was real estate. Working with agent James Gallagher at Century 21-Gallagher/Scanlon, Blue Bell, and, later, at Bristol Real Estate for 30 years, she won countless professional awards. (Courtesy of the Mayron family.)

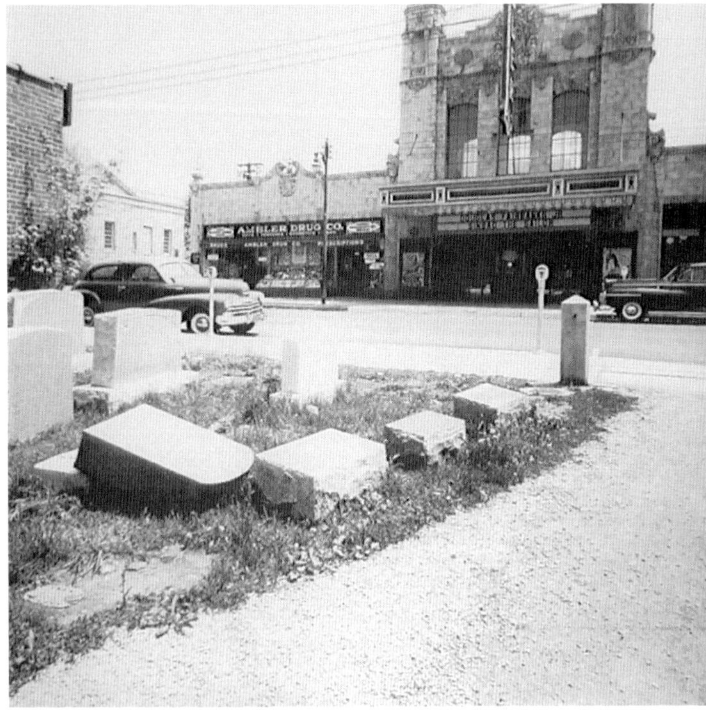

Sinbad's in Town

Here is a vintage look at the Ambler Theater, probably in 1947, judging from the marquee, announcing that Douglas Fairbanks Jr. is on the big screen in the Technicolor fantasy *Sinbad the Sailor*, also starring Maureen O'Hara, Anthony Quinn, and Walter Slezak. An old-fashioned Hollywood movie palace, the Ambler Theater, originally owned by Warner Bros., was the seat of entertainment in the borough of Ambler, drawing families, children, couples, and lonely people looking for an escape from the doldrums of daily life. (Courtesy of Ambler Theater.)

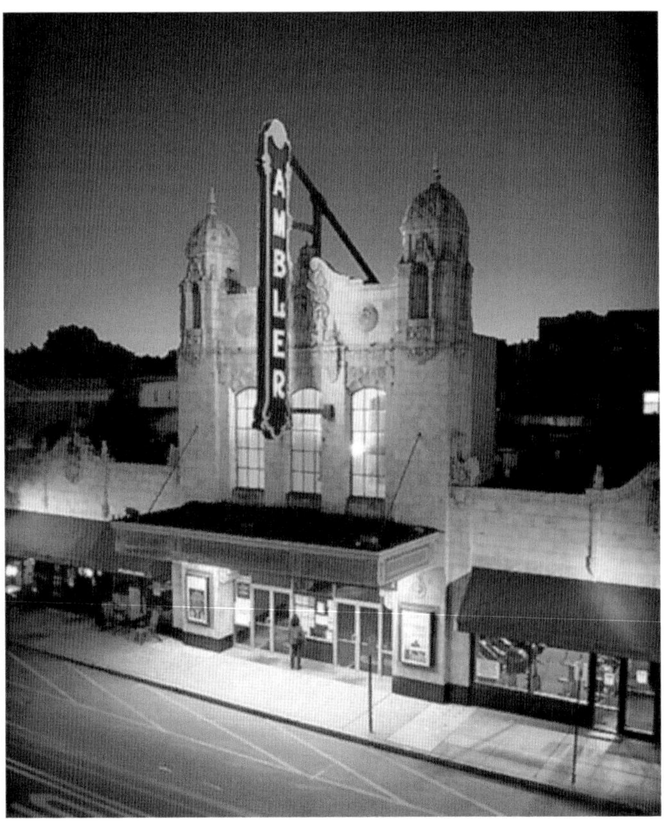

Looking Good

Here is the Ambler Theater in 2008, a year after the borough's popular cinema was again fully operational, offering art-house movie lovers, many of whom are subscribers, at least three or four feature-length film choices on three state-of-the-art screens on any given day. The theater has played a major role in the revitalization of Ambler. (Courtesy of Ambler Theater.)

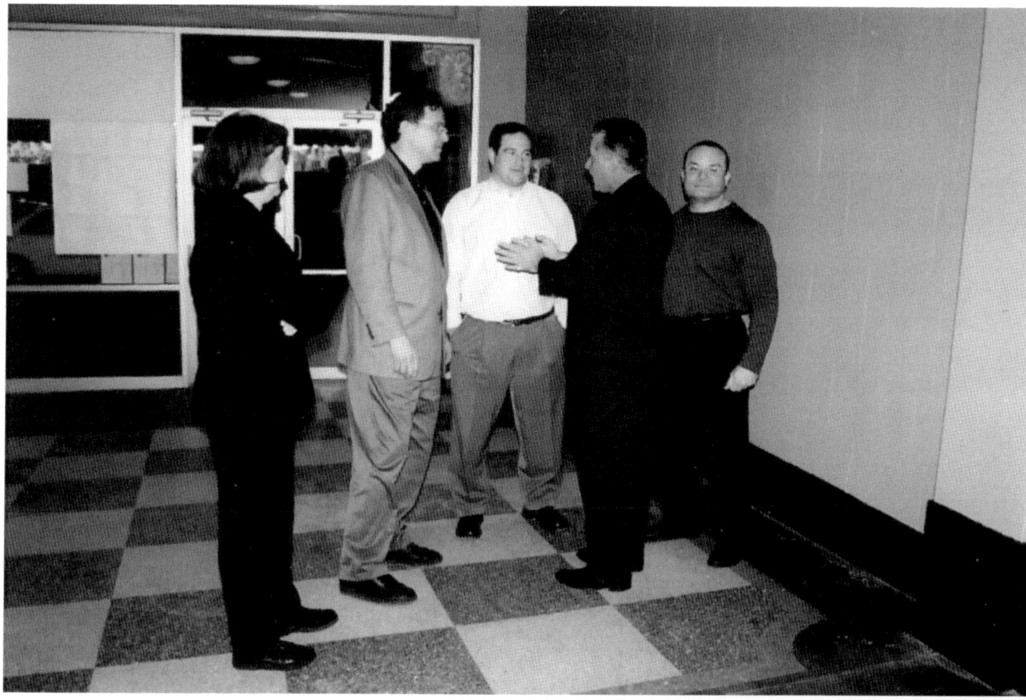

Grand Reopening Night
On February 28, 2003, after several years of renovations, the Ambler Theater reopened. Among the town notables attending the event were, from left to right, Bernadette Dougherty, Ambler Main Street Manager; John Toner, executive director, Ambler Theater; Mike Sloane, president, Ambler Theater; Ronnie Trombino, general manager of Ralph's of South Philadelphia restaurant, which was operating in the Ambler Theater building at that time; and Jimmy Rubino, owner/operator of Ralph's of South Philadelphia restaurant. At right are, from left to right, executive director John Toner and president Mike Sloane, who, working closely with Bernadette Dougherty and Mike Fink, put together a redevelopment plan that led to the popular theater's reopening. (Both, courtesy of Ambler Theater.)

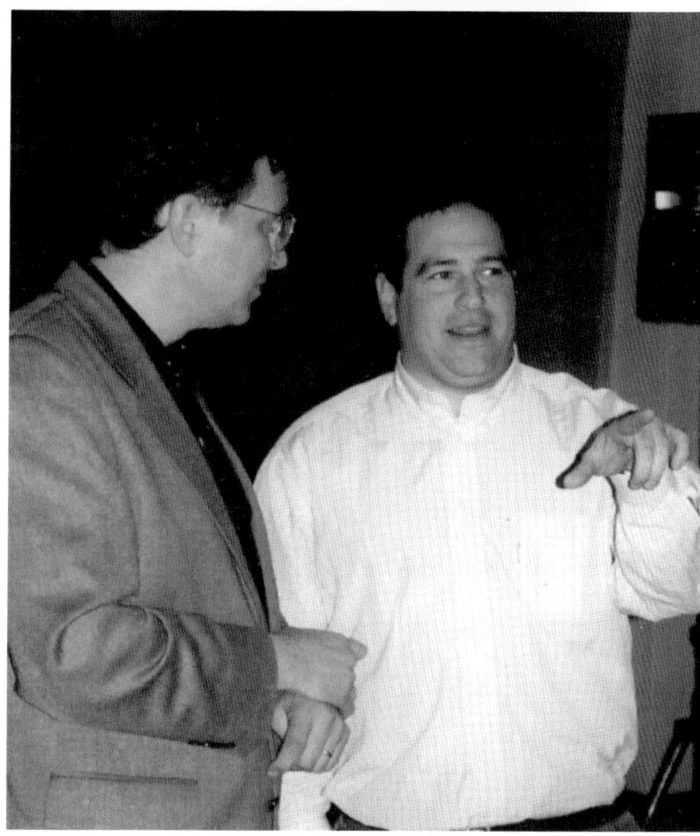

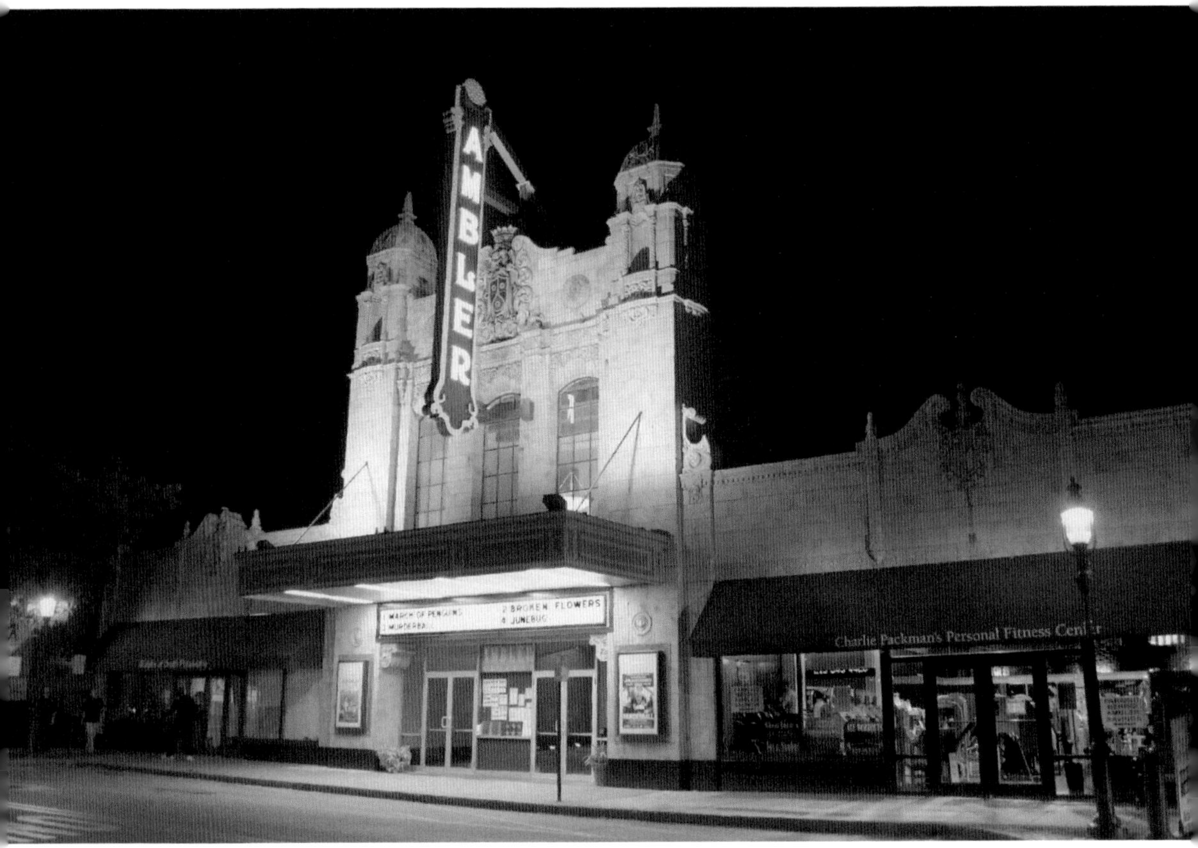

Restored Glory

Here, in all its restored glory, is the Ambler Theater in 2005. In 1928, Warner Bros. built it as a showcase for some of its greatest films; the first film screened there, on New Year's Eve 1928, was *Our Dancing Daughter*, starring Joan Crawford. The cinema was Ambler's entertainment centerpiece for decades. With its twin towers, grand terra-cotta facade, spacious lobbies, and ornate auditorium, the theater could accommodate 1,228 dreamy-eyed patrons who enjoyed watching first-run films there until the 1970s. By then, the theater was showing serious signs of wear, and was sold to a group that turned it into a Christian movie house until 1997, when it finally closed. It was in 1999, when John Toner joined with Bernadette Dougherty ("who struck the match to get it going," he said), Mike Sloane, and Mike Fink to begin plans to restore and reopen the theater. Toner had already opened the successful County Theater in Doylestown, when his Closely Watched Films Society decided it needed a bigger venue to show more than 20 films a year on 16-millimeter film. When Toner, a practicing attorney who loved theater and cinema, moved to nearby Gwynedd in 1999, he began to spend a lot of time in Ambler and realized the potential the shuttered Ambler Theater held. So in 2001, after two years of fundraising and planning, the hard physical work began. The theater reopened to great fanfare in February 2003, with one screen. By 2007, the three-screen cinema was ready to rock. Along with Act II Playhouse, it has given Amblerites and visitors from miles around plenty of reason to return in force to Butler Avenue to enjoy an evening out. Toner today is the head of the Renew Theater group, which also owns and operates the County Theater in Doylestown, the Hiway Theater in Jenkintown, and the newly built Princeton Garden Theatre in Princeton, New Jersey. (Courtesy of Ambler Theater.)

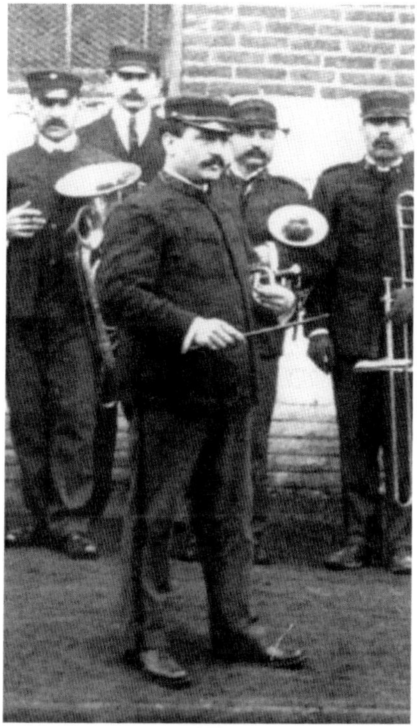

Band Leader

At the turn of the 19th century, entertainment at the town bandstand by the railroad tracks was quite popular. One day, as well-known conductor Frank Palumbo was leading the Ambler Band, a stranger in town was creating a disturbance by imitating train whistles and such—until Police Chief Dick Ford intervened, offering the offender 40 days in jail or a ticket out of town. Naturally, he chose the latter. (Photograph from the Newt Howard Collection; courtesy of Buck Amey.)

By the Old Op'ry

Richard V. "Doc" Mattison, Ambler's "first citizen," brought not only employment and housing opportunities but also culture to the newly incorporated borough, building the town's first opera house in 1890. It was there that popular theatrical productions and concerts took place, including George S. Fister's fife-and-drum corps. (Photograph from the Newt Howard Collection; courtesy of Buck Amey.)

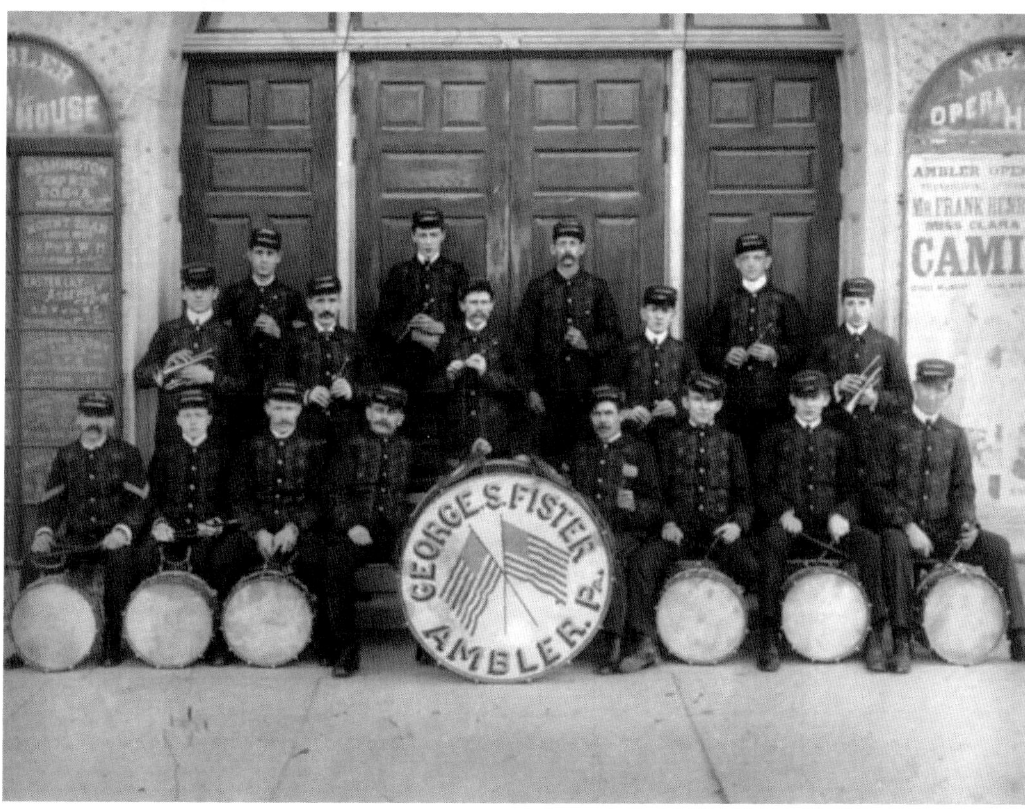

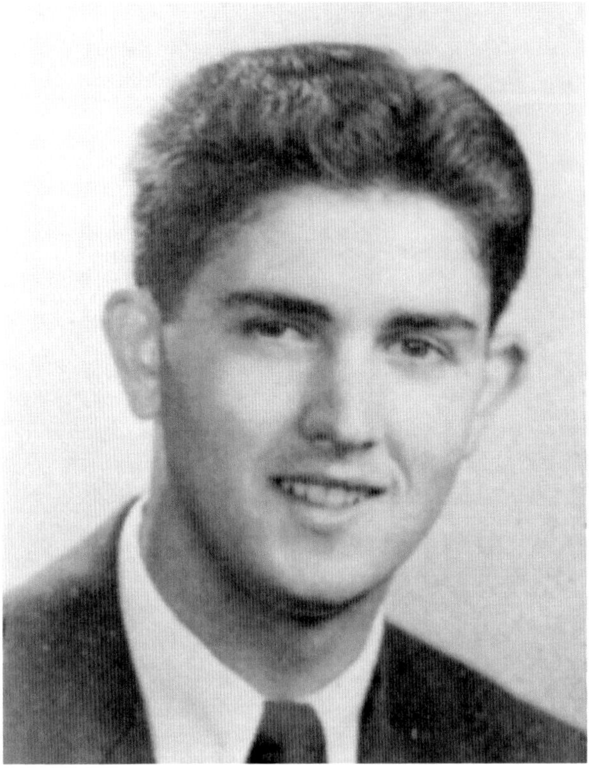

Underwater Photographer

Recognized as one of the world's leading underwater photographers, Ambler's Frank Pugliese has produced many films for civic, industrial, and scientific use. Among the most memorable were those he produced as an aquanaut, camera man, and director for several space, oceanographic, and environmental projects, one of which was a simulation of living in a space capsule. Pugliese was also an International Film Festival award winner. (Courtesy of Wissahickon High School.)

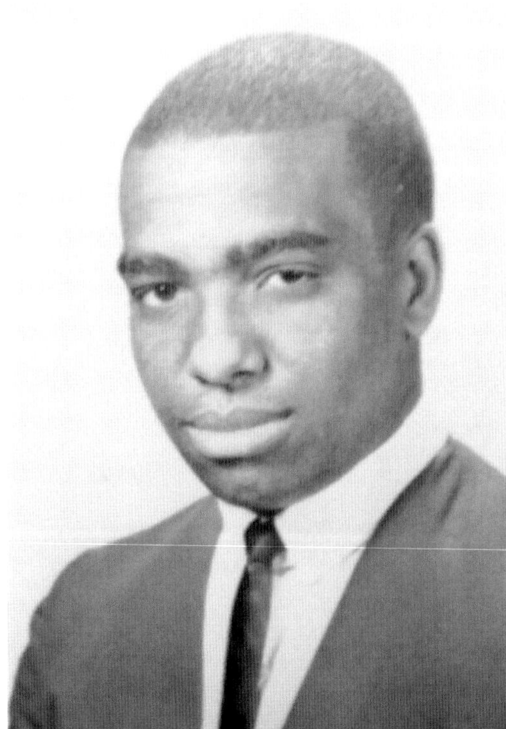

From Jazz to Jesus

Although this music-minded graduate of Wissahickon High School's class of 1964 got his start as a jazz drummer, eventually playing with the likes of Gene Krupa, Sammy Davis Jr., Liza Minnelli, Patti LaBelle, and Dave Brubeck, Phillip Henry is more likely to be remembered for his successful founding of the "Bridging the Gap between Addiction and the Church" program as a deacon at Yardley's First Baptist Church. (Courtesy of Wissahickon High School.)

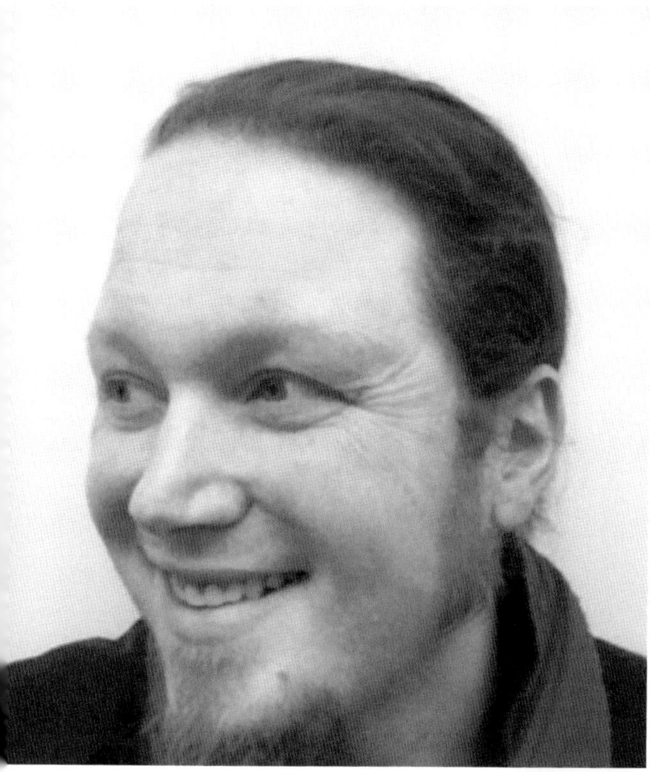

Ambler's Music Man
From Beethoven to the Beatles, his style is a distinctive amalgam of many harmonic forms—classical, jazz, soul, rock—all of which he lovingly employs in his courses in music theory, composition, and performance at Wissahickon High School. Teacher, composer, performer, and recording artist, pianist/vocalist John Conahan says that music begets everything he does, from playing jazz and improvisational music in Big Apple cafés to recently composing classical pieces with the late Maestro Lorin Maazel. (Courtesy of John Conahan.)

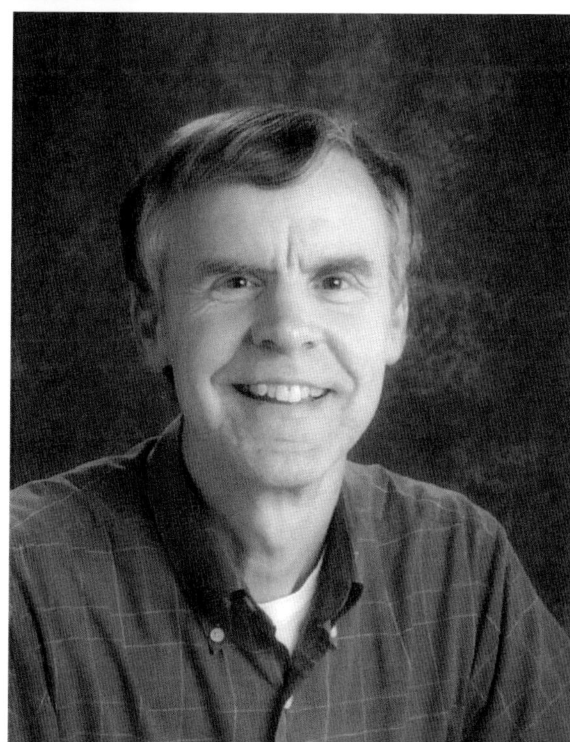

Musician/Environmentalist
Passionate about music, the library, and the environment, David Morgan typifies Ambler's community spirit. Concertmaster for the Ambler Symphony (and freelancer with regional orchestras), coffeehouse organizer for the Church of the Brethren, and longtime elementary, middle, and high school music teacher for the Wissahickon School District, Morgan has also been a spokesperson for the Wissahickon Valley Public Library. He also works on Open Space grants, tree plantings, and other community environmental projects. (Courtesy of David Morgan.)

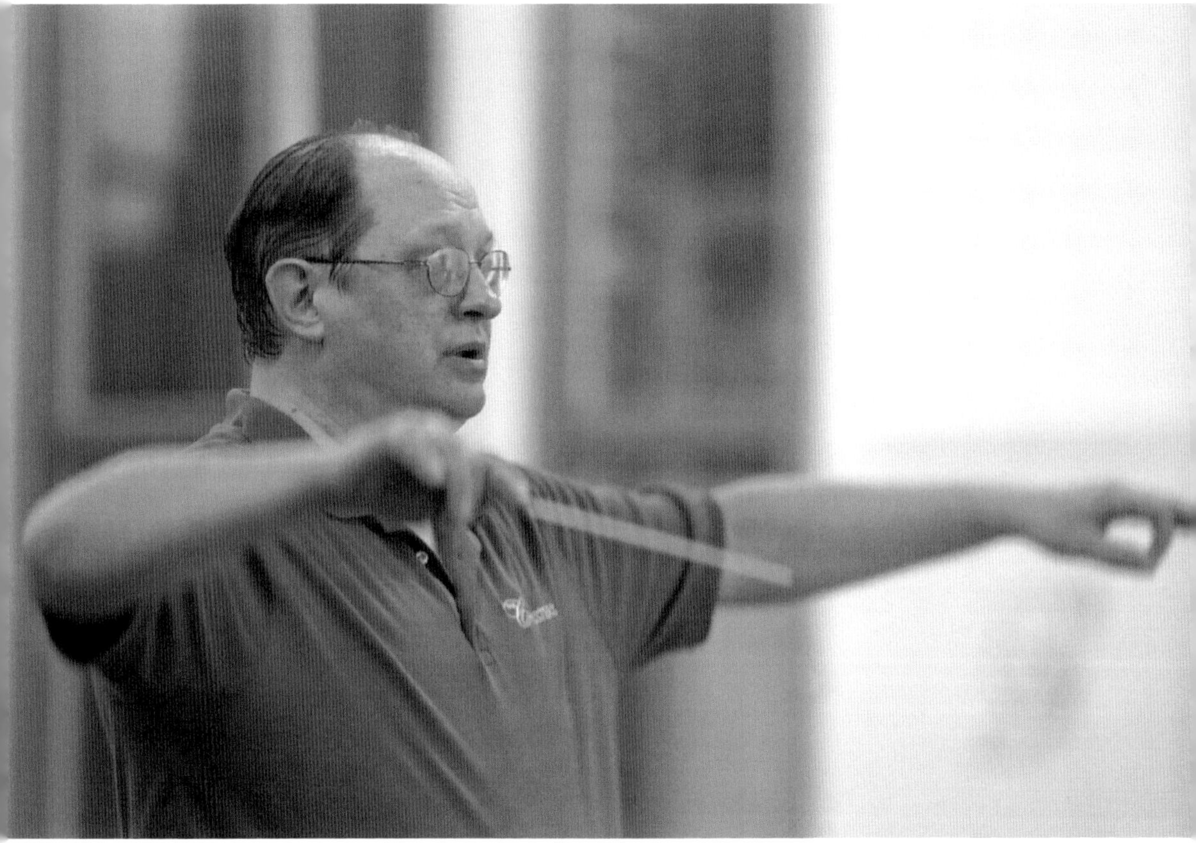

Heavenly Voices
By day, he practices law in Montgomeryville, but David Spitko's real passion is choral music. In 1978, the longtime pianist, choral singer, and theater lover was named organist/choir director at Upper Dublin Lutheran Church; at the same time, he founded The Choristers of Upper Dublin, to prepare and perform undeservedly underperformed classical choral works in the community, which includes Ambler, where he grew up. He continues as The Choristers' artistic director to this day. (Courtesy of David Spitko.)

Music Ministers

Pianist, cellist, composer, and arranger Jim Holton and flutist Cindy LeBlanc, partners for 19 years, serve as music ministers at St. John's Lutheran Church of Ambler, leading the congregation in jazz vespers the first Sunday of every month. Holton's obsession with music has led to his performing and recording with such jazz greats such as Tyrone Brown, Orrin Evans, Larry McKenna, Bootsie Barnes, Clifford Adams, and John Swana. (Courtesy of Jim Holton.)

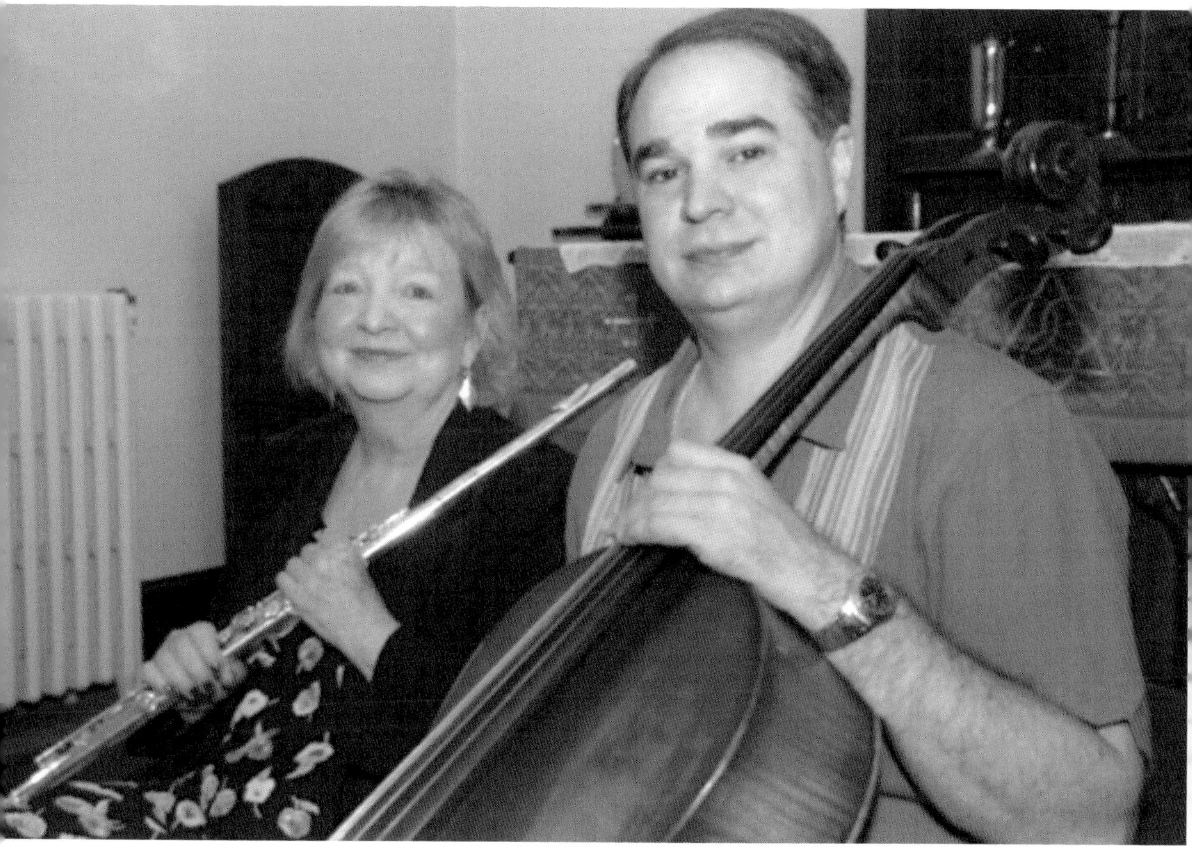

Music of the Spirit

Bill Bloom still remembers the now defunct Temple Ambler Music Fair, which he frequented years ago. Today, ironically, the pianist/composer graces the clubs of Ambler with his musical stylings and rich baritone. But as his musical breadth ranges from opera/classical to jazz and pop, Bloom also performs with the Philadelphia Boys Choir and Chorale. Ordained by the Interfaith Ministry, he takes special pride in his role as a mentor to these young singers because he is also the minister of music at United Christian Church in Levittown, Pennsylvania. As a staff writer and producer for Philadelphia International Records, home of "The Sound of Philadelphia," Bloom penned and produced, with Frankie Smith, the seminal platinum-selling hip-hop recording "Double Dutch Bus." He says he straddles his two careers easily because his intention is simply to do his best with both his music and the church. (Both, courtesy of Bill Bloom.)

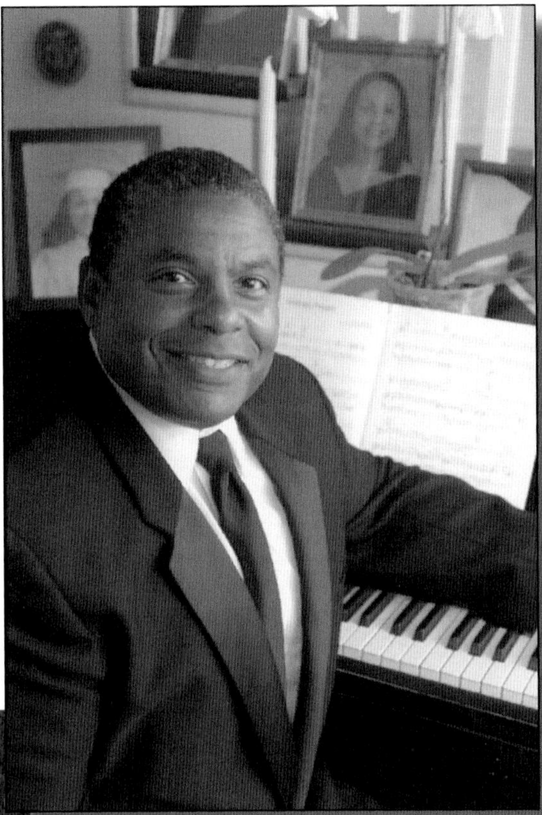

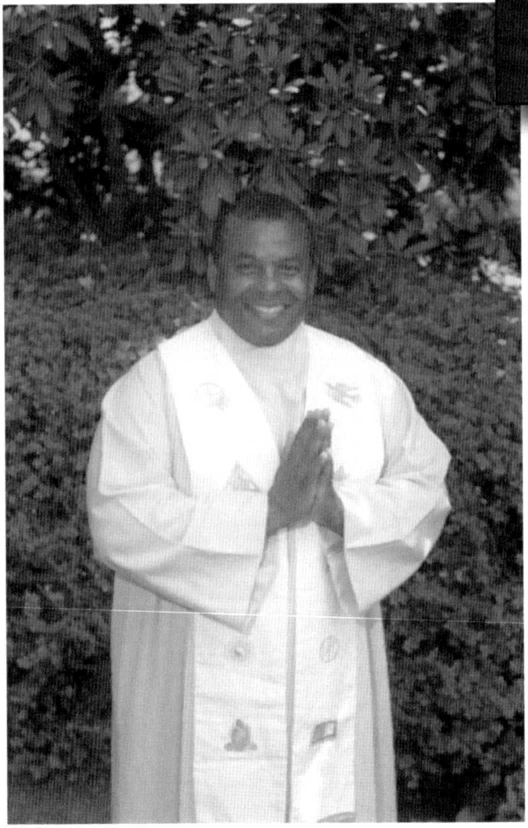

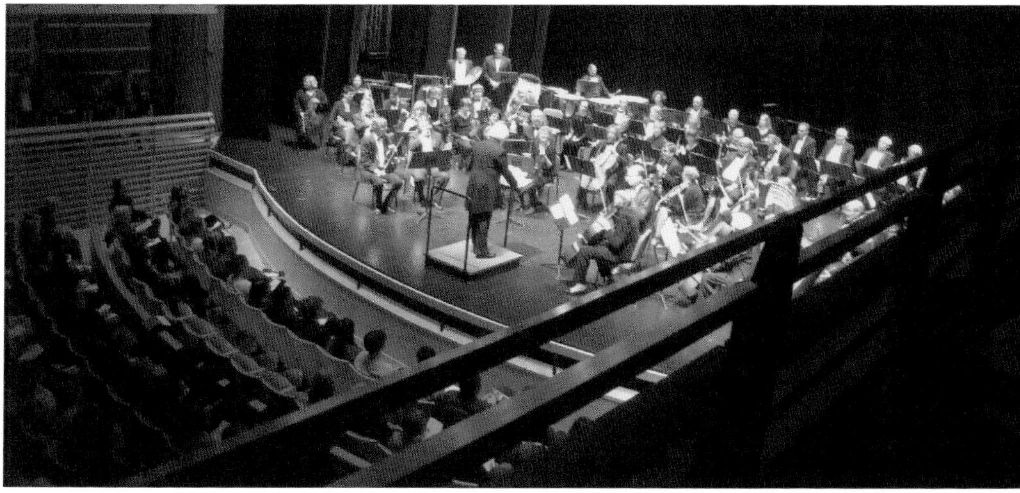

Classical Gas and Jack Moore

With enough energy to daunt a youngster half his age, Jack Moore divides his days (and nights) between his 30-year career in radio—he is the classical music host (since 1997) and program director (since 2002) of WRTI, Temple University's Public Radio Network—and music. The violist, who majored in music at Glassboro State College (now Rowan University), has been the music director of the Ambler Symphony Orchestra since 1995, the principal conductor of the Orchestra Society of Philadelphia since 1997, music director of the Olney Symphony Orchestra, and has made guest appearances with other orchestras in the Philadelphia area, including the Bucks County Symphony, Rose Tree Pops, and Bux-Mont Chamber Orchestra. Abroad, he has conducted the acclaimed Bohuslav Martinu Philharmonic in the Czech Republic and served, in the 2001–2002 season, as principal guest conductor of the Vidin State Philharmonic in Bulgaria. (Both, courtesy of Jack Moore.)

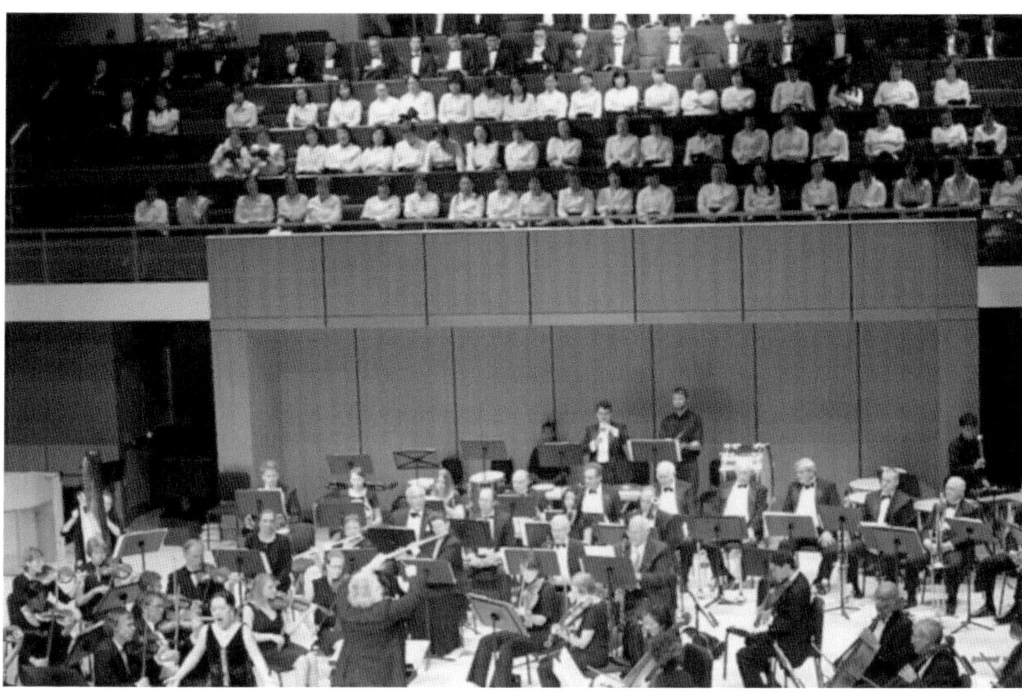

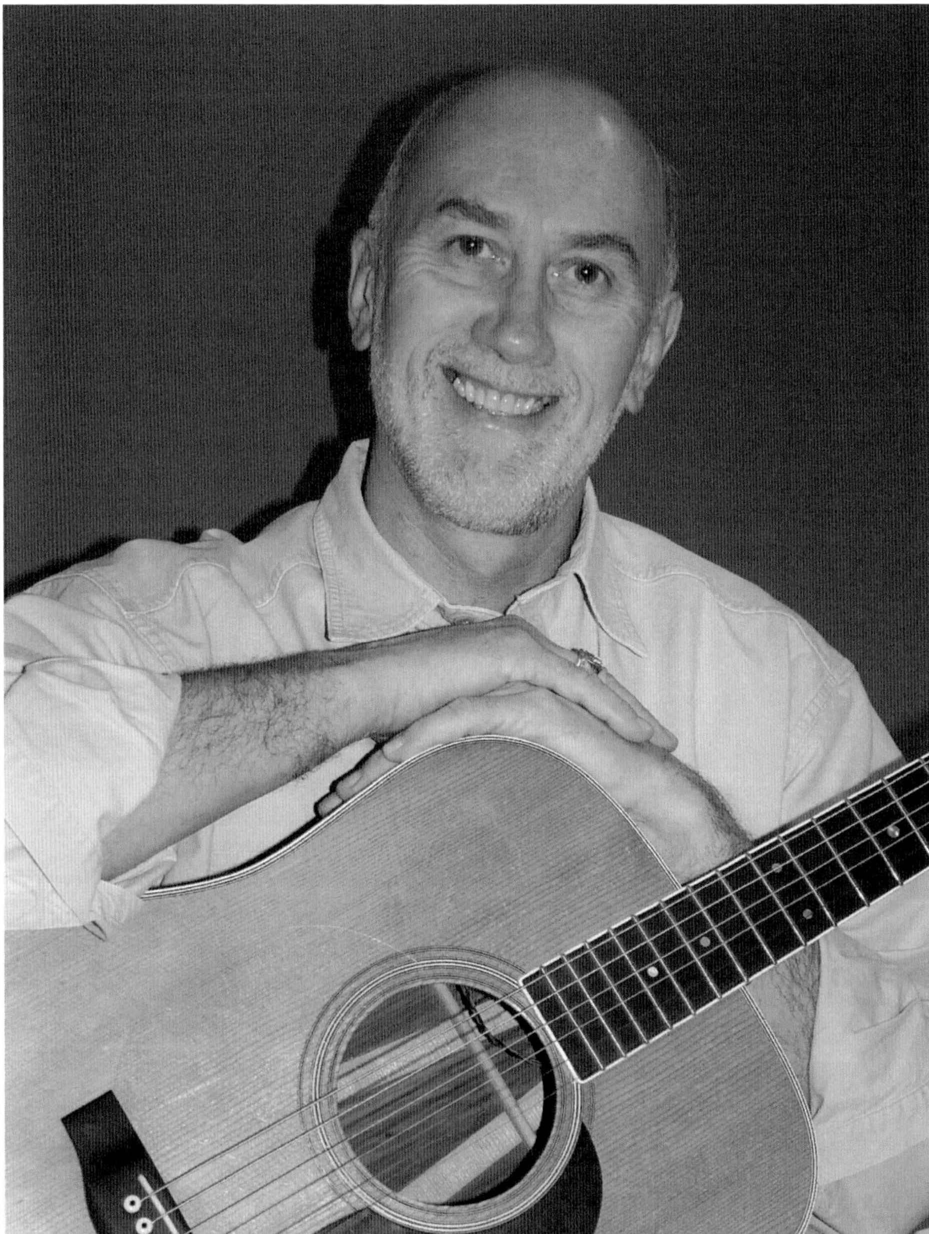

Irish Troubadour

Gregarious troubadour Gerry Timlin brought Celtic music to Ambler when he opened the Shanachie Irish Pub & Restaurant in October 2004. He went onstage with Tommy Kane, his singing partner of four decades, singing at the Capitol Building in Washington on March 14, 2014. Timlin and Kane had been invited to perform as part of the Friends of Ireland luncheon for an audience that included Pres. Barack Obama, Vice Pres. Joe Biden, Prime Minister Enda Kenney of Ireland, and some ministers from his native Northern Ireland. It was a heady moment for the folk-musician from County Tyrone, who still leads tours to the Emerald Isle every year. The Shanachie is now closed, but Timlin continues to perform at concerts and music festivals throughout the United States and around the world. (Courtesy of Gerry Timlin.)

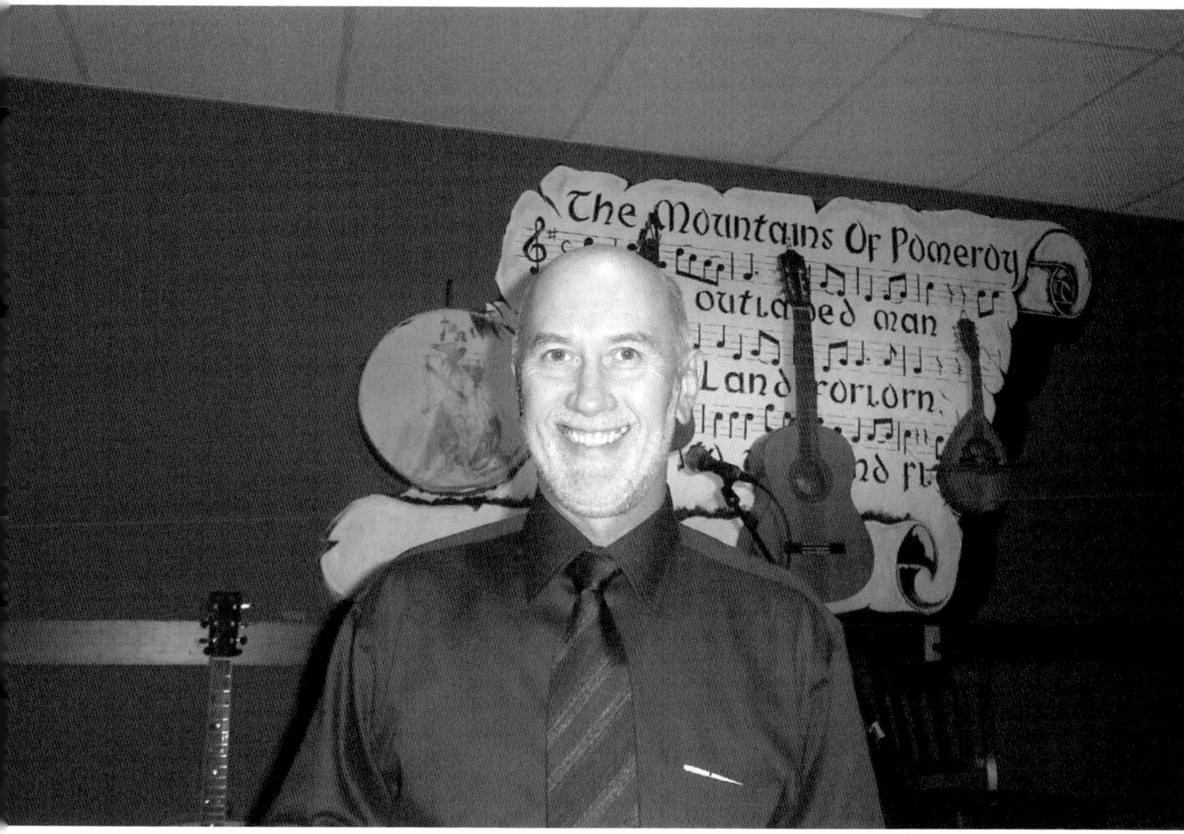

Gerry at Shanachie

The Shanachie, which means storyteller in Irish, brought a new wave of excitement to Butler Avenue, Ambler's main street. With Act II Playhouse already established in its first five years of operation and the Ambler Cinema fully functioning again, drawing people in from miles around to see superb art-house movie fare, the Shanachie provided yet another boost for Ambler's music lovers. Co-owner Gerry Timlin (his business partner was attorney Ed Egan) offered not only the best in underrated Irish cuisine but also the opportunity, sometimes several times a week, to hear live Irish music performed on the restaurant's cozy stage. Far from being a neighborhood tavern, the Shanachie proved to be a magnet for families. The convivial atmosphere, fired by Timlin's folksy warmth and Egan's relaxed hand at the helm, made the Shanachie the musical center of town. Timlin, sometimes with his pal Tom Kane, and other famous or otherwise talented Celtic musicians made their way to Ambler to entertain the townies. And during Ambler's many street fairs and festivals, Timlin was often the lead performer and willing borough booster. He still performs in concerts and festivals around the world. (Photograph by Eve M. Quattrone.)

Sustainable Rock

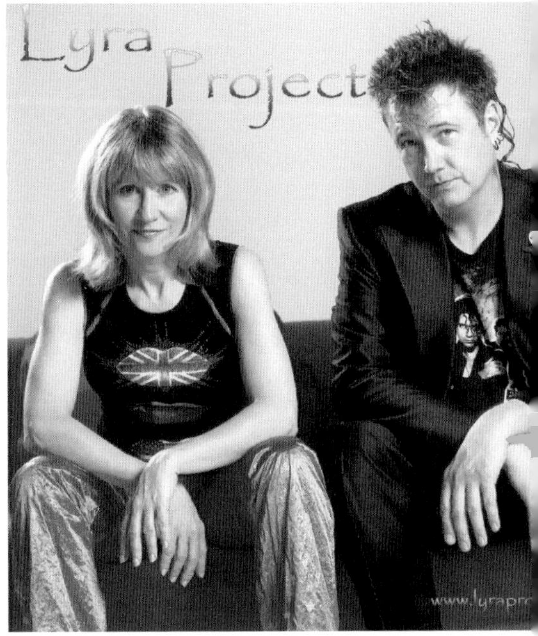

Integrating their twin passions for music and sustainability, Ambler's indie-music rock stars Rick Denzien and Debra Lee, seen here as the Lyra Project, have made an impact. Their meticulously green, lovingly handcrafted Slot-1 production studio provides tracklaying, recording, and postproduction services for regional and national recording artists. Rick and Debra offer music workshops and house concerts (even electric car tours) all across the country, where they raise the issues of sustainable living in their words and music. While Rick works with the borough of Ambler to seek suitable sites for solar energy panels, Debra runs a popular music school at their home and serves as regional workshop coordinator for the Nashville Songwriters Association International. Below, they are performing at the 2014 Ambler Music & Arts Festival with cellist Michael Ronstadt. (Right, photograph by Lauren Lyons Photography; below, photograph by Eve M. Quattrone.)

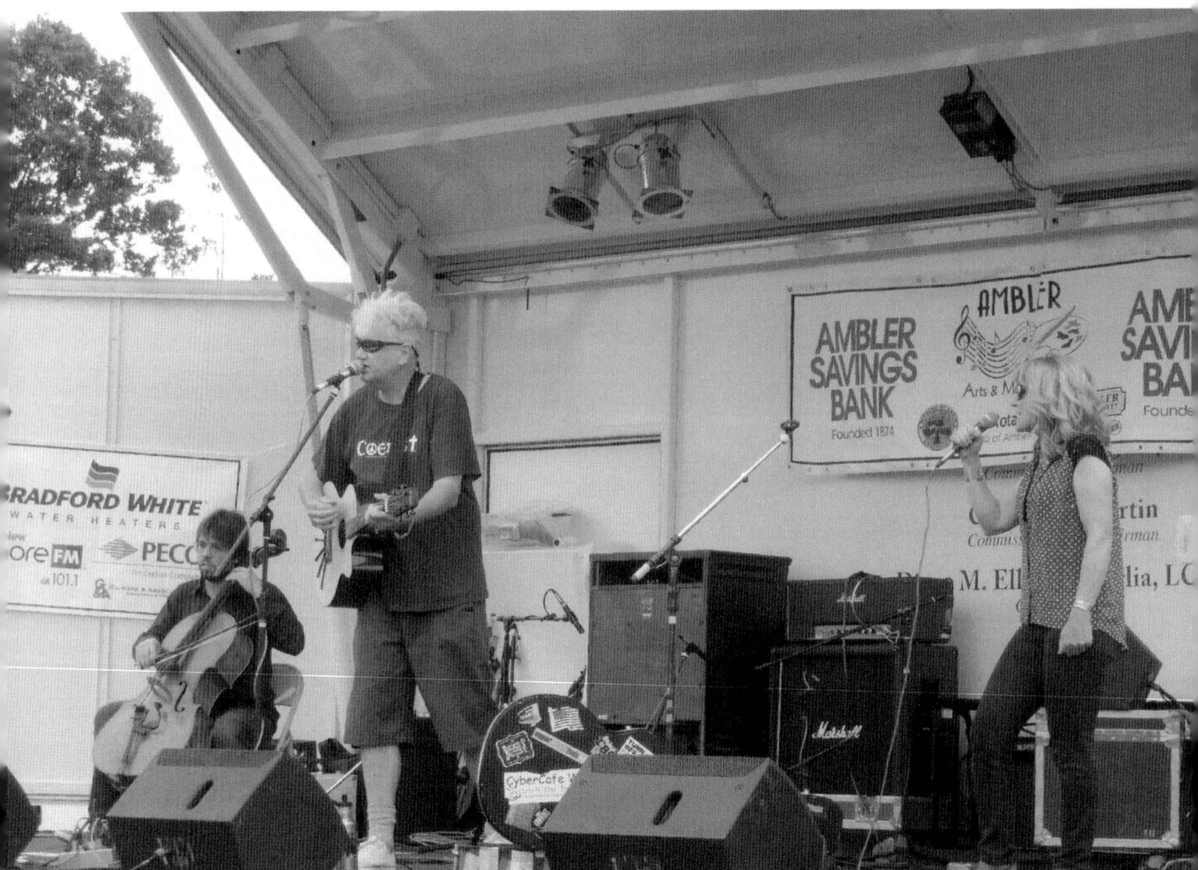

Vocal Health

Taking a short break from their music are, from left to right, Lisa Popeil, Debra Lee, and Rick Denzien. Popeil, the half-sister of Ron Popeil (so-called "King of the Infomercials" and creator of the Veg-O-Matic—the original model is now in the Smithsonian), is one of the country's foremost researchers on vocal health for singers. In that role, she has visited Ambler several times to teach master class vocal workshops, bringing in talented vocalists from across the East Coast. (Courtesy of Rick Denzien.)

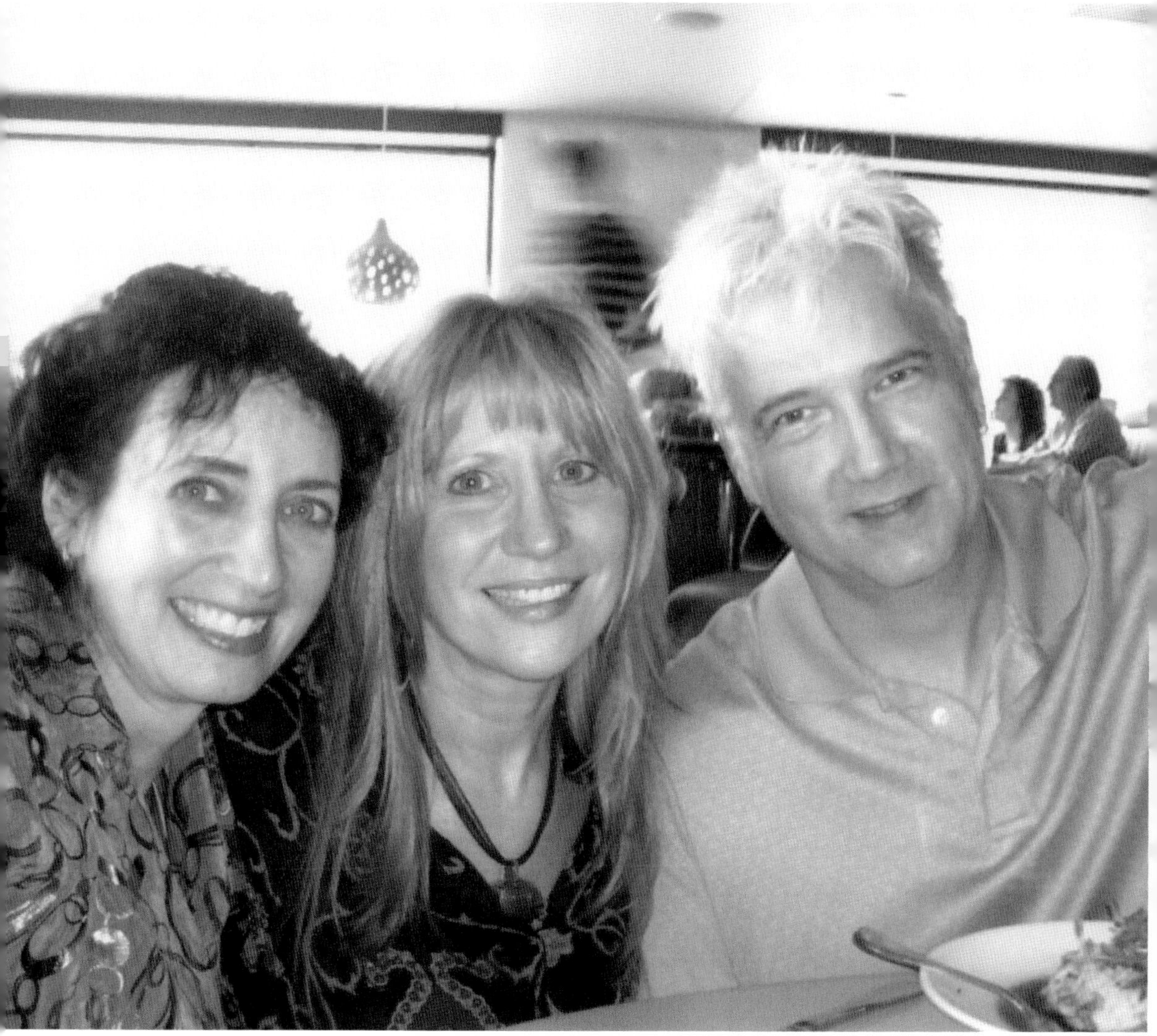

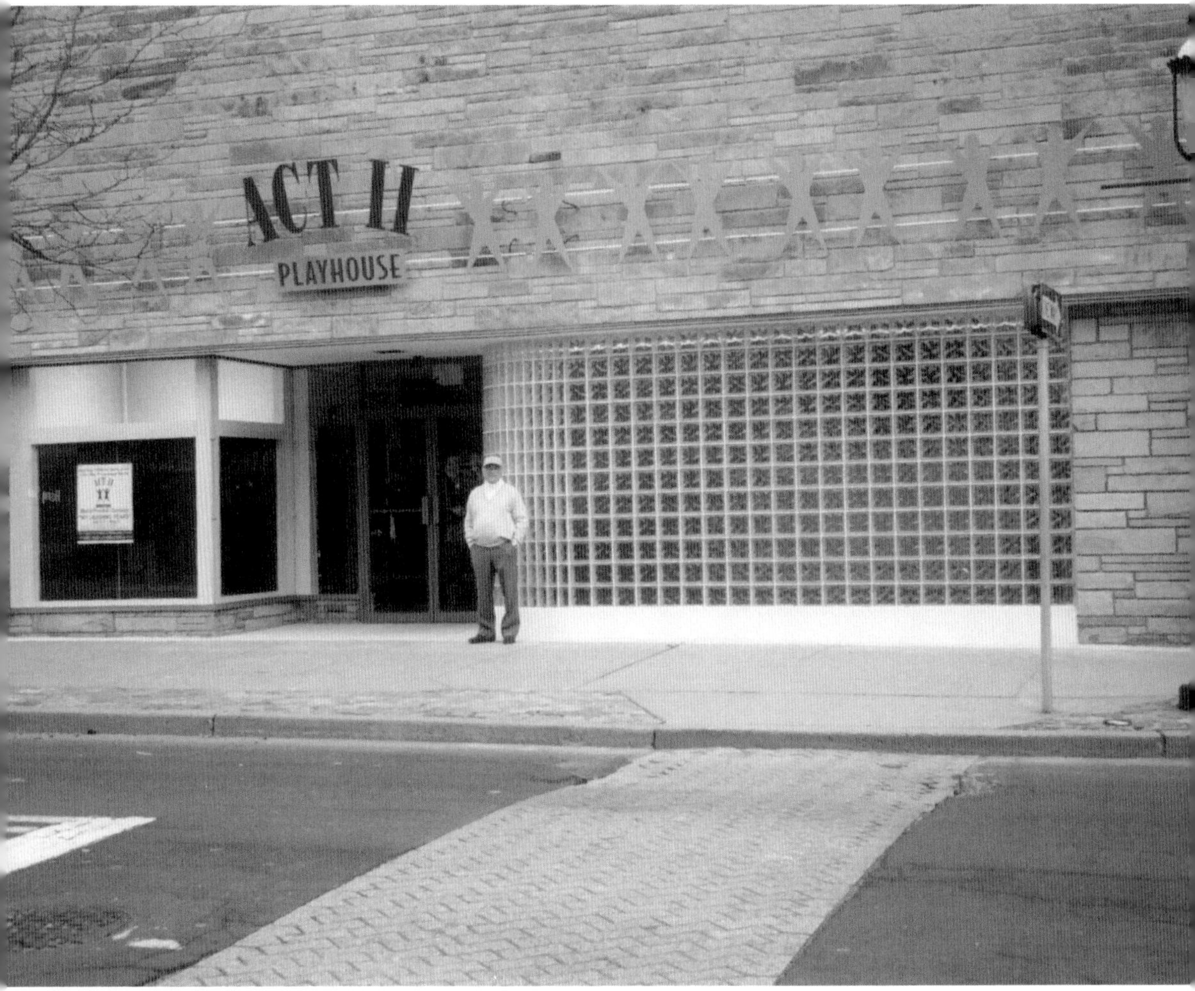

Opening Night
On opening night, April 21, 1999, founder and artistic director Stephen D. Blumenthal stands before the entrance to Ambler's Act II Playhouse, the first professional theater to be built in Montgomery County. The theater's initial production was the premiere of *My Laughing Years*, a comedy by William Missouri Downs about four elderly New Yorkers facing eviction from their run-down apartment building. This historic occasion nearly got derailed when Blumenthal and associate artistic director Alan Blumenthal (strangely enough, no relation) discovered that the cleaning crew had been a bit too ambitious. Because they had not been informed that the set would be strewn with graffiti and trash, they cleaned up the stage as well as the auditorium. Before panic could set in, the Blumenthals quickly rounded up some suitable trash and re-created the set just minutes before the audience arrived. Blumenthal is still on the board of the playhouse, with Ambler attorney Berne Siergiej serving as its president. Since Steve Blumenthal has retired from his post as producing artistic director, the playhouse has been fortunate to have the services of Bud Martin, who brought in actors from New York City as well as productions rarely performed in this area, and Tony Braithwaite, a staple on the Philadelphia stage, who has fully realized Blumenthal's vision. Blumenthal has said, "The theater can't be dark too often." Today, in addition to five or six productions per year, Braithwaite's Act II Playhouse also offers cabaret, comedy nights, musical performances, children's shows, holiday shows, and other productions that assure that the bright lights seldom go dark. (Courtesy of Stephen D. Blumenthal and Act II Playhouse.)

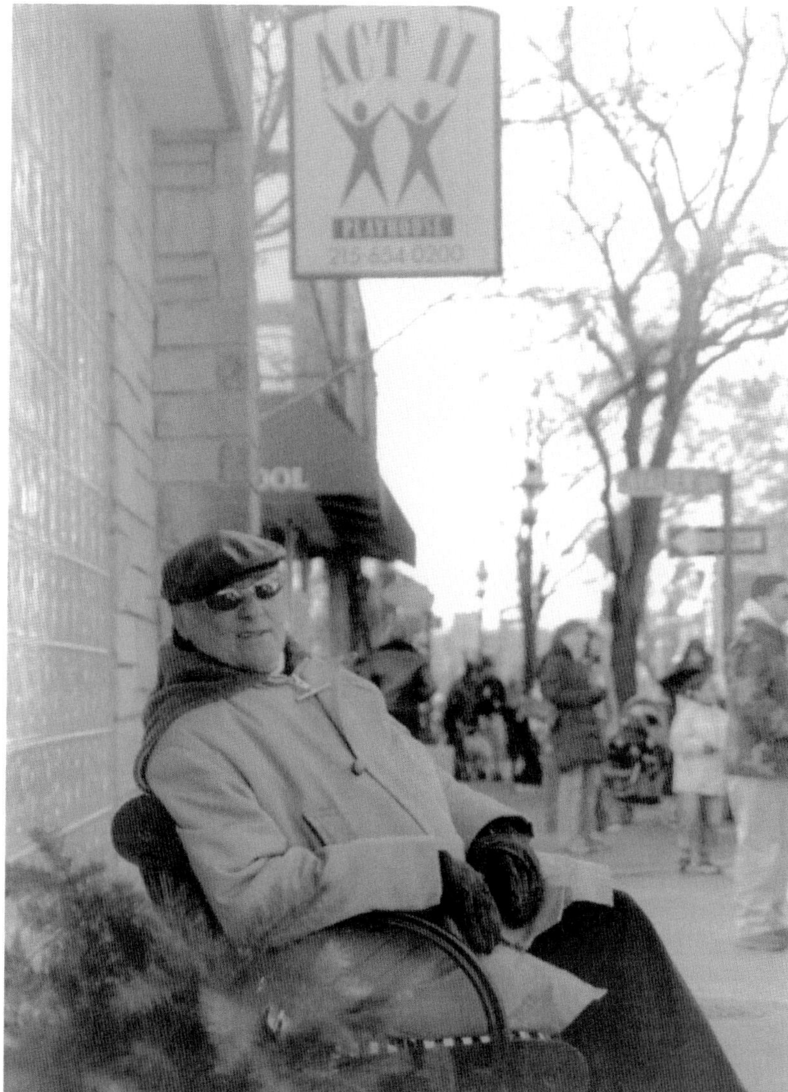

Blumenthal's Second Act

As Act II Playhouse sparked the revival of Butler Avenue, Ambler's main street, Blumenthal sits in a calmer mood with plenty of passersby in view in 2001. When asked how he got his start in theater, Blumenthal laughed. He said he was in his mid-20s when he heard that an actor was needed to play "the husband" in a production of *The Mousetrap* at Cheltenham Playhouse. He had never taken an acting course and had never been in a play before, but Blumenthal was hooked. Since then, he has performed in various local theaters. In 1992, he decided to form his own theater company, the Actors' Community Theatre, which performed at Gwynedd Mercy University and at Abington Friends. By 1998, Ambler's real estate community knew that he was looking for a theater site and that the building housing a former karate studio was up for sale. Looking at its gorgeous floor, Blumenthal knew exactly where his stage would go. So the deal was struck, and Ambler has benefitted from the transaction ever since. Since its opening in 1999, Act II Playhouse has received more than 30 Barrymore nominations (the standard for excellence in the Philadelphia-area theater scene) and earned six and continues to be a beacon for rejuvenated Ambler. (Courtesy of Stephen D. Blumenthal.)

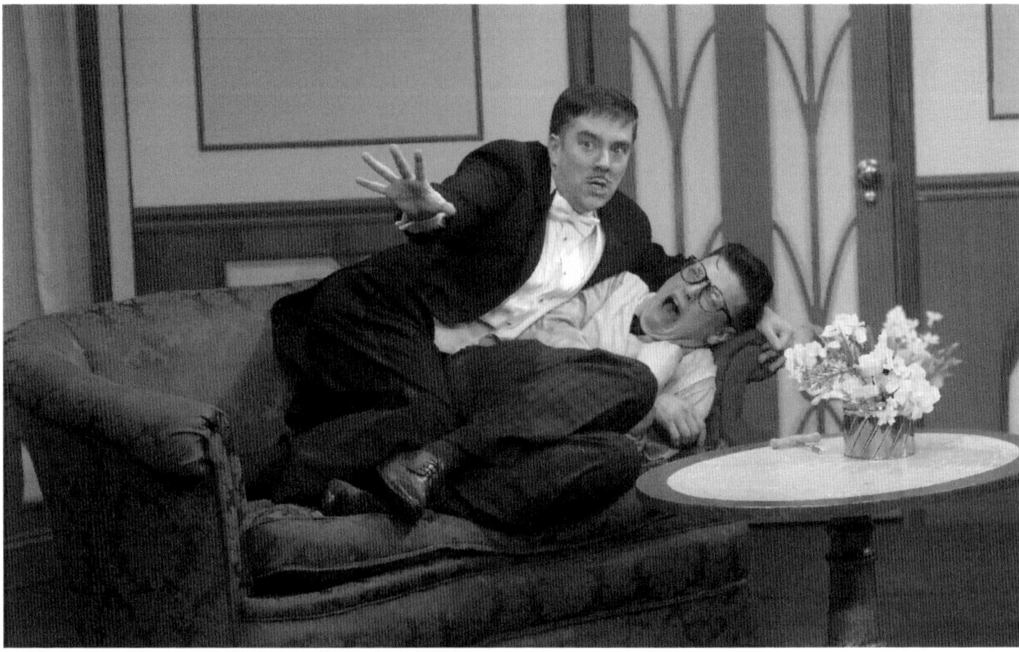

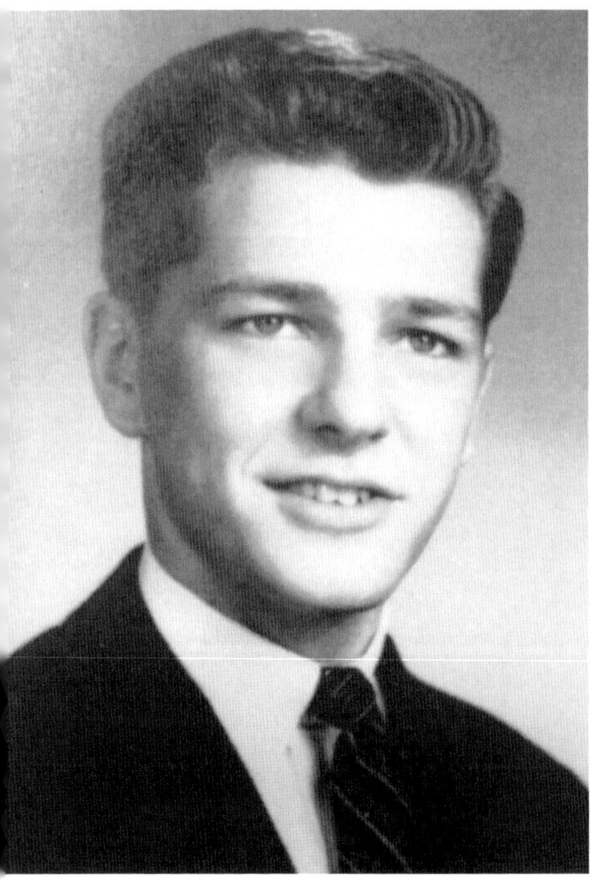

Comic Mayhem

Pictured here, Tony Braithwaite (with hand outstretched), the present producing artistic director of Act II Playhouse, and Michael Doherty (in glasses) create comic mayhem in the Act II Playhouse production of *Lend Me a Tenor*, which ran at Ambler's popular professional theater during the 2012–2013 season. Braithwaite, one of the Philadelphia area's most acclaimed actors, is also a playwright and a master of the one-man show, like *Didn't Your Father Have This Talk with You?* (Photograph by Bill D'Agostino; courtesy Act II Playhouse.)

International Correspondent

A high school sports star as well as a member of the *Trojan Times* newspaper, Ronald Miller (class of 1959) went on to make quite a name for himself as an ABC-TV international correspondent. He covered the fall of Saigon in 1971, investigated POWs and MIAs for *Nightline* and *20/20*, and, in 1985, left the air to become a fine-dining restaurateur in Union Pier, Michigan. (Courtesy of Wissahickon High School.)

Ambler-Maui Connection

Frustrated working as an illustrator/freelance artist for various advertisers, book publishers, magazines, and interior decorators in Philadelphia, Ambler's Eddie Flotte (pronounced "float") began "painting old abandoned buildings and neighborhood characters," the kind of art he found much more natural and rewarding. When people began buying his paintings, he felt he could exercise his talent anywhere. So he decided (almost on a whim) to move to Maui, where he still lives and paints for a living today. On his many weeklong or summerlong return visits to Ambler, Flotte started painting architectural scenes and details, mostly buildings with character and spirit, places whose imagery often brought tears of remembrance and joy to his old friends and neighbors when they saw them. (Courtesy of Eddie Flotte.)

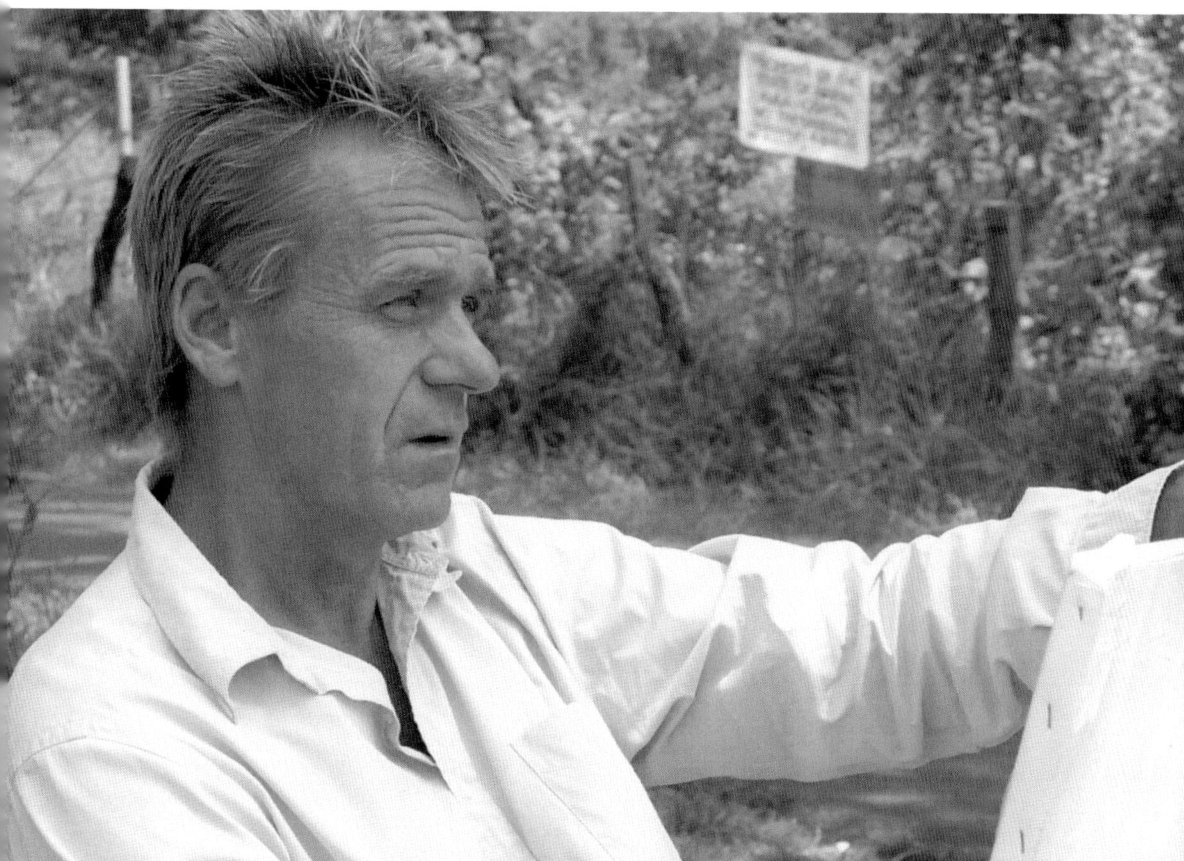

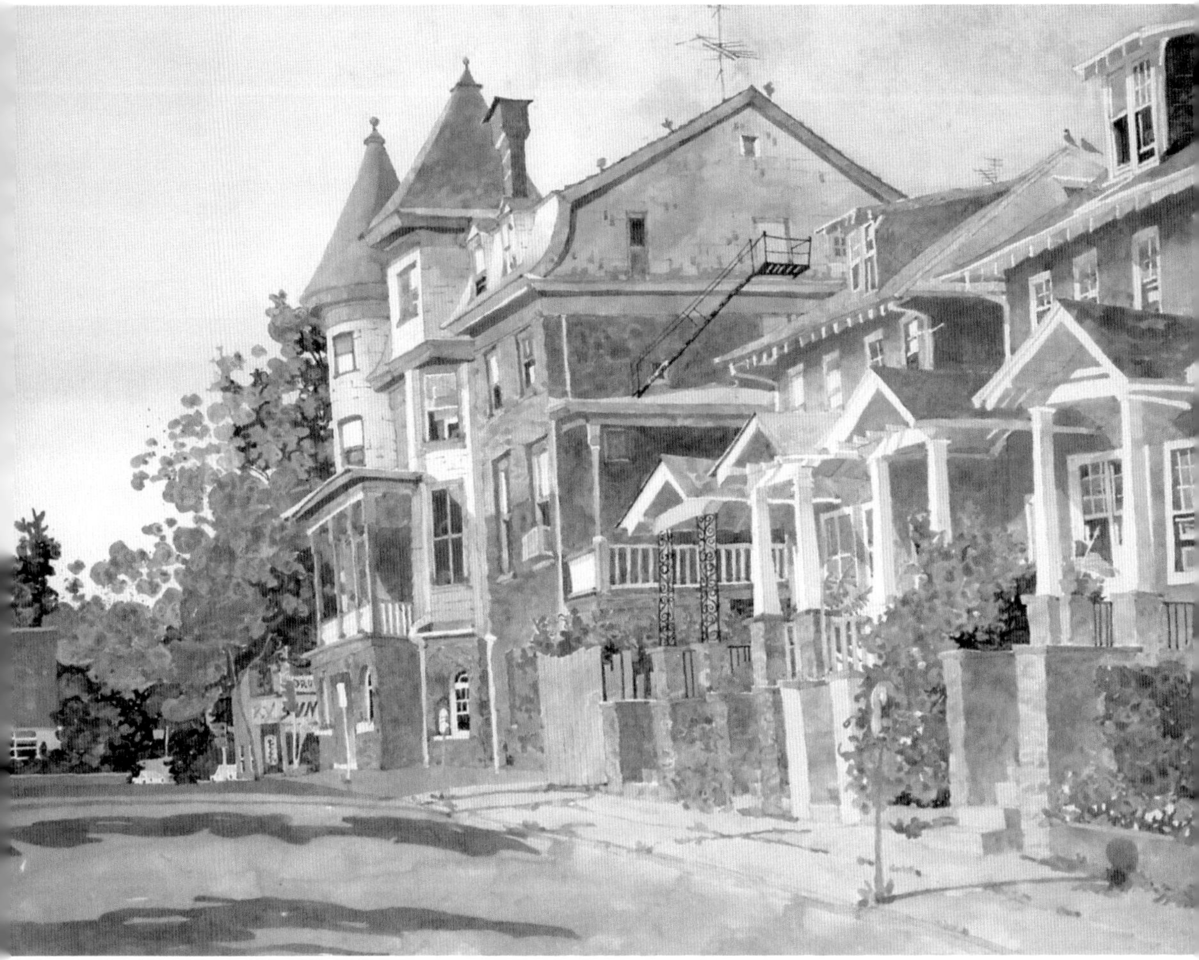

"Ridge and Butler" (OPPOSITE)
During a return visit to Ambler from his home on Maui, Eddie Flotte, sitting at a booth at the borough's annual Oktoberfest, finally showed his paintings. It was a seminal moment, as a huge turnout of the festival patrons stopped by and, moved by his impressions of their hometown, bought every painting he had brought. This is a painting of the intersection of Ridge and Butler Avenues, now a Rita's Water Ice. (Courtesy of Eddie Flotte.)

"Wyndham Hotel" (OPPOSITE)
One of Flotte's favorite paintings is this, of the Wyndham Hotel, built in 1893 and soon to become Gypsy Blu restaurant. The Wyndham, built in 1893, at the beginning of the Keasbey & Mattison era, was a charming Queen Anne Victorian that boasted 45 rooms in its heyday, 28 of which were bedrooms. Because the hotel had extensive stables in the rear, able to accommodate up to 40 horses, it was a popular rest stop for travelers before the advent of the automobile. (Courtesy of Eddie Flotte.)

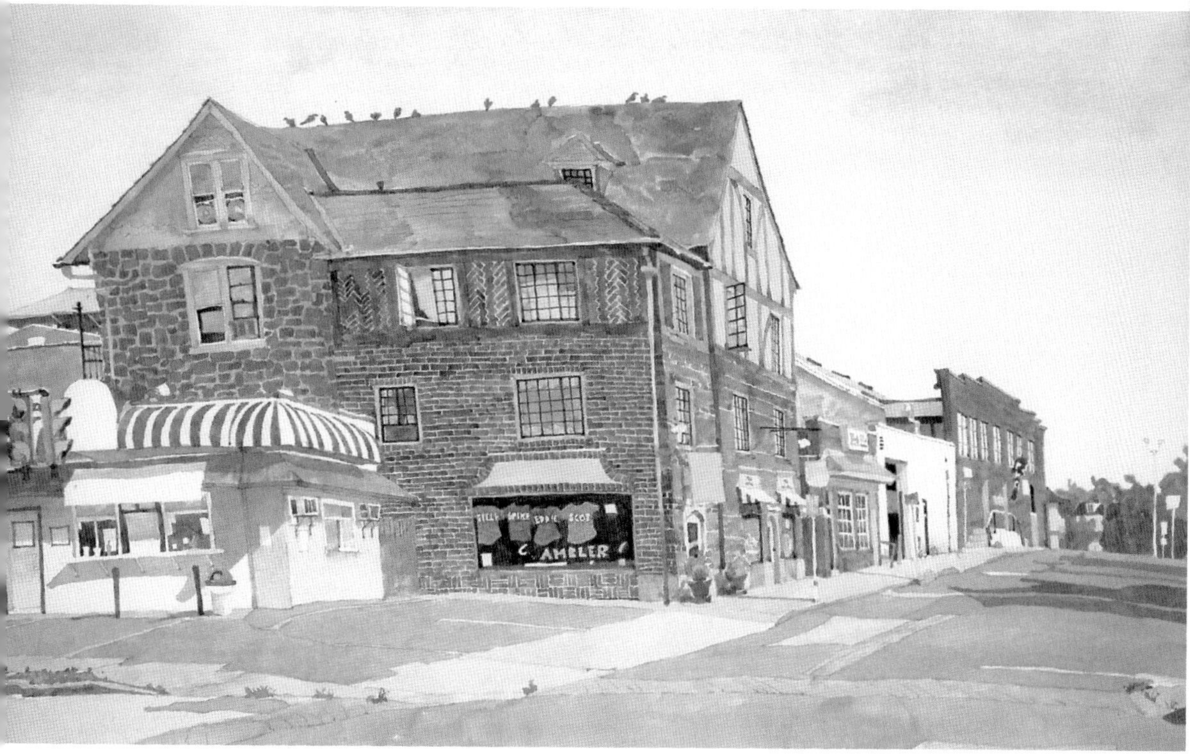

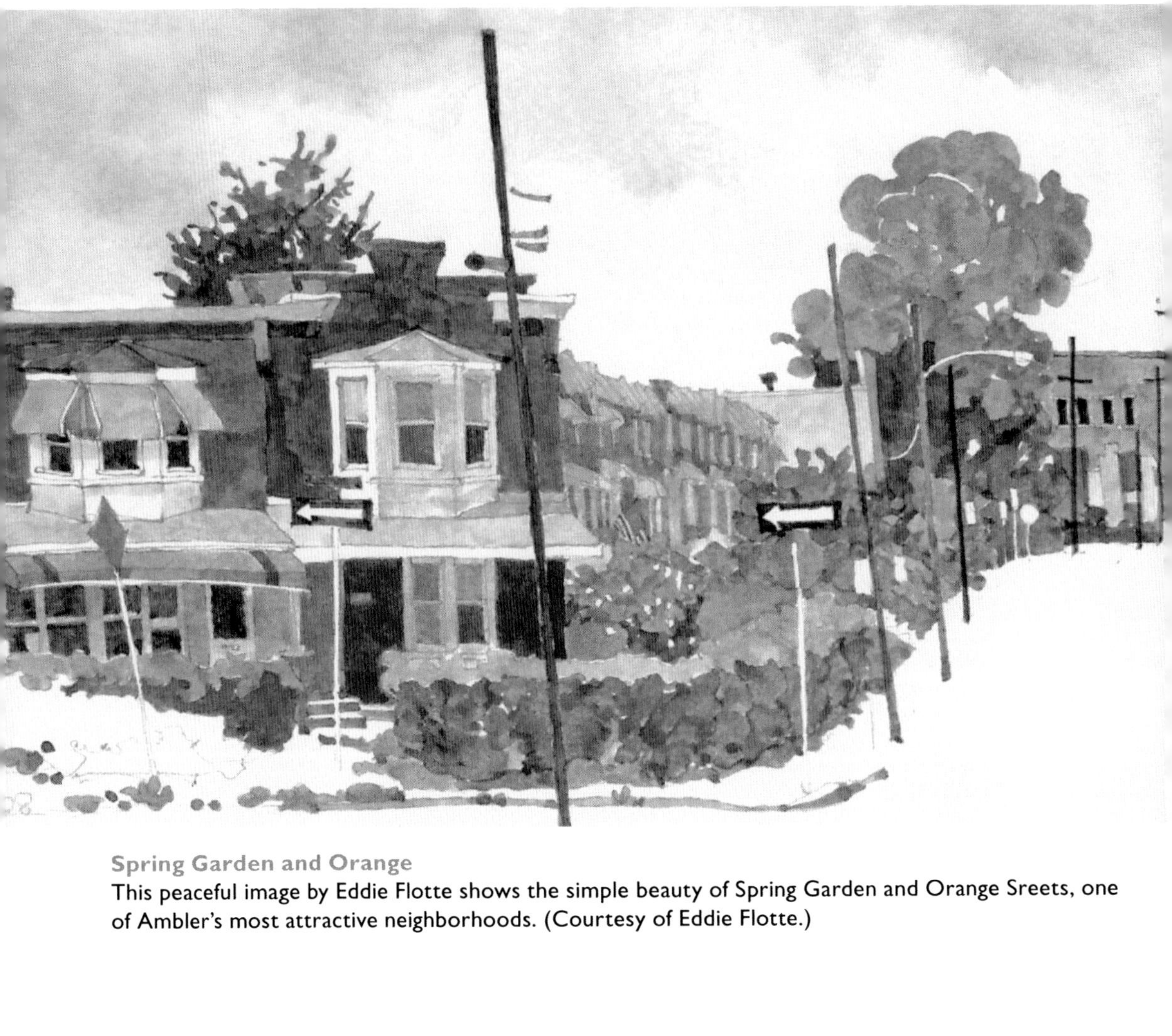

Spring Garden and Orange
This peaceful image by Eddie Flotte shows the simple beauty of Spring Garden and Orange Sreets, one of Ambler's most attractive neighborhoods. (Courtesy of Eddie Flotte.)

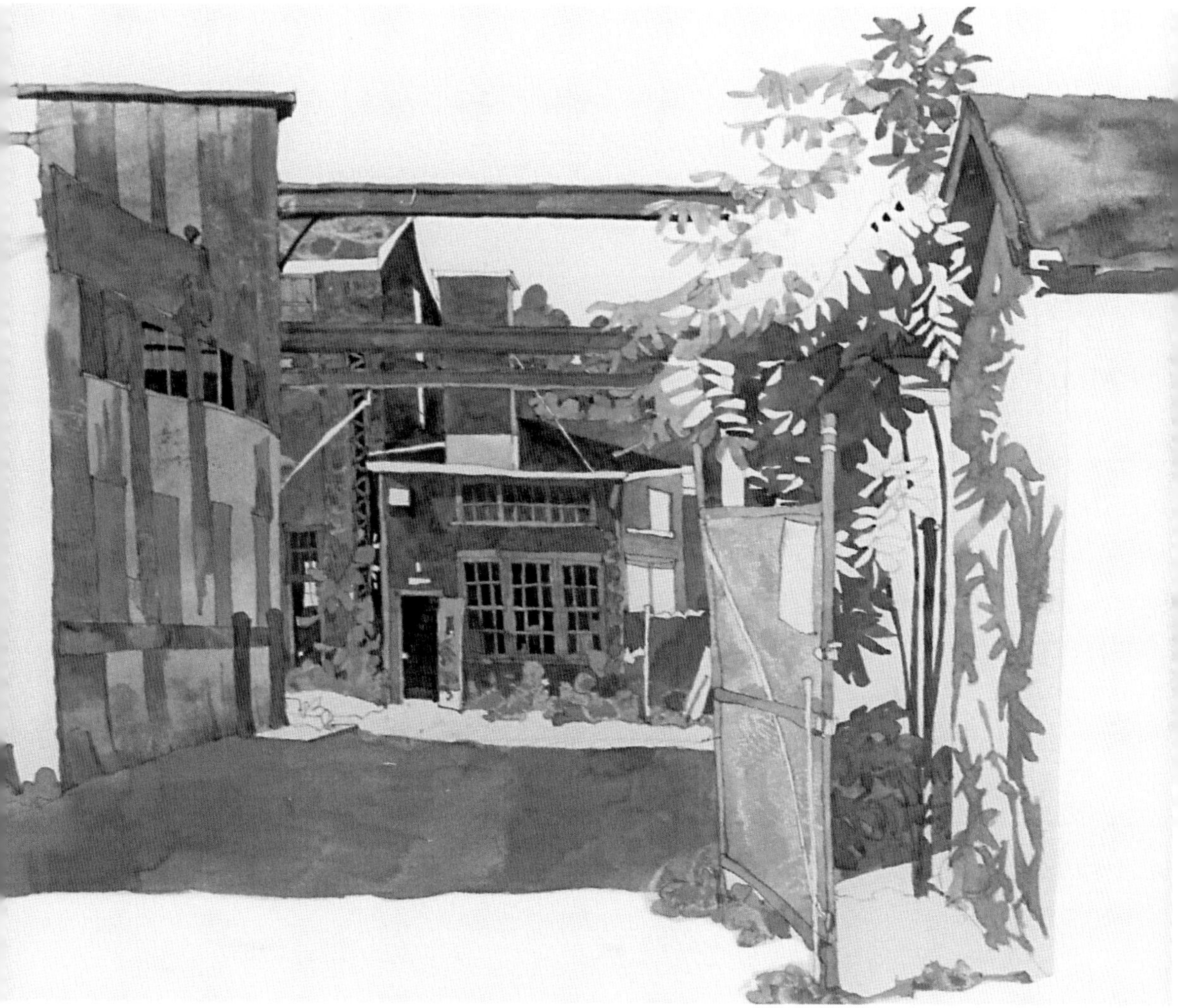

Boiler Plant II
Although this boiler plant was not part of the Keasbey & Mattison Company operations, it shows the remnants of the Industrial Revolution before the lights on most of the factories dimmed. Artist Eddie Flotte almost makes it seem pleasantly nostalgic. (Courtesy of Eddie Flotte.)

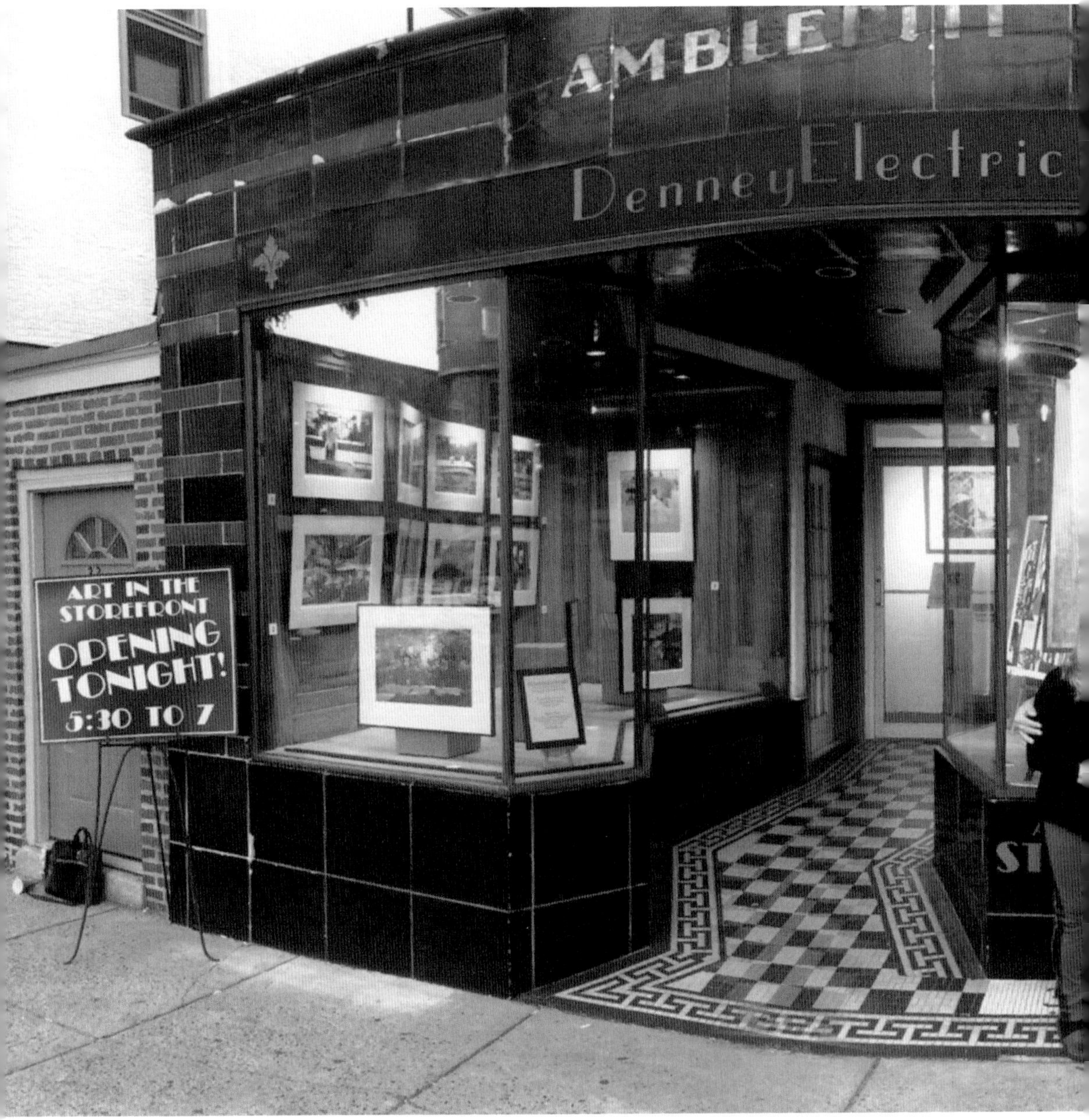

Art in the Storefront

This incredible image reveals one more reason that Ambler's main street, Butler Avenue, has become such a magnet for locals and people from miles around. The former Harris' Department Store and storage area for Denney Electric has been transformed by local artists Karen Kieser and Mark Elliott (seen here) into Art in the Storefront, a showcase for the works of talented artists from the region. At any given time, framed by the stunning 1920s Art Deco storefront, a panoply of images reaches out at passersby and nearly distracts drivers rolling slowly by along busy Butler Avenue. One month, it might be the figurative photography of artist Anthony Casasanto—inviting shore points and dreamy pastels of the Italian countryside. Another month, the brilliant graphics or motion design of Ambler freelance photographer Laura Kicey might stop a person in her tracks. And yet another month, it might be the fanciful

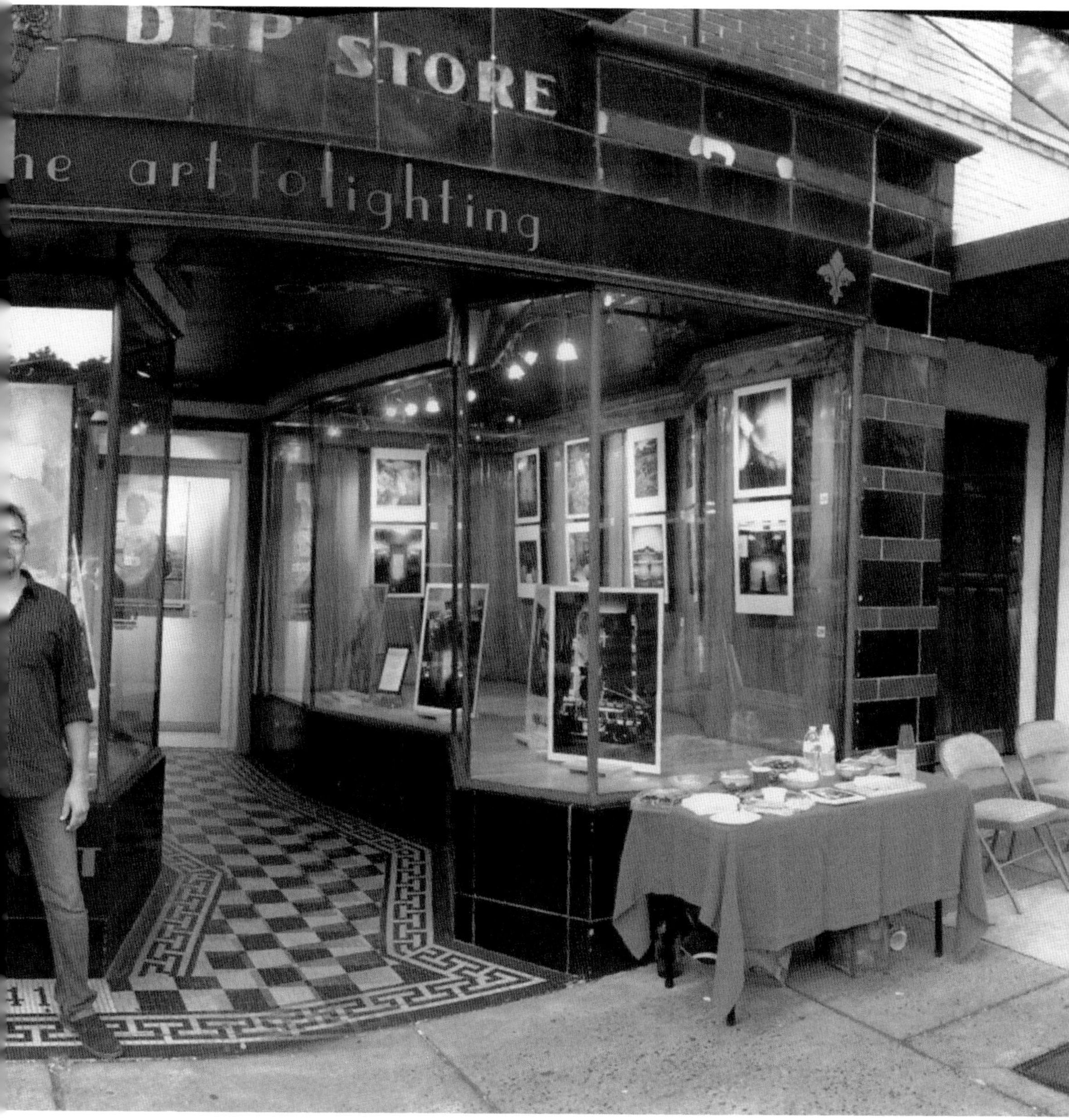

archetypes of mixed-media artist Lynette Shelley—sweetly symbolic animals, snake-headed goddesses, and other interpretations of folkloric figures. Whatever one sees, it has been a welcome addition to Ambler's burgeoning arts scene. Since sculptor/artist Kieser set her concept in motion in 1999, Art in the Storefront has not only brightened Ambler's lively main street, but it has also provided mostly local artists with opportunities to showcase their works at solo and/or group exhibitions, generally lasting two months. One of the artists featured in the very first exhibition in 1999 was Mark Elliott, owner of Ambler's No Bare Walls custom frame shop. He and Kieser hit it off immediately; since then he has been her curating partner in this creative enterprise—just one more example of Ambler's growth as an artistic community. (Photograph by Dan Marcolina.)

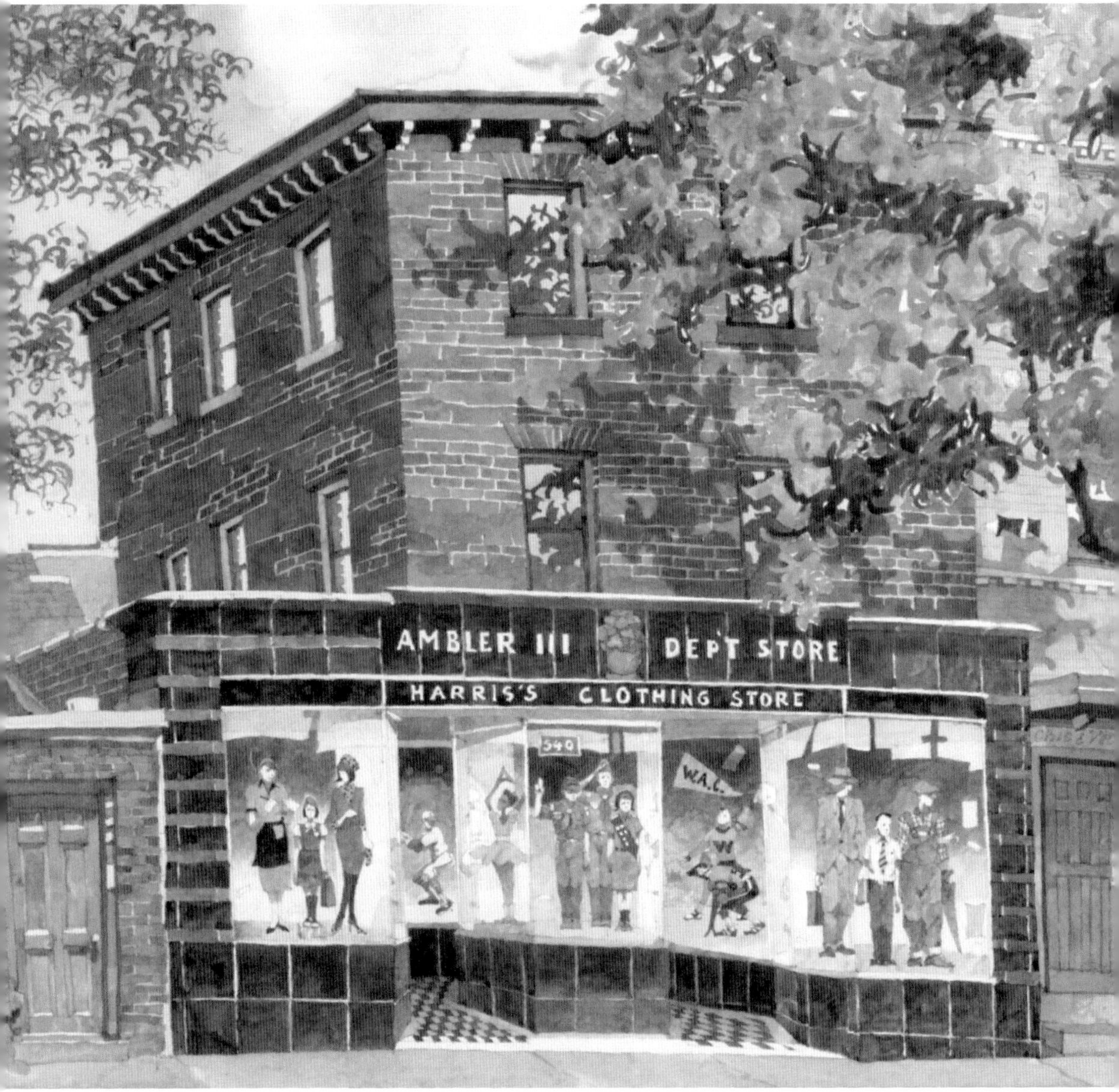

Harris's Department Store

Eddie Flotte did not know it at the time he painted the front of Harris's Department Store that the 1920s-era Art Deco facade would soon serve as the setting of Ambler's unique exhibition space. Called Art in the Storefront and cocurated by Karen Kieser and Mark Elliott, the space offers local artists the opportunity, every two months, to show their works to a public that has truly begun to appreciate and support its burgeoning arts community. (Courtesy of Eddie Flotte.)

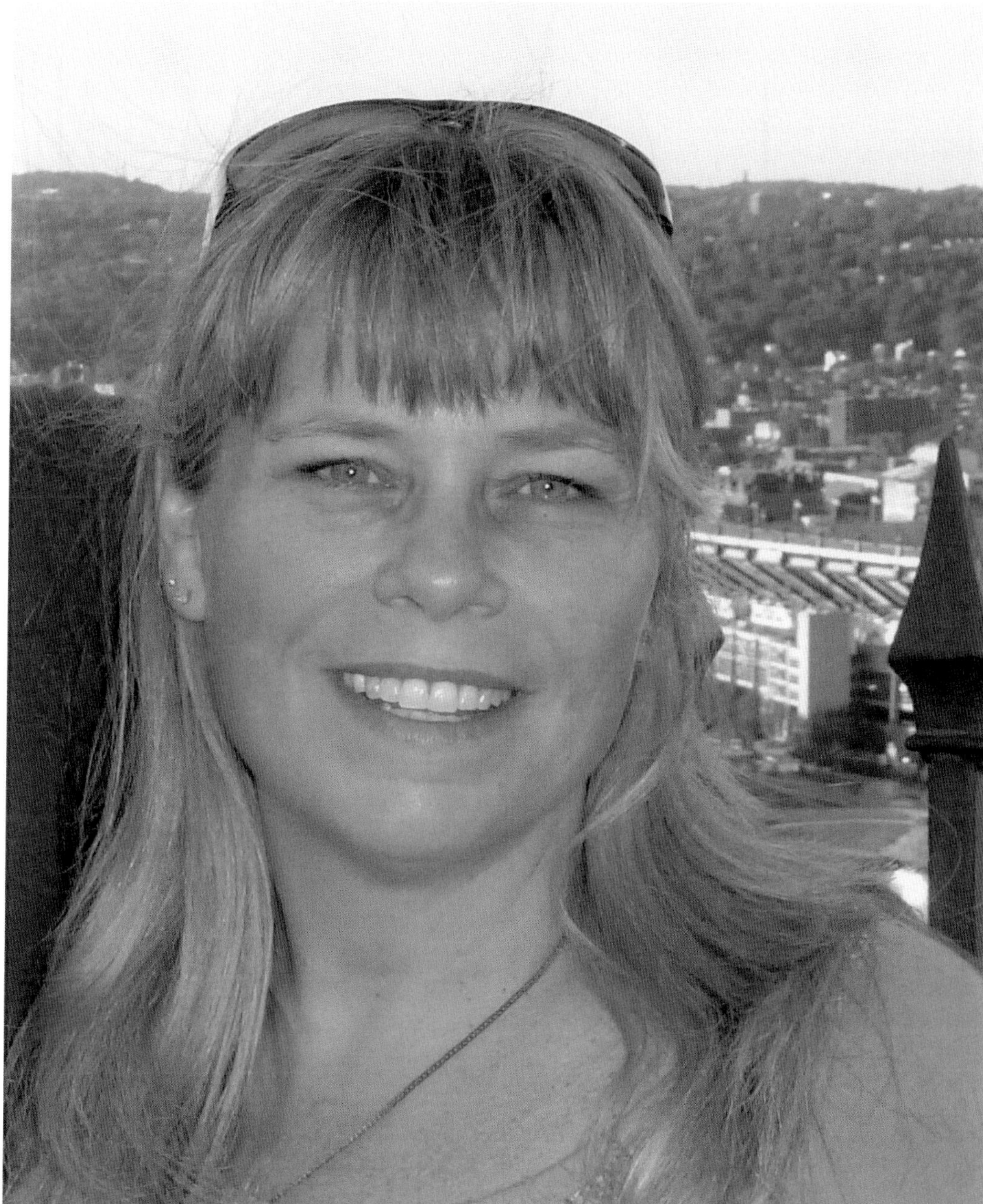

Storefront Artist

She had participated for years in art exhibitions in abandoned or occupied buildings in Buffalo, New York, and when she moved to Ambler, energetic sculptor/artist Karen Kieser approached the owners of Denney's Electric on Butler Avenue to gauge their interest in having art exhibitions in the storefront of their 1920s Art Deco building. After their approval, and some subsequent renovations, Art in the Storefront was launched (cocurated with Mark Elliott) in 1999 and continues to feature local artists' work every two months. Kieser has also been an adjunct professor of fine arts at Gwynedd Mercy University since 1999. (Courtesy of Karen Kieser.)

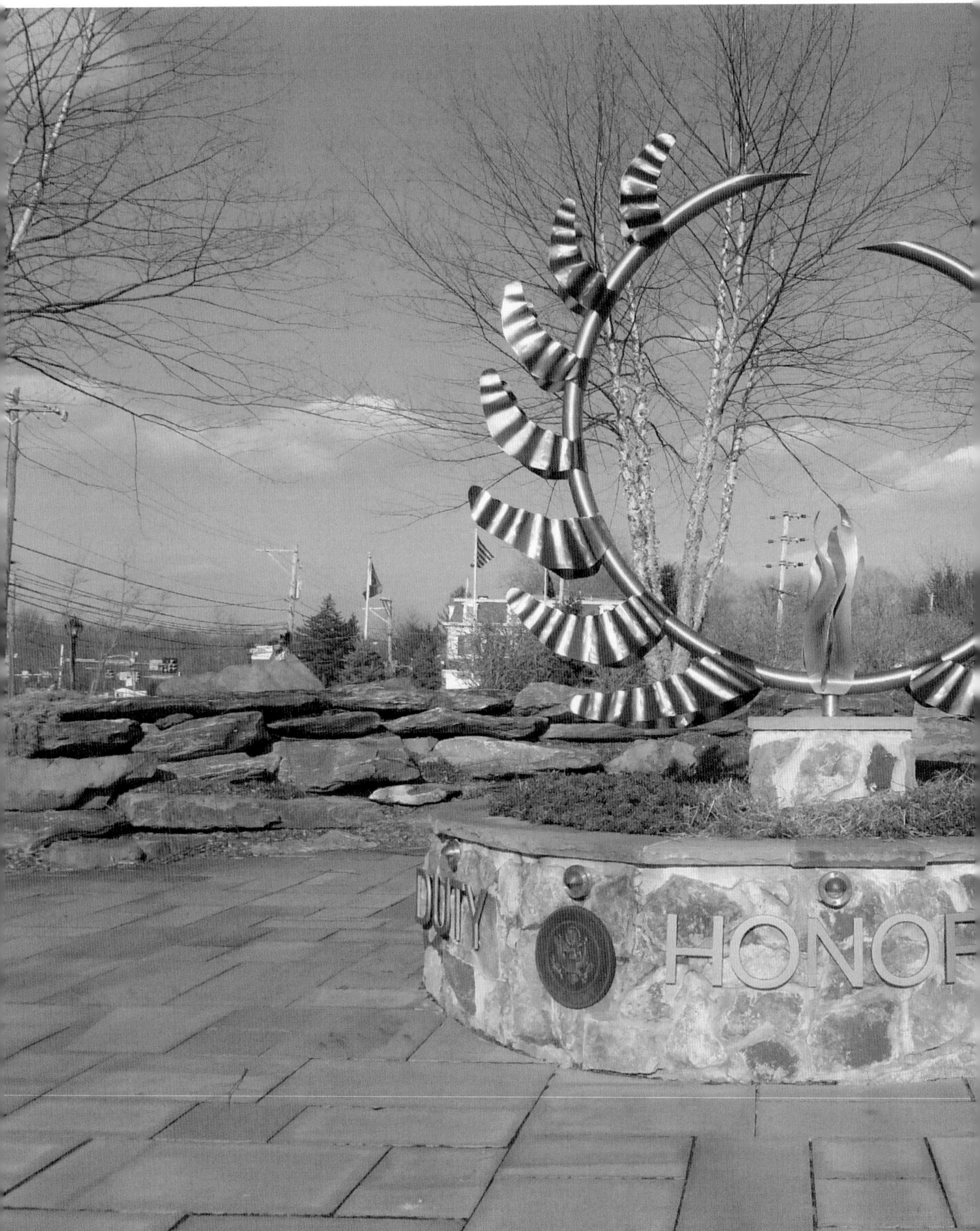
DUTY
HONOR

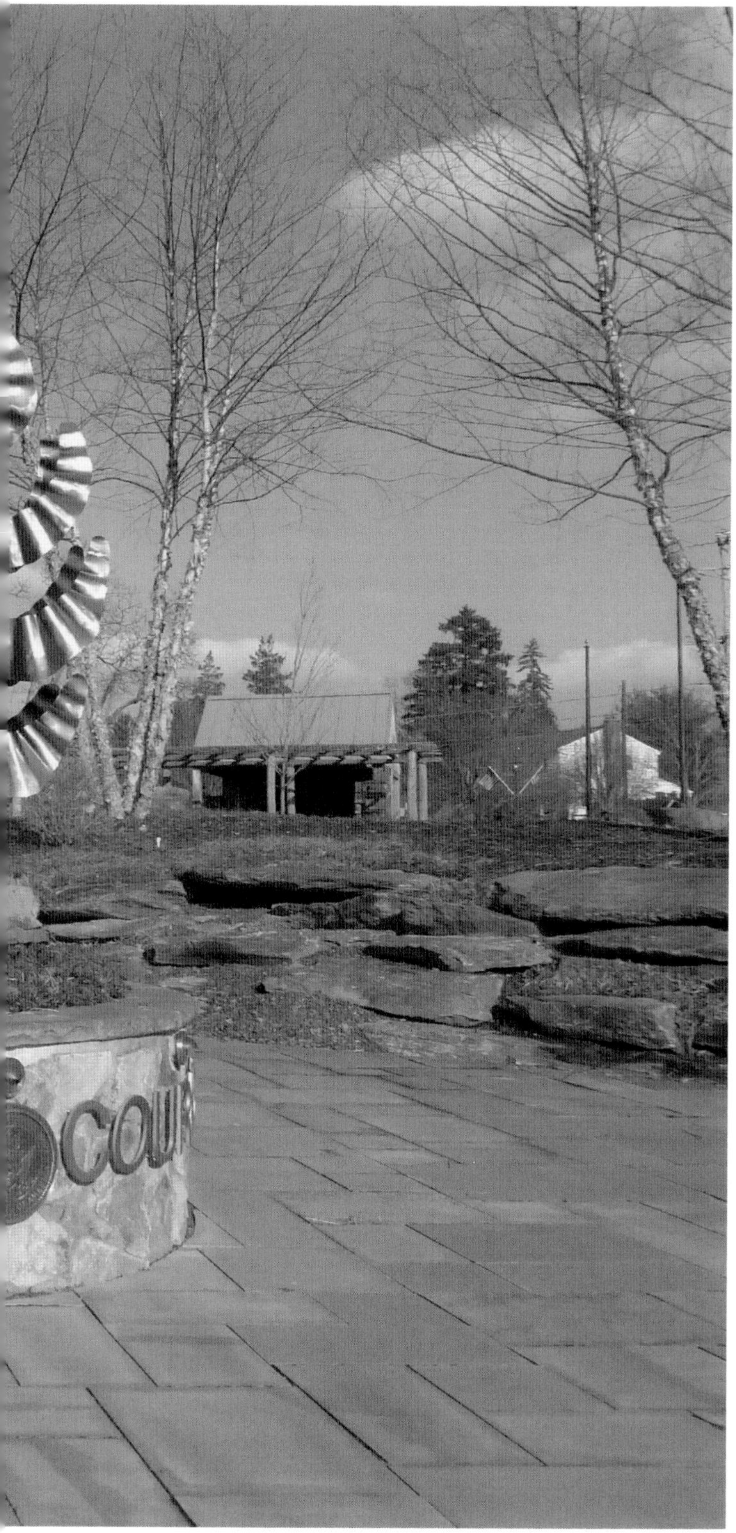

Wreath of Honor
In 2006, Lower Gwynedd Township commissioned Karen Kieser's monumental "Wreath of Honor" for its Veterans Park to honor veterans from all wars. Kieser, who served on Ambler's Borough Council from 1996 to 1999, was appointed chair of its revitalization and parks and recreation committees. She has also been on the board of trustees of Wissahickon Valley Public Library since 2007. (Courtesy of Karen Kieser.)

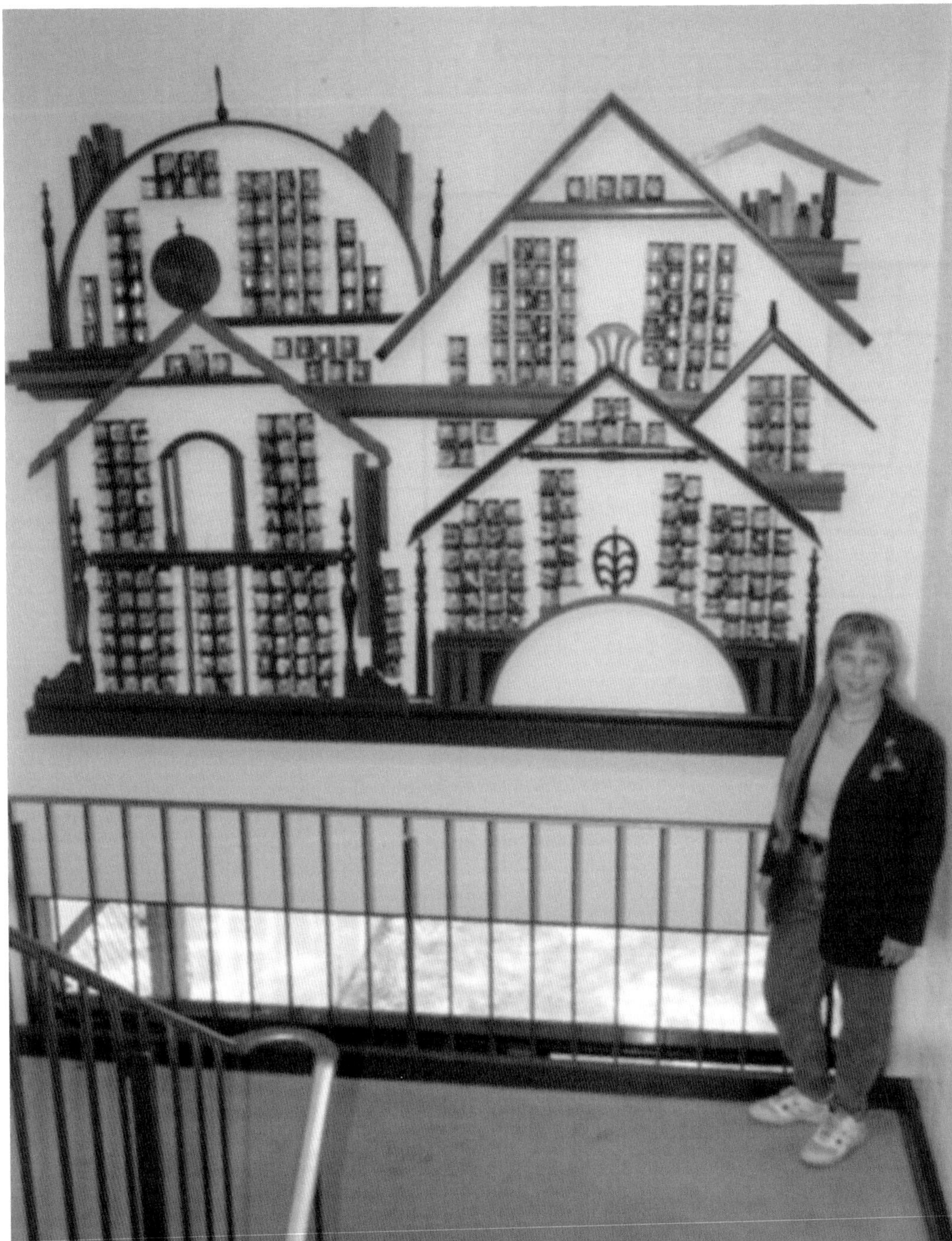

"Hopes and Dreams"
One of Karen Kieser's favorite artworks is the glass-block wall sculpture "Hopes and Dreams," a public project she worked on with students from the now shuttered Mattison Avenue Elementary School. (The school building is soon to become the new headquarters for Ambler Borough and its police department). The "Hopes and Dreams" wall depicts the students' life goals. (Courtesy of Karen Kieser.)

"There Were Others"
Mark Elliott, the owner of No Bare Walls, a custom framing studio in Ambler since 1999, is a graduate of the Pennsylvania College of Art & Design in Lancaster, Pennsylvania. He was one of the first five artists whose works graced the refurbished space now occupied by Art in the Storefront in 1999. Since then he has teamed with Karen Kieser to curate the exhibition space. Their mission, he said, has been to work closely with Ambler's borough council to bring art to the citizens of Ambler, which they all felt would contribute mightily to the revitalization of the borough. Elliott's evocative oil on canvas called "There Were Others" is a striking piece of social commentary. Anonymous, timeless, universal, its depiction of a barbed-wire fence, a makeshift crown of thorns, and a prisoner's stripes—not to mention a mysterious "monocle"—reveals much about the endless cycle of violence committed in the name of politics, religion, and other social forces. (Courtesy of Mark Elliott.)

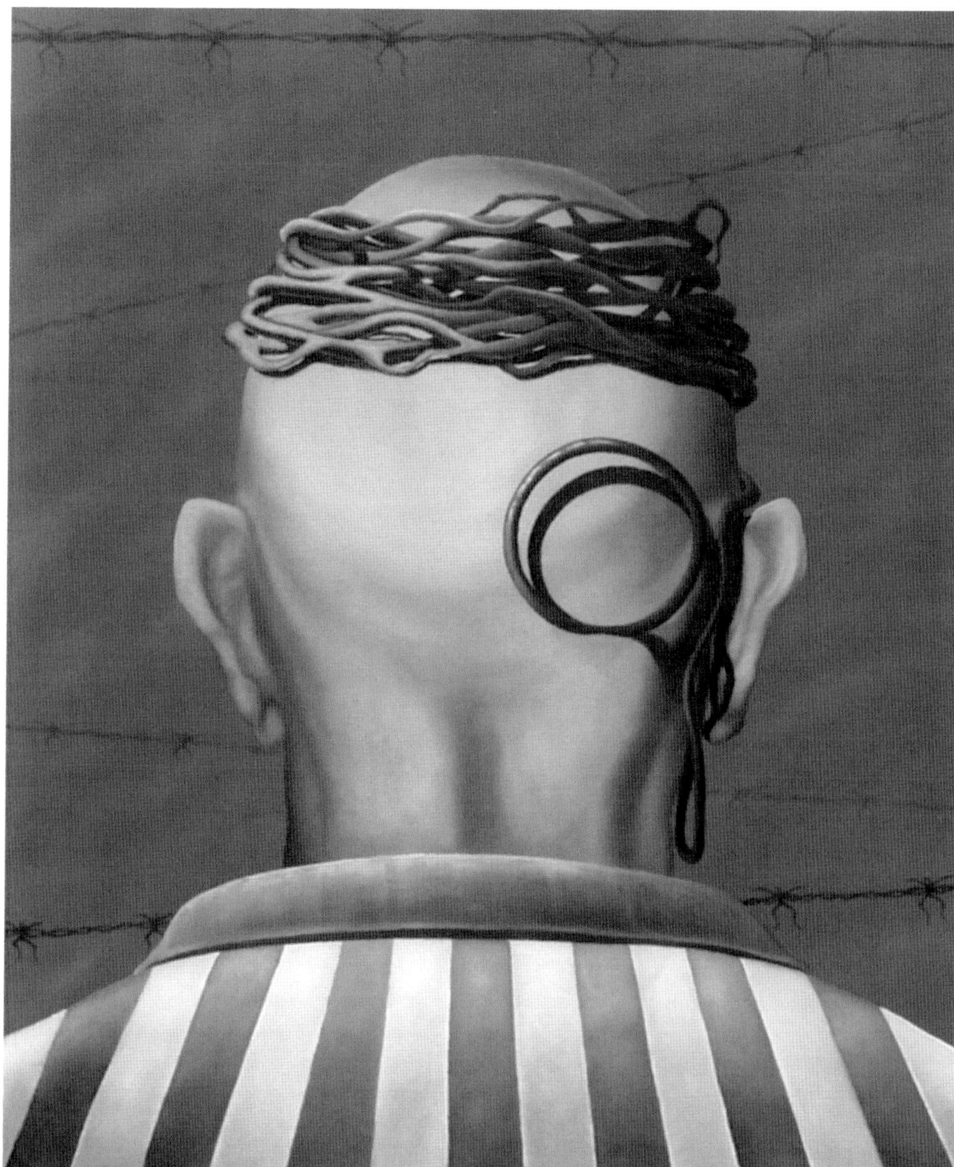

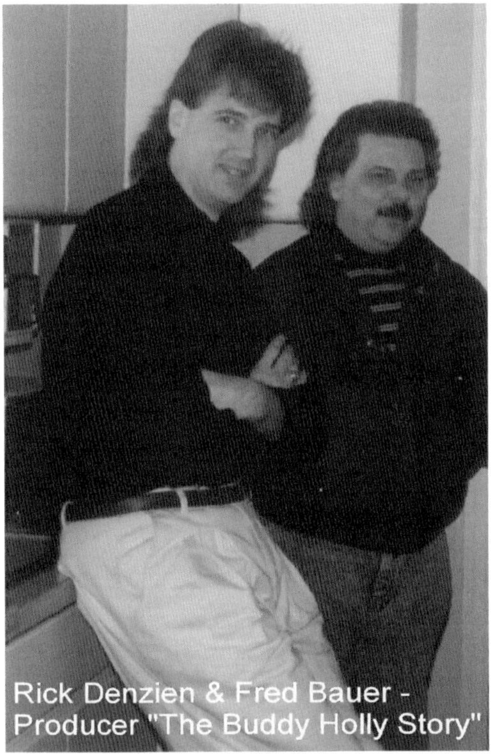

Calling the Shots

Musician Rick Denzien (left) welcomes Fred Bauer to Ambler. Bauer, the producer of the 1978 hit movie *The Buddy Holly Story*, arrived as Denzien was producing his *Laser Writing on the Moon* CD. Bauer helped Denzien to produce the Songwriters' Original Showcase at Ambler's Act II Playhouse, serving as the video line producer, calling out the shots from a five-camera set-up for the live concert event. (Courtesy of Rick Denzien.)

Fleetwood Mac Vibe

Joining Ambler's Rick Denzien (second from right) for a session on his song "Dream That Far" (on his *Green Sky* CD) are, from left to right, Jamie Cohen, Andy Kravitz, and Kjell Benner. Cohen, who was one of the leading artists-and-repertoire experts in the music industry (he has signed or worked closely with artists like Ringo Starr, George Harrison, Santana, and Whitney Houston), was in the control room during the session and exclaimed, "Man, this is just like a Fleetwood Mac session! What a vibe!" (Courtesy of Rick Denzien.)

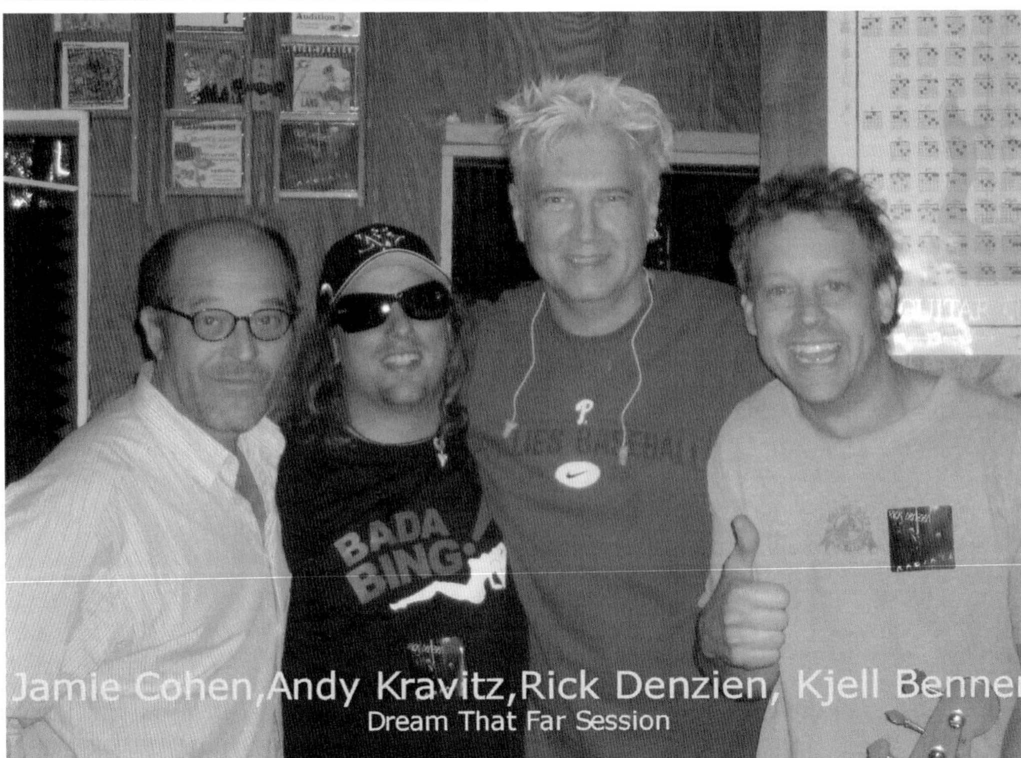

CHAPTER SIX

Restaurateurs and Restaurant Revival

For years, Ambler was a town where people generally ate at home. Aside from Costa's Delicatessen at the crossroads of Bethlehem and Butler pikes, the Ambler Diner, and some taverns (where food was not necessarily the main attraction), there were not any restaurants of note to draw Amblerites from their homes. But things have changed!

The restaurant revival began in 1998 and 1999, when Steven Waxman opened his charming Trax Restaurant & Café adjacent to the SEPTA tracks, offering innovative twists on new American cuisine, and when the entrepreneurial Kevin Clib opened KC's Alley, bringing eminently affordable upscale comfort food to a borough that really needed it. In 2004, Clib also opened Bridget's, which has settled nicely into its role as a modern American steakhouse. It is not so long ago that Trax and KC's were virtually the only places in town one could get a meal worth remembering.

In the first decade of the new millennium, Ralph's of South Philadelphia came to Ambler. So did Gerry Timlin and Ed Egan's always popular Shanachie, an Irish restaurant and pub offering live Celtic music to whet the appetite. The boom had begun in earnest.

In 2011, Ambler Main Street mainstay Allison Wolf introduced the highly anticipated semiannual Ambler Restaurant Week, featuring special prix fixe menus from the area's top restaurants, including the Shanachie, now closed and replaced by the Lucky Well.

Foodies can now sample the tangy subcontinental flavors of Saffron Indian Kitchen, the Greek/Mediterranean/Portuguese fare of Massa, and the great barbecue of the Lucky Well. They revel in Dettera, a restaurant as renowned for its wine list, architectural features, and stunning decor as the inspired upscale contemporary cuisine of executive chef Jeffrey Power, who was honored by being invited to cook at the prestigious James Beard House in 2012. They can also find Italian (From the Boot, Costa's Deli), Mexican (El Limon and El Jefe), sports bar/grill fare (Fireside Bar & Grille), a brewpub (Forest & Main Brewing Company), casual fare (Sweet Briar Café), and more, including two very fine restaurants right outside Ambler's door—Cantina Feliz (contemporary Mexican) and Zakes Café (Mediterranean with touches of Vietnamese).

And then there is Ambler resident Michael Wei, the Taiwanese restaurateur who owns and operates four of the best restaurants in the Greater Philadelphia area.

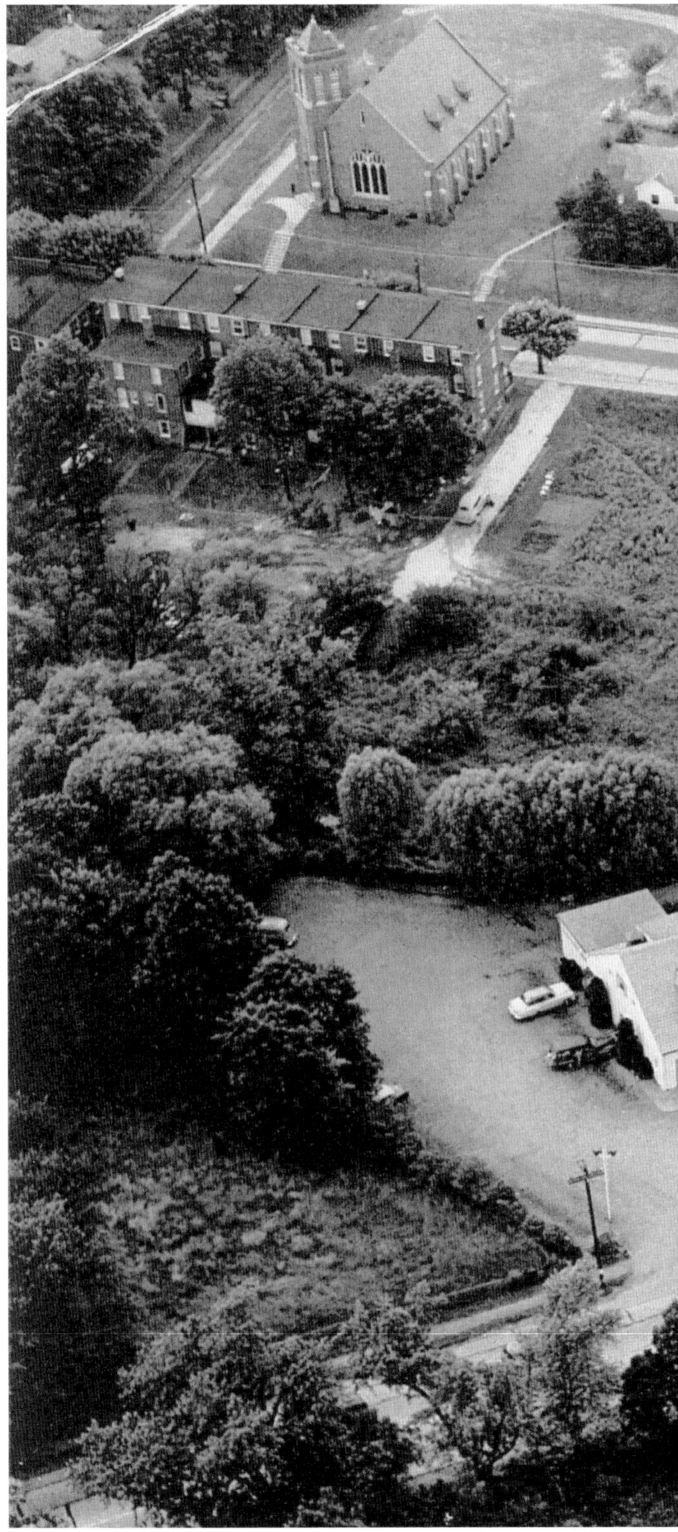

Mid-Century View
The busy intersection where Butler Avenue meets Bethlehem Pike looked pretty sleepy in 1952, when this aerial view was taken. Costa's Delicatessen, still standing, is in the upper right. Across from the deli is the Mullin Motor Company. In the upper left is the Church of the Brethren, still standing, as well as the row houses across the road. The Howard Johnson's in the lower right burned down in the early 1960s; today, the Ambler Extended Care Center exists in that location. (Courtesy of the Costa family.)

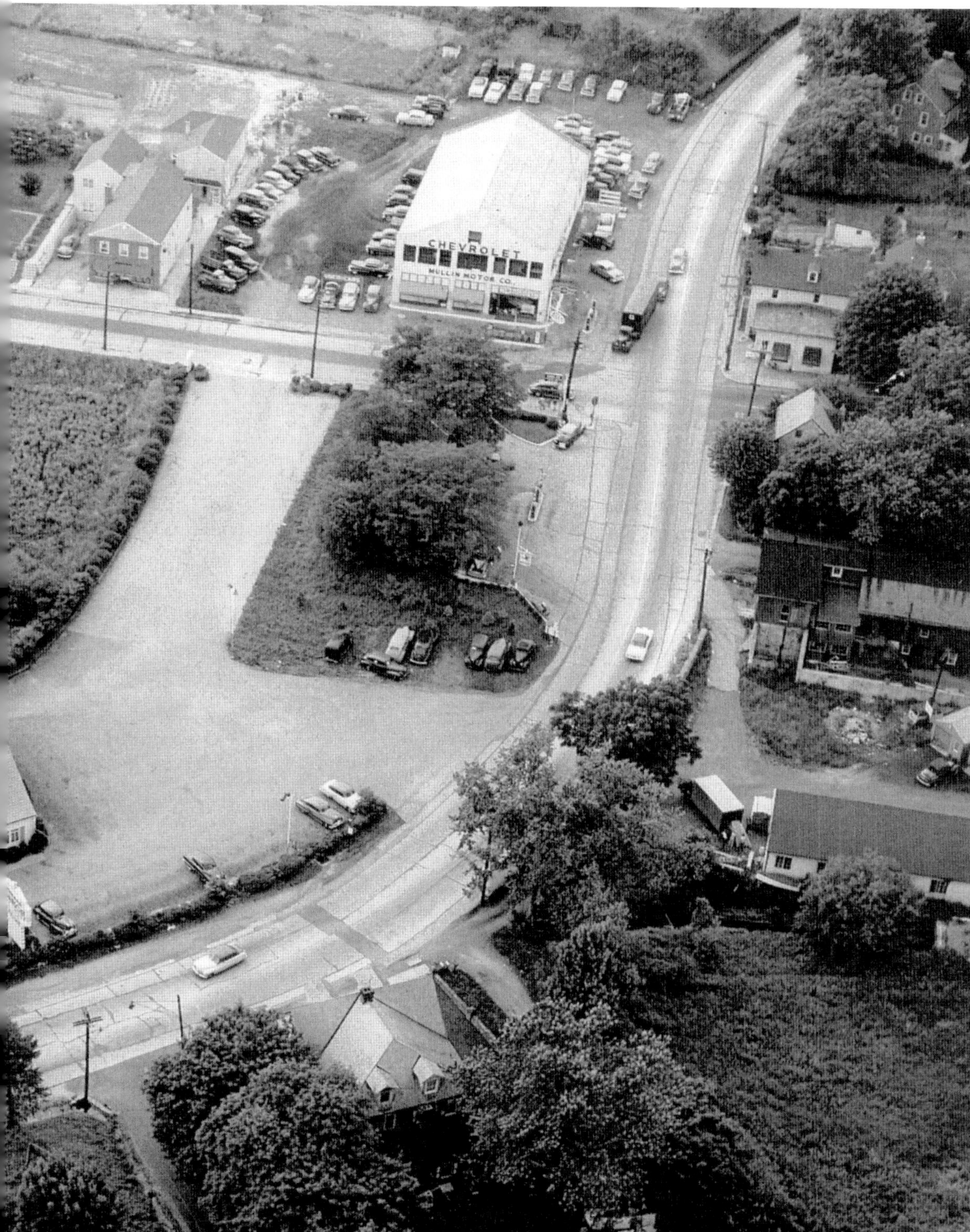
CHEVROLET
MULLIN MOTOR CO.

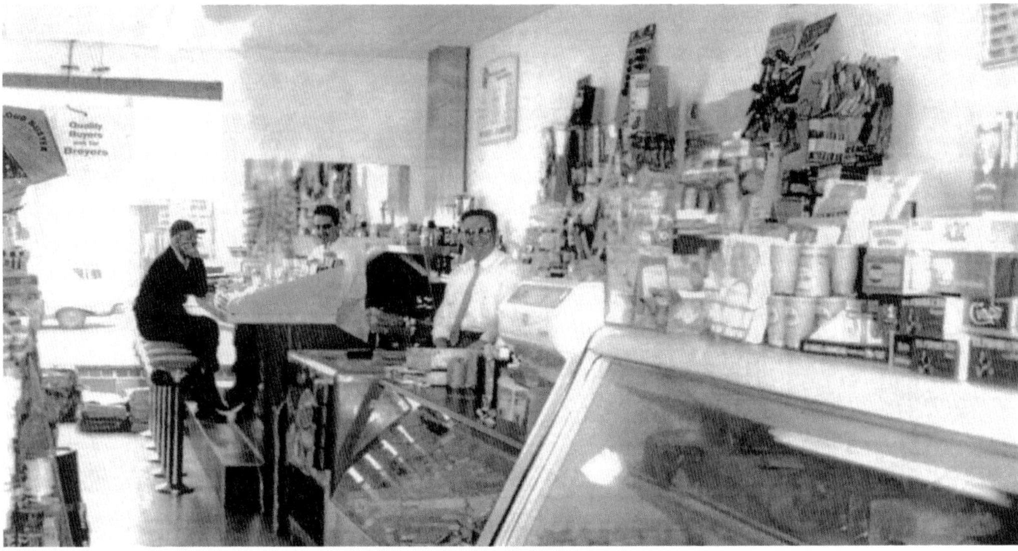

A Deli Smiles
When Italian immigrant Rocco Costa (center) bought the old Rose Valley Delicatessen in 1950, located at the intersection of Bethlehem Pike and Butler Avenue, it had already served Ambler since the American Revolution. He and his family, who lived in the apartment above the store, greeted customers like family as they offered steaks, hoagies, and world-class milkshakes in their charming soda fountain/luncheonette. (Courtesy of the Costa Family.)

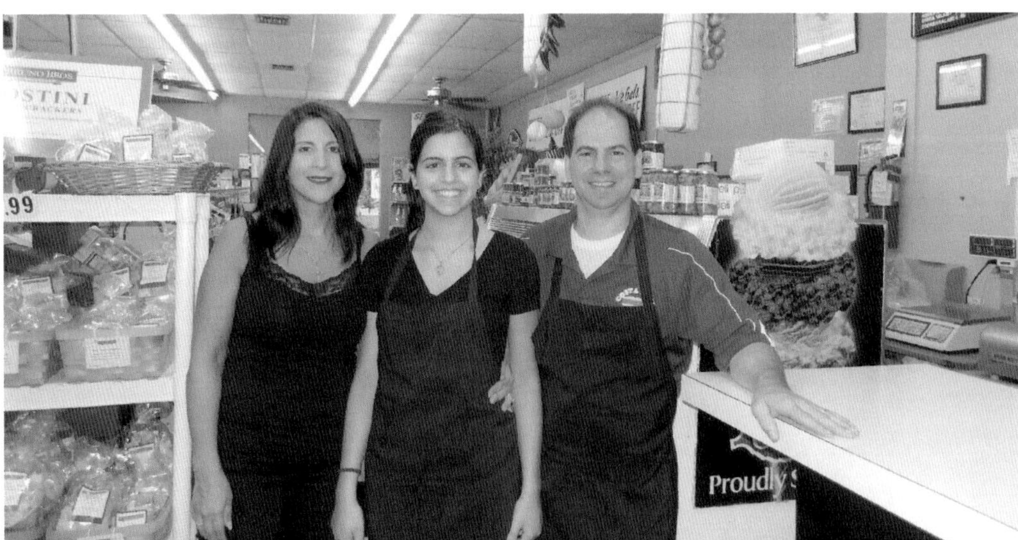

Costa Family Today
In the 1970s, when Rocco's son Michael and his wife, Marie, took over the family business, the deli got a facelift, retaining its round swivel chairs and milkshake machine, adding groceries and lunchmeat to its offerings. Present owners David and Gina Costa (with daughter Victoria between them) have retained the deli's Old World charm and warmth. When community tastes shifted, they added high-end Italian products from DiBruno Brothers and Talluto's, plus Gina's Amazing Cupcakes. (Photograph by Eve M. Quattrone.)

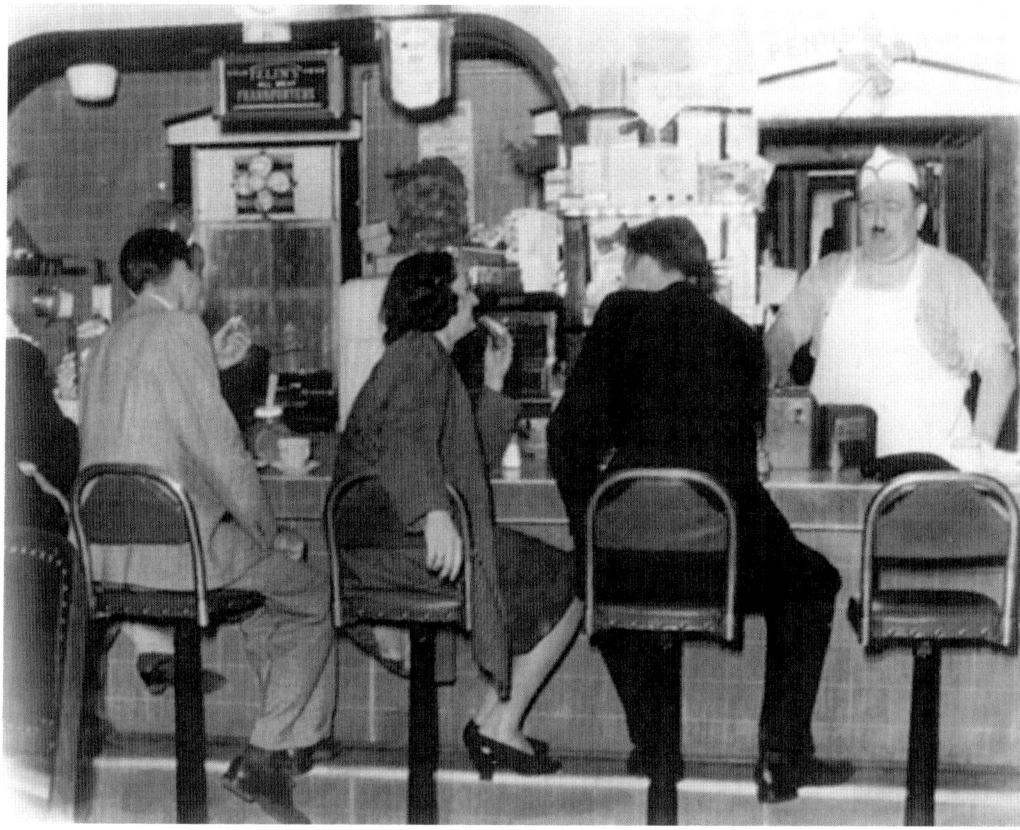

Inside the Diner

Amblerites are enjoying a quick bite inside the Ambler Diner during the Eisenhower era, the 1950s. The diner was located adjacent to the railroad tracks. When it was finally torn down, it was replaced by a parking lot. When KC's Alley opened in 1999, it signaled the beginning of a genuine restaurant revival in Ambler. (Photograph from Newt Howard Collection; courtesy of Buck Amey.)

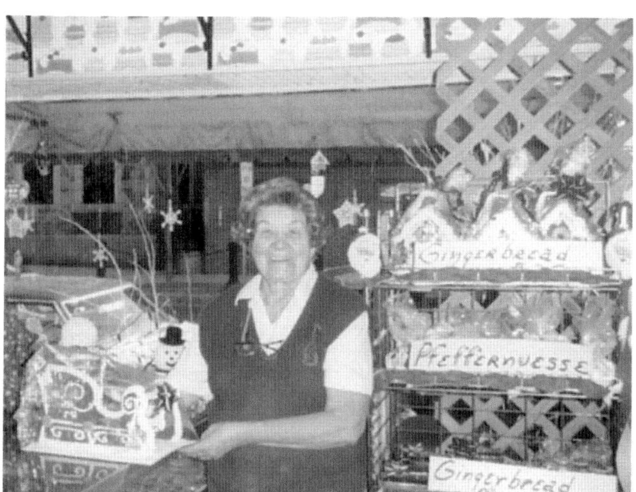

Happy Helen

Did they come for the coffee and donuts, the pfeffernüsses, the house specialty gingerbread houses, or to say hello to Helen Simanaitis, who enjoyed her golden years at Goettner's Bakery, greeting regular patrons and outsiders alike as if they were family. Simanaitis loved to wear funny hats for Halloween, Philadelphia Eagles' caps, or anything that would make the customers smile. She left the venerable bakery in 1984, when she was 80. It was sold three years later. (Courtesy of Louise Galyo.)

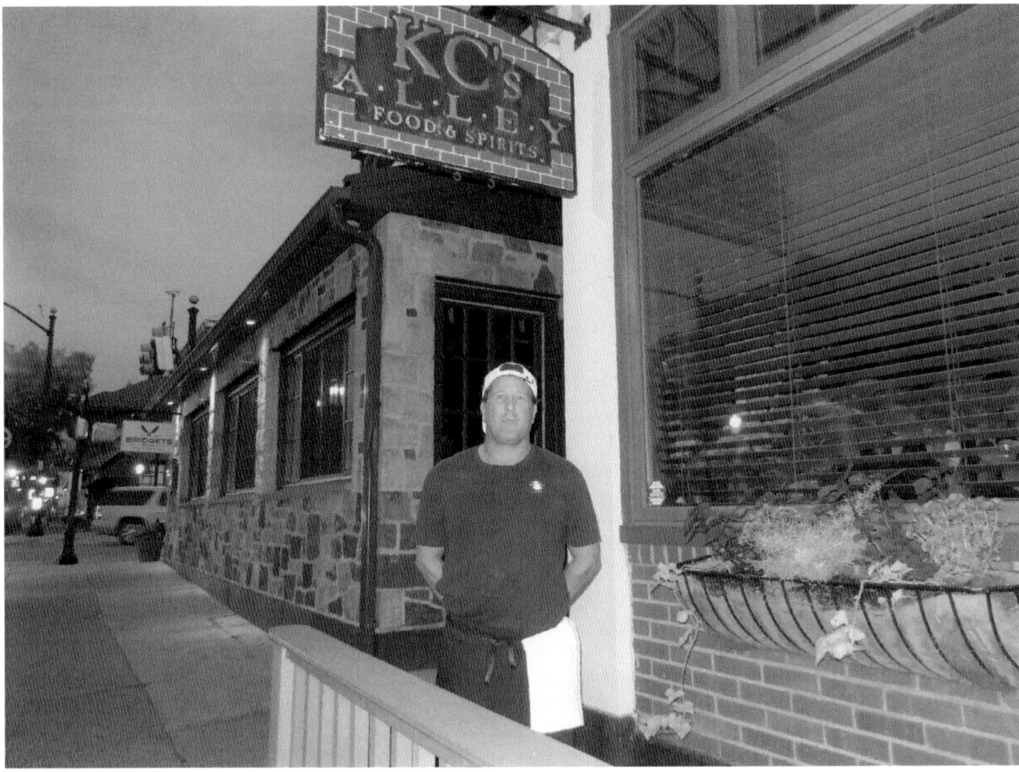

Pioneering Restaurateur

Like Ambler itself, which had become a "dark and difficult" place after the malls had decimated local businesses, Kevin Clib (seen here in front of his two Ambler restaurants, KC's Alley and Bridget's) has come a long way since he ran Lee's Hoagies at the Willow Grove Naval Air Station in the 1990s. A courageous and respected restaurateur, Clib says he saw working-class Ambler as "a nugget in the midst of the more affluent" surrounding communities and took a chance on opening KC's Alley near the train station in 1999. For a while, it looked as though the naysayers, who had gotten used to the eyesore Ambler had become since the 1960s and 1970s, might be right. It took about 18 months before KC's Alley really began to click, but now Clib's cozy gastro pub, filled with fanciful pop artwork (like "The United Plates of America," a map of the United States fashioned from license plates from every state) and friendly staffers, is packed every night—with singles, couples, friends and families dropping in to enjoy affordable, creative, mostly homemade comfort food, with daily specials to keep the regulars returning again and again. Although he still cooks some nights at KC's and at his more-upscale, modern steakhouse Bridget's (opened in 2004), right next door, the gregarious Clib enjoys coming out to meet his guests.

Recently, he and longtime business partner Scott Dougherty became co-owners of the iconic Blue Bell Inn in nearby Blue Bell. Serving families since its founding in 1743, it was once the restaurant where every regional function had to take place. After its yearlong refurbishing and modernization, the venerable inn where Clib and his wife had their rehearsal dinner in 1991 has regained its stature as one of the premier destinations in the Philadelphia suburbs.

Meanwhile, Clib notes that his "three mom-and-pop restaurants have been doing great business, even during the dead of summer, because we don't believe in cutting corners. My staff, like me, truly enjoy what we're doing. We treat our guests like friends, not customers. Our aim is to maintain the highest standards in quality of food, service, and atmosphere." (Photograph by Eve M. Quattrone.)

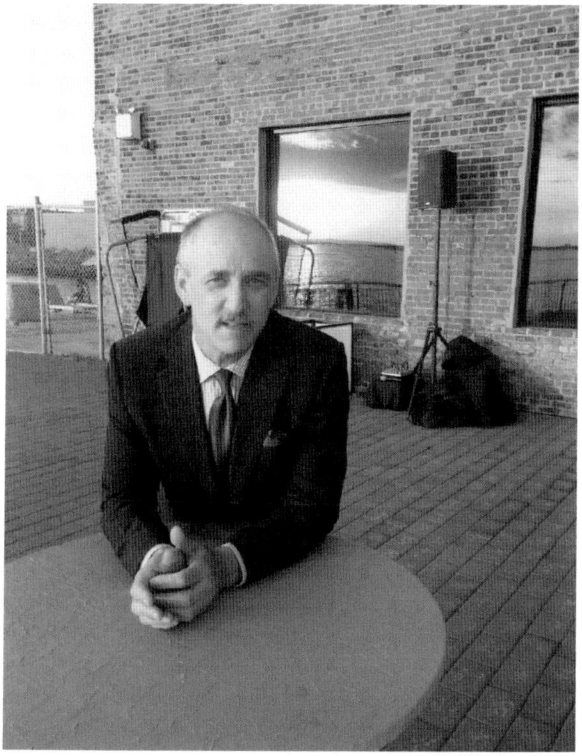

American Beauties

Steven Waxman, chef-owner of Ambler's charming Trax Restaurant & Café, is one of two restaurateurs whose courage, imagination, and vision helped put Ambler on the map as a destination for food lovers throughout the region. His "new American" restaurant, located adjacent to SEPTA's busy R5 rail line, is ringed with Waxman's grape vines and aromatic herb gardens. Through the tenacity and determination of Waxman and Ambler Main Street president and realtor Allison Wolf, the Ambler Farmers' Market, the first of its kind in the cozy borough, got off to a rousing start during the summer of 2013. Waves of local residents can be seen ambling up Butler Avenue, the borough's main street, to check out the fresh produce, unique products and services and live music available at the market from late spring through just before Thanksgiving. (Left, courtesy of Steven Waxman; below, photograph by Eve M. Quattrone.)

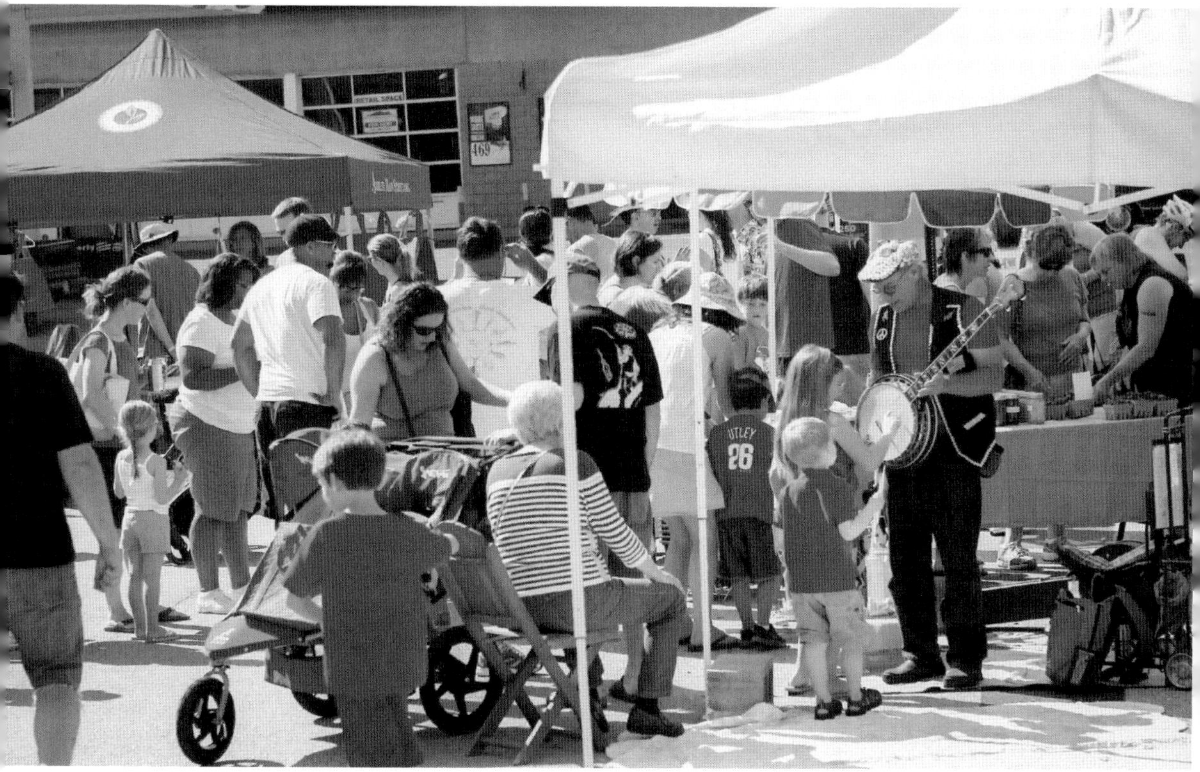

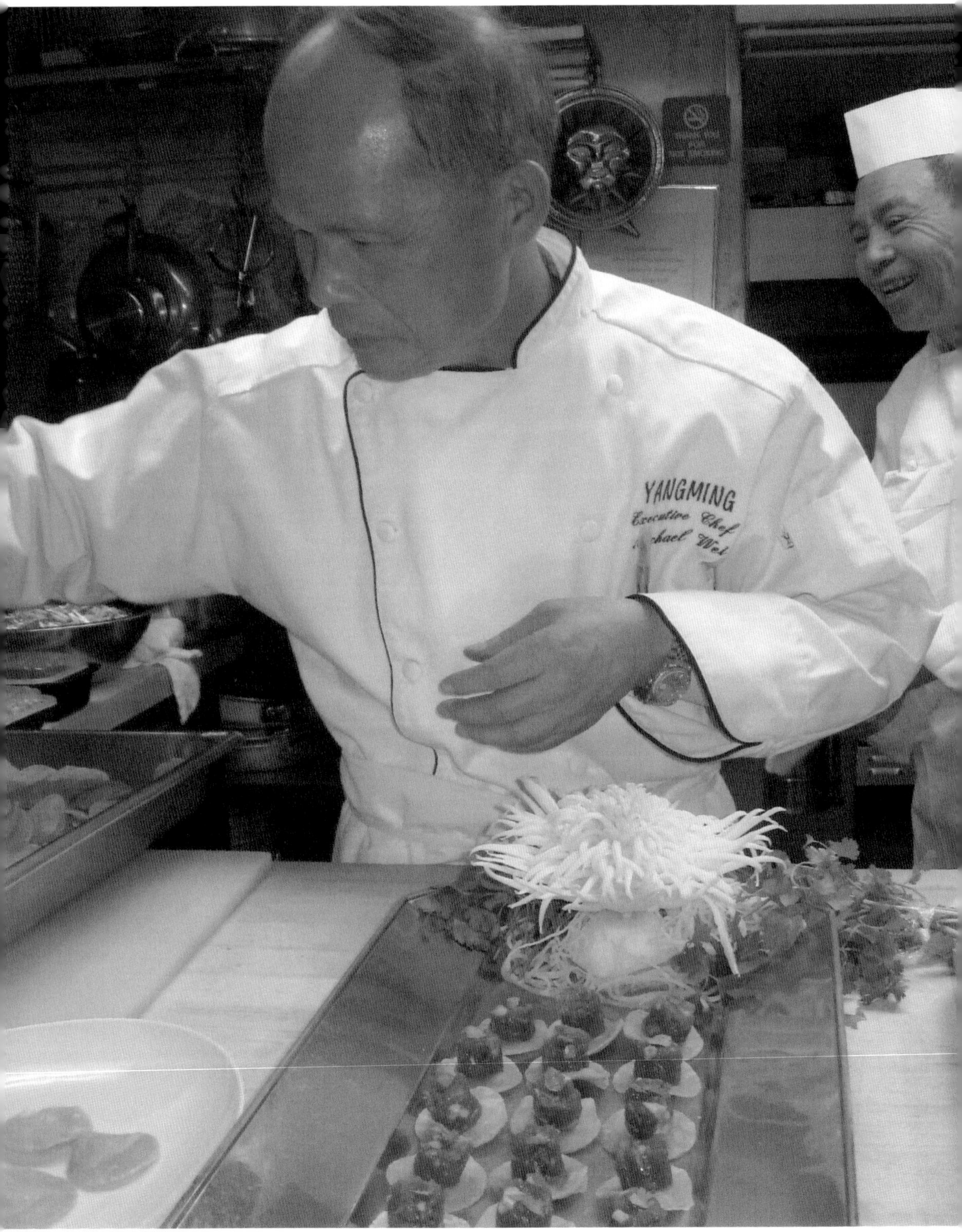
YANGMING
Executive Chef

Humble Restaurateur

Michael Wei, the humble, eloquent native of Taiwan and resident of Ambler, seen here preparing a feast at the prestigious James Beard House in New York, has been a gentle if powerful force in the restaurant industry since he arrived in America in 1970 to study journalism at the University of Missouri. Presently the owner or co-owner of four acclaimed restaurants in suburban Philadelphia—Bryn Mawr's Yangming, Willow Grove's Mandarin Garden, Chestnut Hill's Cin Cin, and Berwyn's Nectar—Wei and his restaurants were honored twice by the James Beard Foundation. Wei was lauded by the *Chinese Restaurant News* as one of the 20 "Most Influential Personalities in American Chinese Restaurant Industry" for 2010. Yangming was named by San Francisco's *Chinese Restaurant News* in 2010 as the No. 1 restaurant in its seventh annual "Top 100 Chinese Restaurants Competition." And in 2013, it was honored as one of the top 25 Chinese restaurants in the country (out of 44,000) by *Travel + Leisure* magazine, one of the bellwethers of the hospitality industry. These accolades are not difficult to understand, as Wei made Yangming one of the first restaurants in the country to champion a fusion between Eastern and Western cuisines. Although his usual regimen is to work a 15-hour day, seven days a week, visiting as many of his restaurants as he can along the way, the genial restaurateur also loves dining out when he can—sometimes in Philadelphia, sometimes in New York City. "I love Italian food, but I also love French, Indian, and other kinds of cuisine." Employing one of the most sound and savvy business models possible, Wei works with trusted partners at each of his restaurants, granting them a strong measure of autonomy, even as he helps plan the menus with each of his chefs. Asked about the key to his success, Wei graciously spreads the praise: "Everyone who works in my restaurants becomes part of my family," he said, "and they take pride in the quality of the food and service and want to keep our customers happy. I couldn't do this by myself. My partners and coworkers have contributed so much to make this possible." (Photograph by Eve M. Quattrone.)

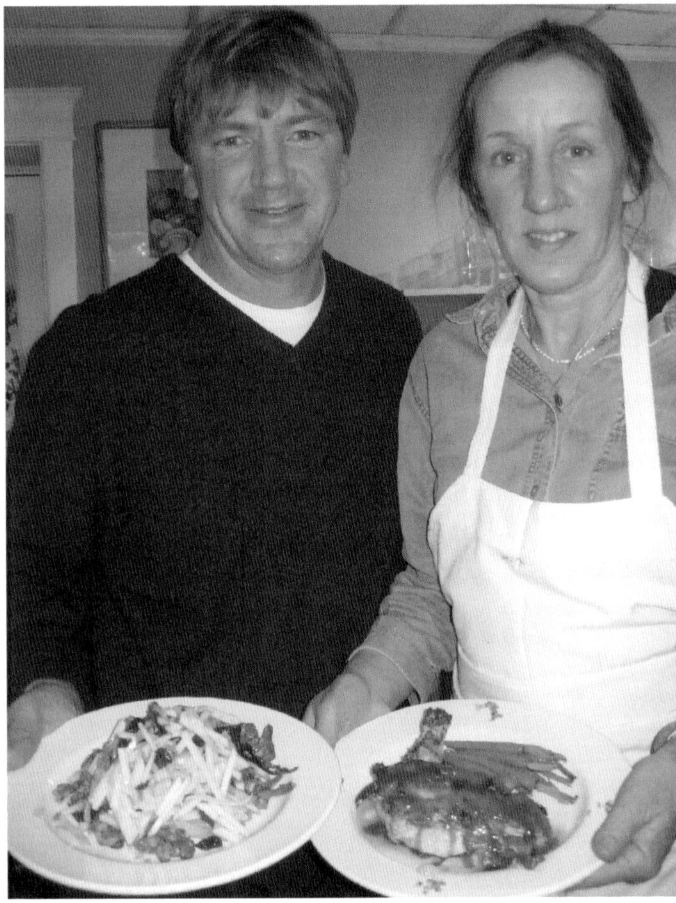

Cozy Café

With a crack kitchen staff headed by sibling co-owners/executive chefs Marlene Zakes and Joe McFadden (pictured here holding two of their delectable dishes), their creative American and Vietnamese cooks, and a buzz that easily transcends the rush of trains zipping by at nearby Fort Washington Station, Zakes does it all!

With outstanding daily morning treats like two poached eggs on wheat toast, topped with freshly roasted sweet red peppers lightly dressed with charred tomato vinaigrette and their signature Scottish wedding breakfast of house-cured salmon with scrambled eggs and dill with honey mustard and a side of house-baked whole-wheat toast, one's day is off to a sparkling start. At lunch, a patron can enjoy the likes of grilled Thai chicken or salmon with Thai peanut satay sauce or a Cubana sandwich of grilled pork, sliced ham, provolone, tomato and dill pickle with Cuban citrus dressing on toasted French bread. Dinner is just as enticing, with appetizers like seafood fritto misto, a blend of battered scallops, calamari, shrimp, and assorted vegetables in a lemon caper aioli and entrées like grilled duck breast (best in the country) in dried cherry port wine, served with duck confit fried rice and roasted garlic broccoli. And Zakes's cakes and pastries—from fresh fruit tart (a rainbow of fresh berries, kiwi, and mango on a base of cream cheese and ricotta) to its signature black and white gateaux (light chocolate genoise, filled with white chocolate mousse, topped with vanilla butter cream and chocolate shavings)—are world-class.

These modest and unassuming siblings, who have been serving an adoring and faithful clientele for close to 20 years now and who donate their food to various charities throughout Ambler Borough, Upper Dublin Township, and beyond, offer a constantly evolving menu that never disappoints. Zakes Café is a culinary gem that continually excels as time goes by. (Photograph by Eve M. Quattrone.)

CHAPTER SEVEN

The Great Nonprofits

Some might find it hard to believe that so many nonprofits—charitable organizations with passion, heart, and a can-do spirit—are located within a few miles of each other in the cozy borough of Ambler. Perhaps it is that community spirit that William E. Strasburg has defined so well and sees so clearly in the residents of Ambler.

Sometimes they grow out of obvious need, like the Community Ambulance Association of Ambler, founded in 1941. Sometimes they come to the area from the outside, like the Greater Philadelphia Chapter of the Amyotrophic Lateral Sclerosis Association, which shepherds patients suffering with what is known today as Lou Gehrig's disease.

Whatever the draw, Ambler's nonprofits are making a huge difference in the lives of the disadvantaged, the disenfranchised, the demoralized, and the diseased.

Among the first is the Kelly Anne Dolan Memorial Fund, founded by Peggy and Joe Dolan in 1976 the day after their beloved daughter, Kelly Anne, succumbed to a rare form of leukemia just months before her seventh birthday. The fund comes to the rescue of families put at risk because of serious illness or disease afflicting their children.

Mattie N. Dixon, appalled that so many of her neighbors were living below the established federal government poverty guidelines, created what would soon evolve into the Mattie N. Dixon Community Cupboard to collect and distribute food and services to these families in need.

The National Foundation for Celiac Awareness, founded by Alice Bast in 2003, educates the public about the dangers of food products laden with gluten, and Bast works closely with restaurants and chefs to create gluten-free menus.

The Bonnie Kroll Melanoma Memorial Fund, as in Peggy and Joe Dolan's case, grew out of a tragic death. But Kelly Kroll, herself a melanoma survivor, would not allow her mother's death to uveal melanoma be an end, but the beginning of a courageous fight to learn more about this disease. The funds her nonprofit raises through golf outings, dinner dances, and the like are donated to Thomas Jefferson University Hospital's research arm, seeking a cure.

And Lei Barry, once "homeless" herself, has founded the Inter-Faith Housing Alliance to combat homelessness in Montgomery County.

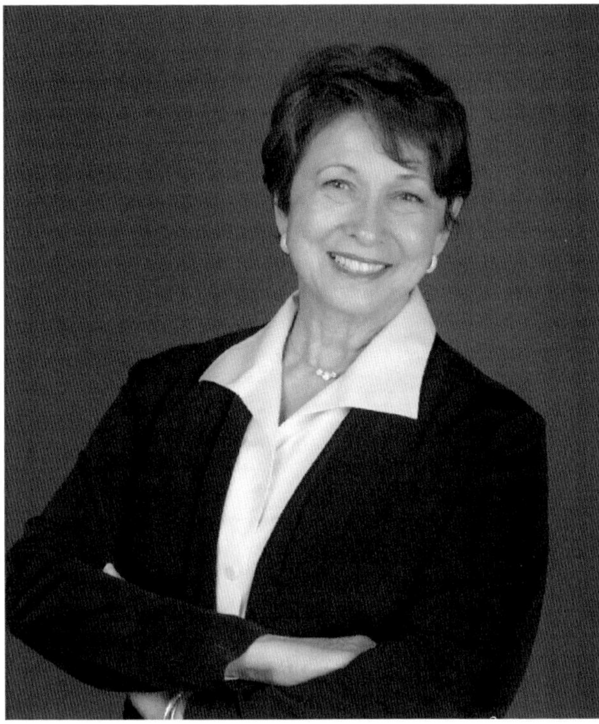

Turning Tragedy into Triumph

Peggy Dolan, the founder and executive director of the Kelly Anne Dolan Memorial Fund, was the devoted mother of Kelly Anne Dolan. Tragically, she lost her beloved daughter to a rare form of leukemia two months before Kelly's seventh birthday. During the weeks that Dolan and her husband, Joe, spent watching over their daughter in her hospital room, they discovered that many families, already overwhelmed with grief, had to deal with crippling costs, including increased medical and out-of-pocket expenses not covered by insurance. They found that many had to contend with lost income and lost jobs because of the time needed to support their ailing children. So on October 6, 1976, the day after Kelly Anne died, they created the Ambler-area nonprofit that has stepped in to provide financial assistance, respite programs, and advocacy for nearly 24,000 families in Pennsylvania, New Jersey, and Delaware whose children are seriously ill, disabled, or severely injured. Because of Dolan's tireless devotion to the cause—she is a wonderful, in-demand speaker at various events for area nonprofits—she has been featured in *People* magazine and the *Philadelphia Inquirer*, earning countless humanitarian awards and milestones for her commitment to seriously ill children and their families, including the following: American Cancer Society's Volunteer Achievement Award (1992); Greater Philadelphia Chamber of Commerce PACE Award for Excellence (1998); Pennsylvania Department of Health and the Special Kids Network, Provider Recognition Award for Improved Child Health in Pennsylvania (2000, 2001, 2002); Miss Philadelphia Scholarship Organization Community Service Award (2002); Dolan became the first woman to hold the office of Chairperson, Board of Directors, for the American Red Cross, Blood Services, Penn-Jersey Region (2002); Philadelphia Business Journal, Women of Distinction Award (2002); GlaxoSmithKline International IMPACT Award (2003); National Caring Award from The Caring Institute (2004); National Association of Home Care & Hospice Humanitarian of the Year Award (2005); Philadelphia Psychiatric Society's Benjamin Rush Award (2010); Lifetime Achievement Award at the Association of Fundraising Professionals' Philanthropy Day Awards, Greater Philadelphia Chapter (2013); and she and the Dolan Fund have been honored by the Philadelphia Phillies and 76ers, among many others, and she has been inducted into the Hall of Fame for Caring Americans (the Caring Hall of Fame) at the Frederick Douglass Museum in Washington, DC (2004). (Photograph by Dara N King Photography.)

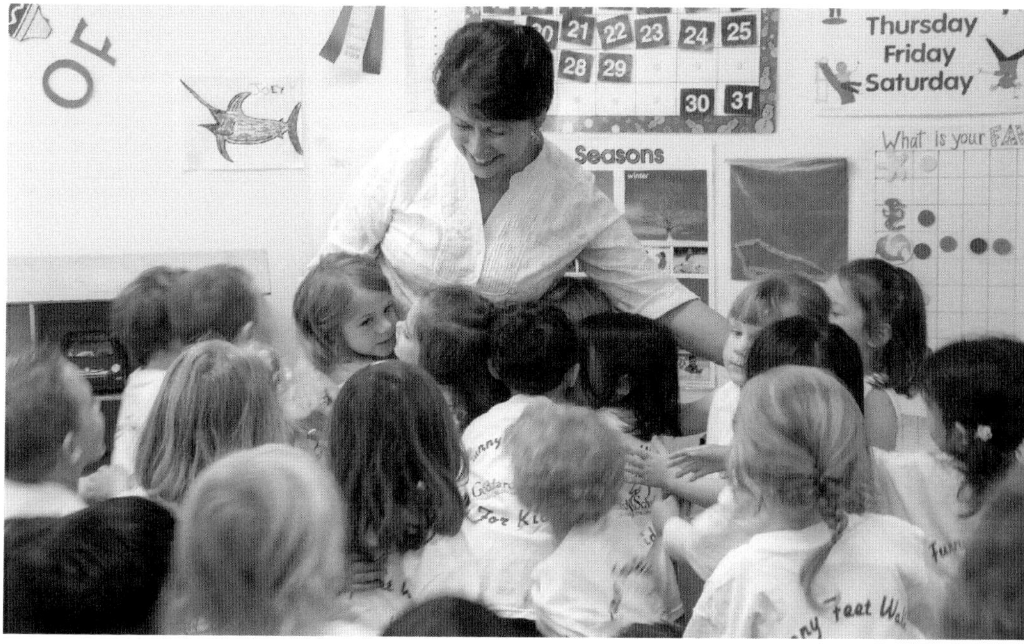

"Mother" to Many

Kelly Anne Dolan Memorial Fund executive director Peggy Dolan, clearly enamored of her role as mother hen to dozens of happy children, laughs during a Funny Feet Walk for the fund held at the Blue Bell Goddard School on May 29, 2013. (Photograph by Dara N King Photography.)

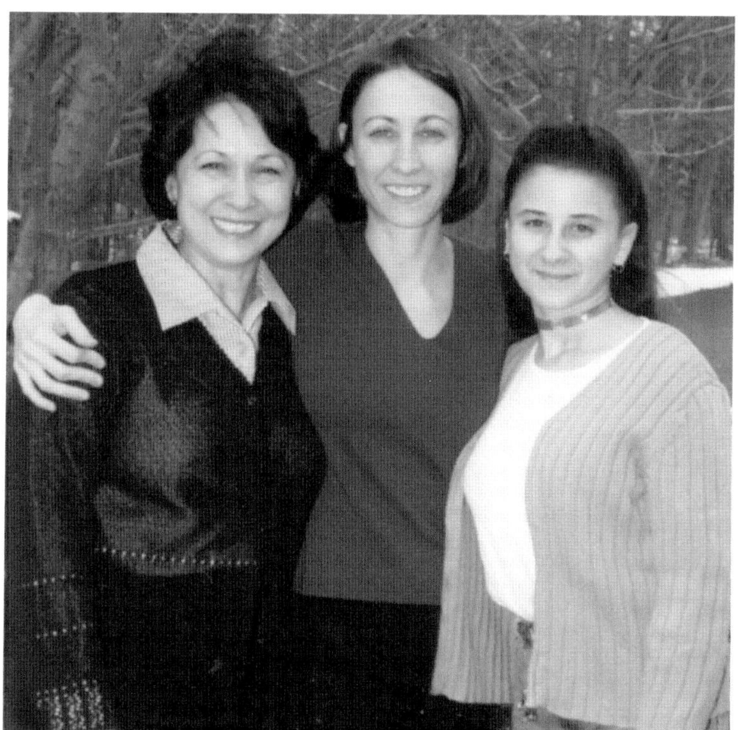

The Girls

Peggy Dolan (left) could not be happier, standing next to her two lovely daughters, Kristen Dolan Murphy and Kimberly Dolan. (Photograph by Carol Kodsi/A Mind's Eye Photograph; courtesy of Peggy Dolan.)

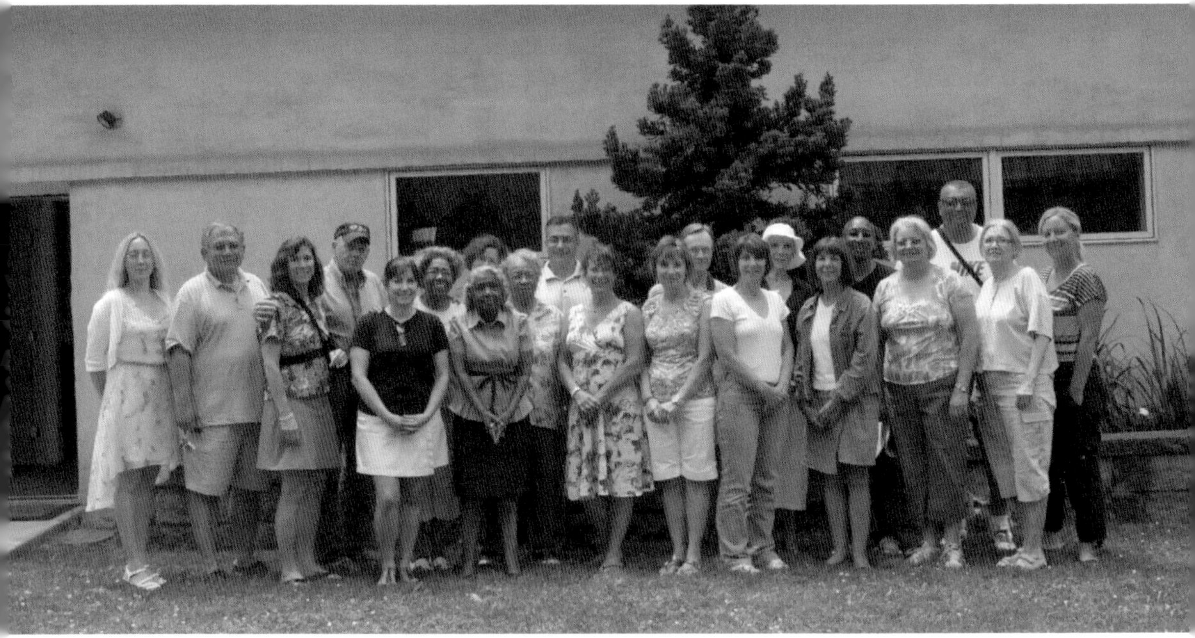

Mattie's New Crew

Some of the key staff, board members, and volunteers who make Mattie N. Dixon's Community Cupboard work go as smoothly as possible are, pictured above, from left to right, executive director Christine Bouley, Dave Herrera, Ellen Sherk, Bobby Dorin, Leslie MacDonald, Annabell Greenidge, Dorothy Thomas (a volunteer for 23 years), Molly Falcone, Thelma Trueheart, board president Ron Maltin, Debbie Derman, Helene Fisher, board treasurer Tom McGready, Amy Yanofsky, Carmine Winters, Sally Benton, Jerry Burgess, Mary Rodriguez, Eleanor Walsh, board member Otis Hightower, and Heather Maltin.

Pictured below at Mattie N. Dixon's Community Cupboard, from left to right are pantry coordinator Steve Toner, Christine Bouley, and pantry coordinator Michael Brown, whose look of astonishment can be attributed to his surprise 63rd birthday party at the cupboard. Bouley, an outstanding grant writer and former housing developer (who has also been a volunteer for the Muscular Dystrophy Association), has served as executive director since 2012. (Both, courtesy of Mattie N. Dixon Community Cupboard.)

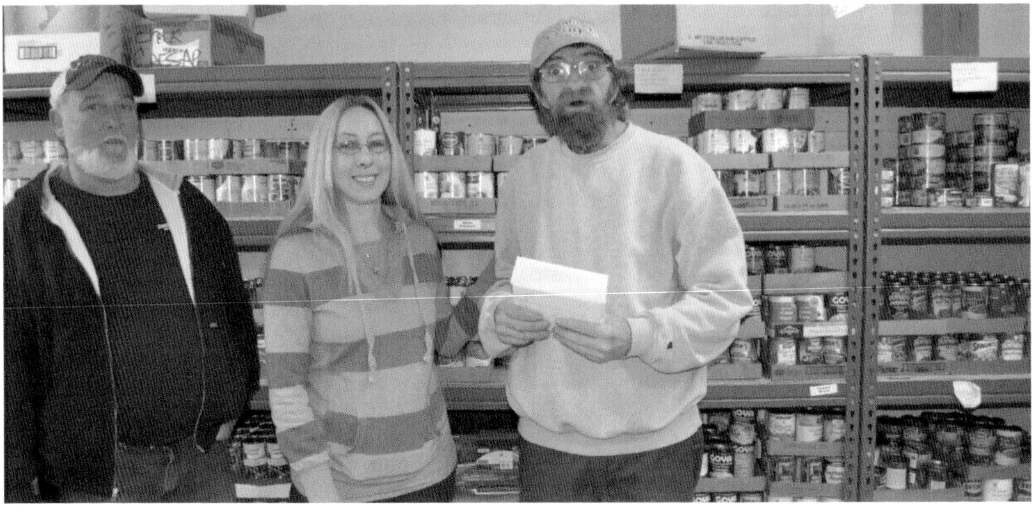

"'No' Is Not a Word"

Mattie N. Dixon, seen here on May 31, 2000, receiving the Outstanding Citizen Award at the 16th annual Upper Dublin Medal Dinner for her work in establishing the Mattie N. Dixon Community Cupboard, is a tough and straightforward soul. At the event, she said, "It's nice to be living in a caring community." Because she does not believe in the word "no," Dixon began responding to requests for help from families with incomes below the federal government poverty guidelines. Starting out in 1973 by feeding families bread and water from the basement of her Ambler home, Dixon, now 92, continued her charitable work at Ambler's Zion Baptist Church, at Church of the Brethren, and at 57 Butler Avenue, until the Ambler Rotary helped secure the organization's present location in 2003. The community cupboard, which has come to the aid of more than 100,000 families since its founding, coordinates the collection and distribution of food, money, clothing, furniture, and household items for roughly 240 families a week and makes medical assistance and advocacy available for families under stress. Living its motto of "neighbors helping neighbors" all year round, the community cupboard strives to keep families together by providing them with basic items and essential services until they are again ready to become self-sufficient. During the holidays (especially Easter, Thanksgiving, and Christmas), the cupboard offers holiday food baskets and gifts. Because of its success in helping families in need, the community cupboard opened its second location in July 2014, in nearby North Hills. It is run with the assistance of Jarrettown Methodist Church, with executive director Christine Bouley overseeing both sites. Bouley explains that the $12,000 allocated each year to help poor families pay their rent and utilities comes entirely from community donations. For medical care, the cupboard relies on a nurse from Abington Memorial Hospital, who joins them on the second Monday of the month to provide blood-pressure screenings, flu shots, flyers explaining where free medical services can be found, and similar assistance. In addition, two counselors are available at the cupboard every Monday morning to provide supportive services, resources, and referrals. Residents of the borough recall that Dixon, tender but tough, would succeed in getting her way (namely, finding ways to help the needy) by never settling for the answer "No." One of Ambler's most respected citizens, Dixon was known for pushing hard until she got what she needed. (Photograph by Bob Raines; courtesy of Montgomery Media.)

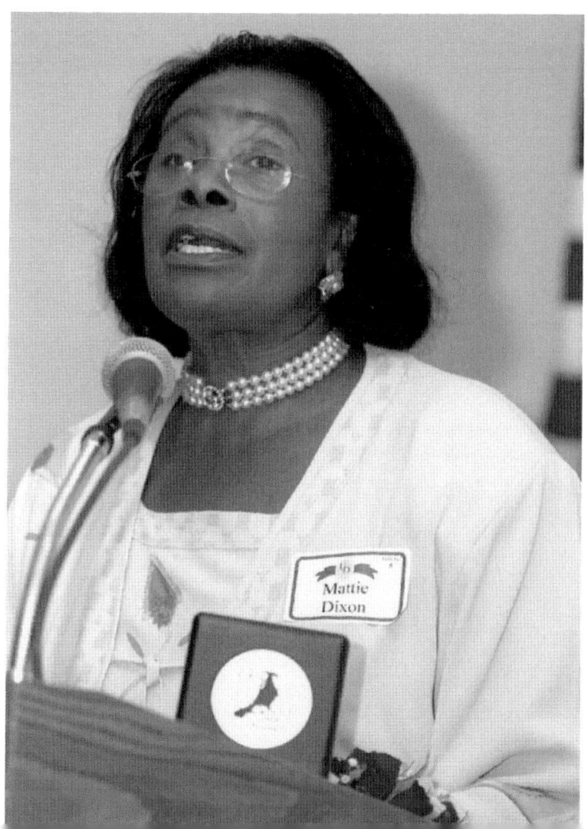

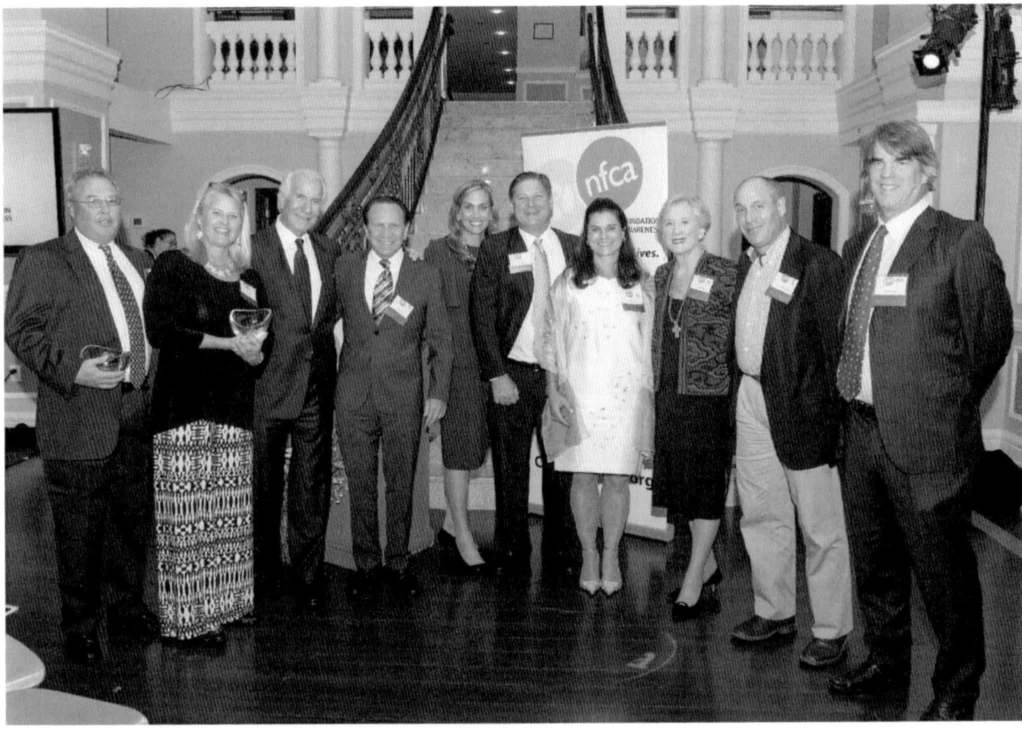

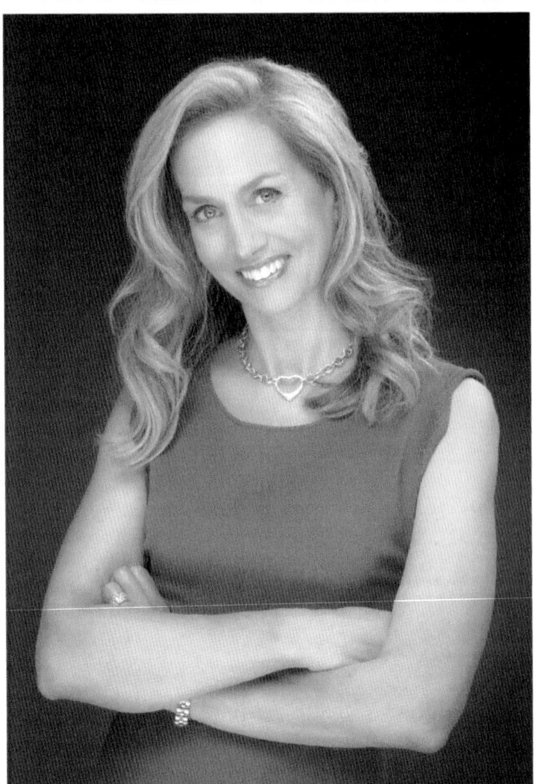

Celiac Awareness and NFCA Champions
Alice Bast (left), the president and chief executive officer of the National Foundation for Celiac Awareness, located in Ambler, suffered through years of physical discomfort, a stillbirth, multiple miscarriages, and a baby born at three pounds before, after consultations with nearly two-dozen physicians, she was finally diagnosed with celiac sprue. There is no known cure, but through the foundation Bast founded in 2003, she has brought significant national awareness about celiac disease, working tirelessly with nutritionists, doctors, chefs, and restaurants to pave the way for the preparation of gluten-free food for the more than three million Americans suffering from the disease. Bast is pictured above at center in 2010 at a reception honoring champions of the cause. From left to right are Don MacMaster, Fran McMaster, Philadelphia Flyers chairman Ed Snider, Bill Green, Alice Bast, Will Bast, Dorothy Binswanger, Anne Waldie, Richard Binswanger, and Peter Vogt. (Above, courtesy of PicturesByTodd.com; right, courtesy of National Foundation for Celiac Awareness.)

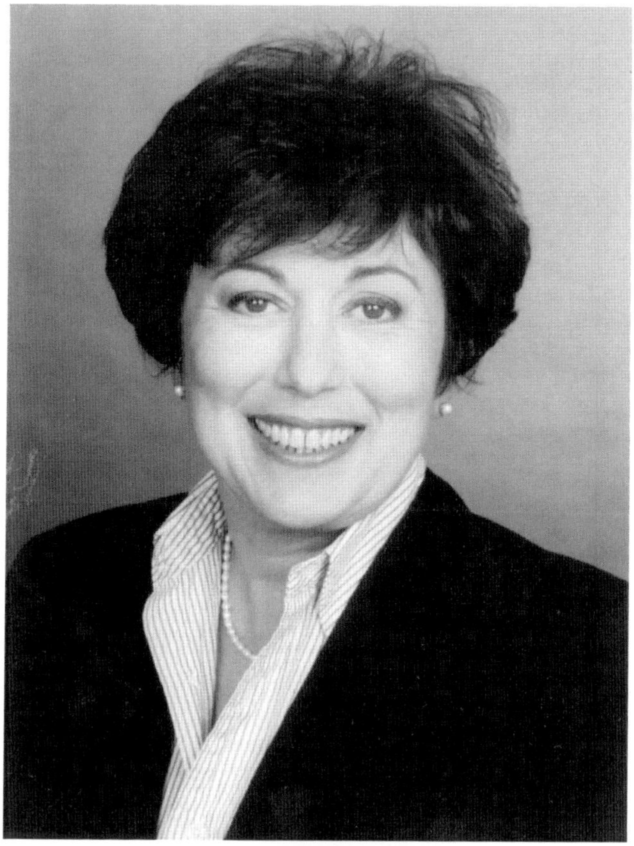

Melanoma Fighters

Bonnie Kroll's legacy as a woman fiercely devoted to the plight of the weak and unfortunate was already firmly established when she discovered she had contracted uveal melanoma, a rare cancer of the eye. A successful real estate agent, she was named best in her field in Pennsylvania in 2000, the year before she died. Kroll was a member of the Ambler Borough Council from 1976 to 1988 and was the first woman to serve as council president. She was also a founding member of the Ambler YMCA and SAGA. In 2001, her daughter Kelly (seen below), also a real estate agent and independent author (*Haikudos for Athletes*), founded the Bonnie Kroll Melanoma Memorial Fund, which has raised $400,000 since 2002. This fund has enabled cutting-edge research into the disease at Thomas Jefferson University Hospital. (Both, courtesy of the Kroll family.)

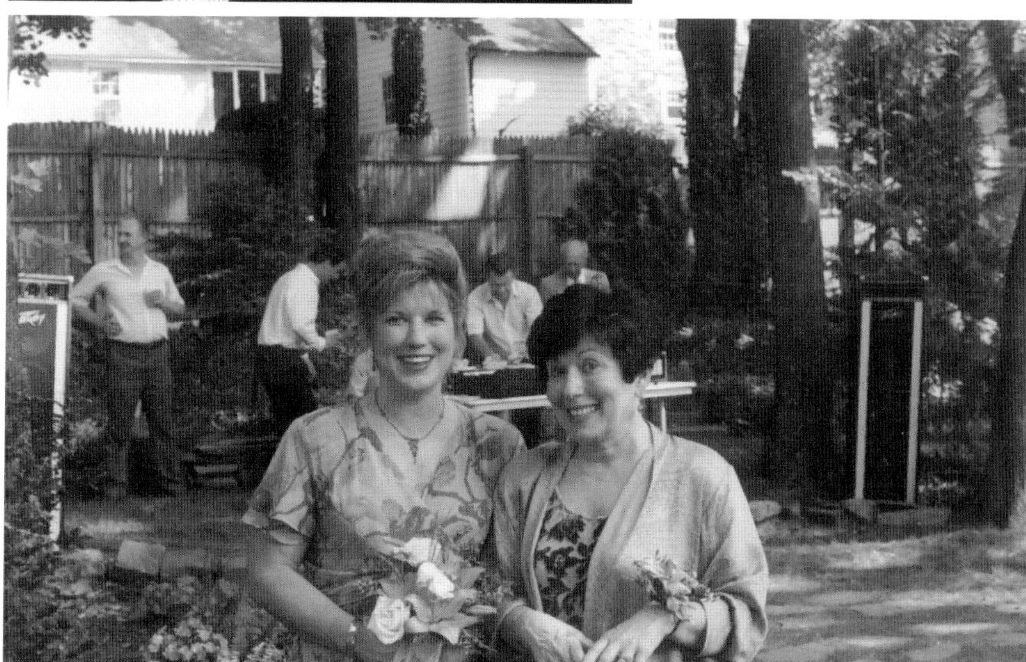

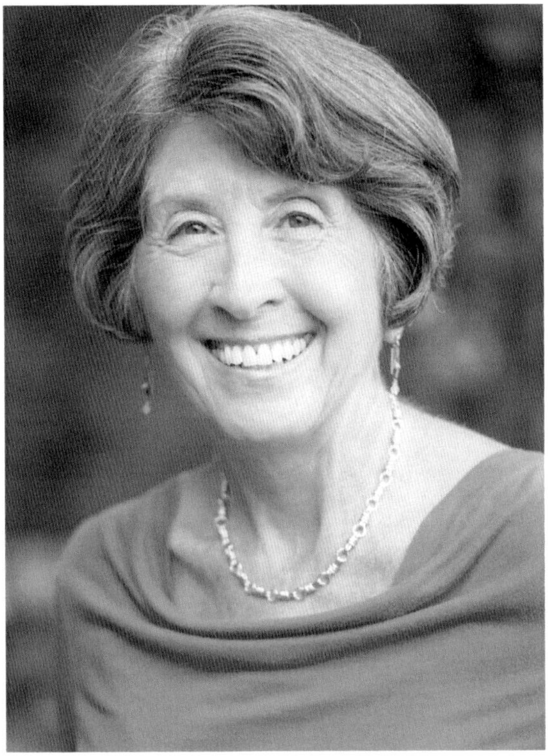

Hope Grows for Homeless and Hope Gardens

Although Lei Barry was named a Five Star Real Estate Agent in the September 2014 issue of *Philadelphia* magazine, an achievement not to be taken lightly, the Blue Bell resident's credentials as an unsung hero stem from her seminal work in founding the Inter-Faith Housing Alliance in 1982 and serving as its director for 25 years. Barry's call to action resulted from the struggles she and her two children faced when they lost their home in 1965. "Homeless doesn't mean being out on the street, having no dignity, style, or choice," Barry said. What the Ambler-based nonprofit does is work with about 20 local religious congregations to provide crucial services to homeless families, including temporary shelter at its eight-unit apartment building called Hope Gardens (see below), as well as guidance in life skills and assistance in locating appropriate housing opportunities. (Both, courtesy of Lei Barry and Inter-Faith Housing Alliance.)

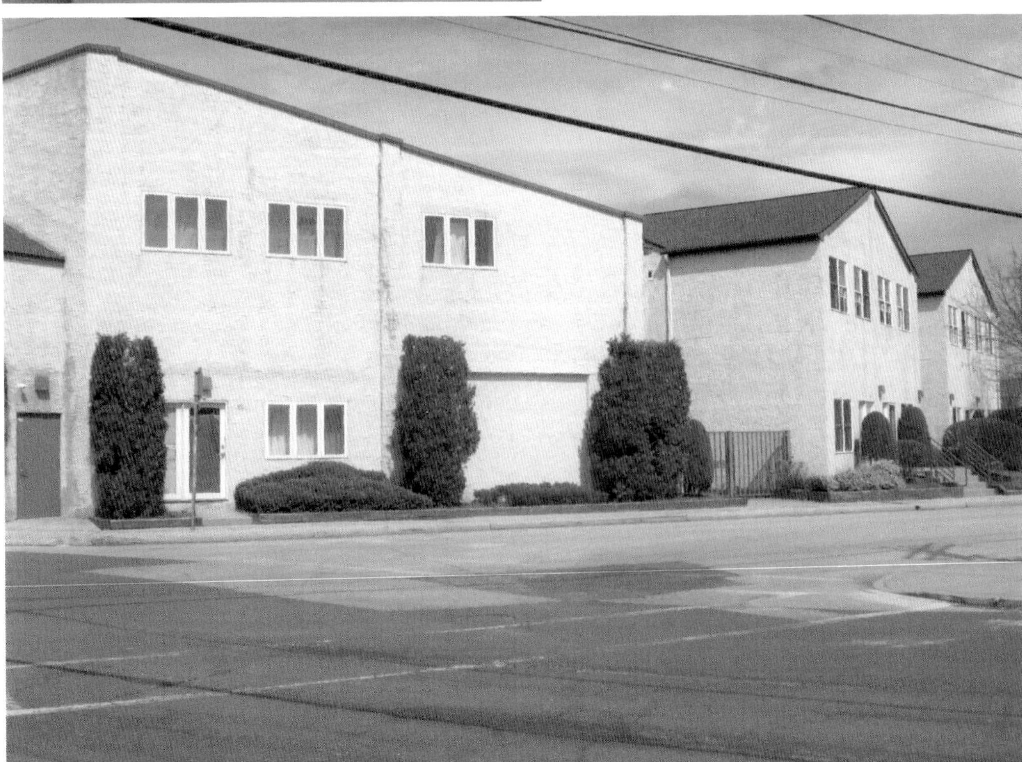

CHAPTER EIGHT

Veterans and Sports Figures

Some of Ambler's most fascinating people cannot be easily classified—any more than the attorneys or tax collectors who help direct the borough's professional theater or movie house, any more than the electricians, roofers, musicians, and advertising executives who still find time to serve their community through the Rotary, the library, the fire company, and environmental groups.

Several of these fascinating people are veterans. But then again, so are so many of the judges, publishers, and ministers who continually choose to serve in some way that benefits the greater good.

Two of these fascinating people, Katie O'Donnell and Kim Gallagher, brought honor to their schools, their teams, and their communities by excelling at their chosen sport with dignity and grace.

It is not just that Thomas J. Morrison served with the 101st Airborne during the ambitious Operation Market Garden invasion of Nazi-held Holland in the waning days of World War II. It is not just that he made more than 9,600 parachute jumps during his career (including several with former US president George H.W. Bush). It is not just that he still runs an advertising agency in Ambler at the age of 90.

Maybe it is just the following: Tom's daughter Suzanne Morrison reflects on the day her father was throwing a big party at his home just outside Ambler. By the time all the guests had arrived, and the host was nowhere in sight—just before panic began to set in—Suzanne recalls hearing that familiar fluttering roar overhead. It was a plane. There was a man in a parachute zoning in on the lawn for a perfect landing.

Guess who?

Suzanne said, "Gee, dad, did you always have to make such a dramatic entrance?"

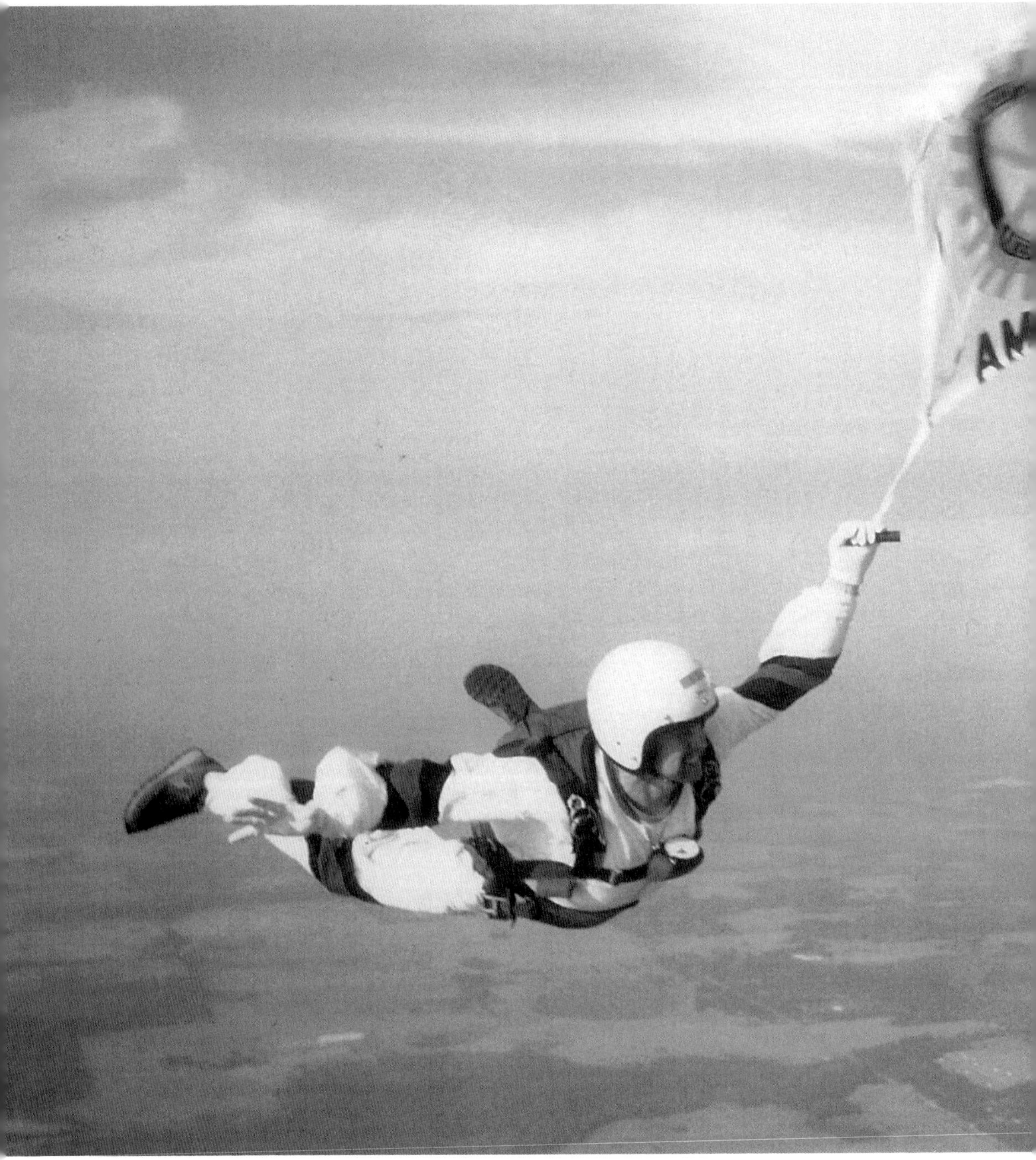

Flying High

Ambler Rotarians Bob Deen (left) and World War II veteran Thomas J. Morrison are pictured floating gracefully over Montgomery County, holding the banner of the Ambler Rotary between them. This was Morrison's 4,533rd jump. The avid skydiver was a witness to history when the 101st Airborne in which he served landed behind enemy lines on D-Day. During his career as an advertising executive, Cub Scout leader, and active member of the community, Morrison made 9,665 jumps in all, including

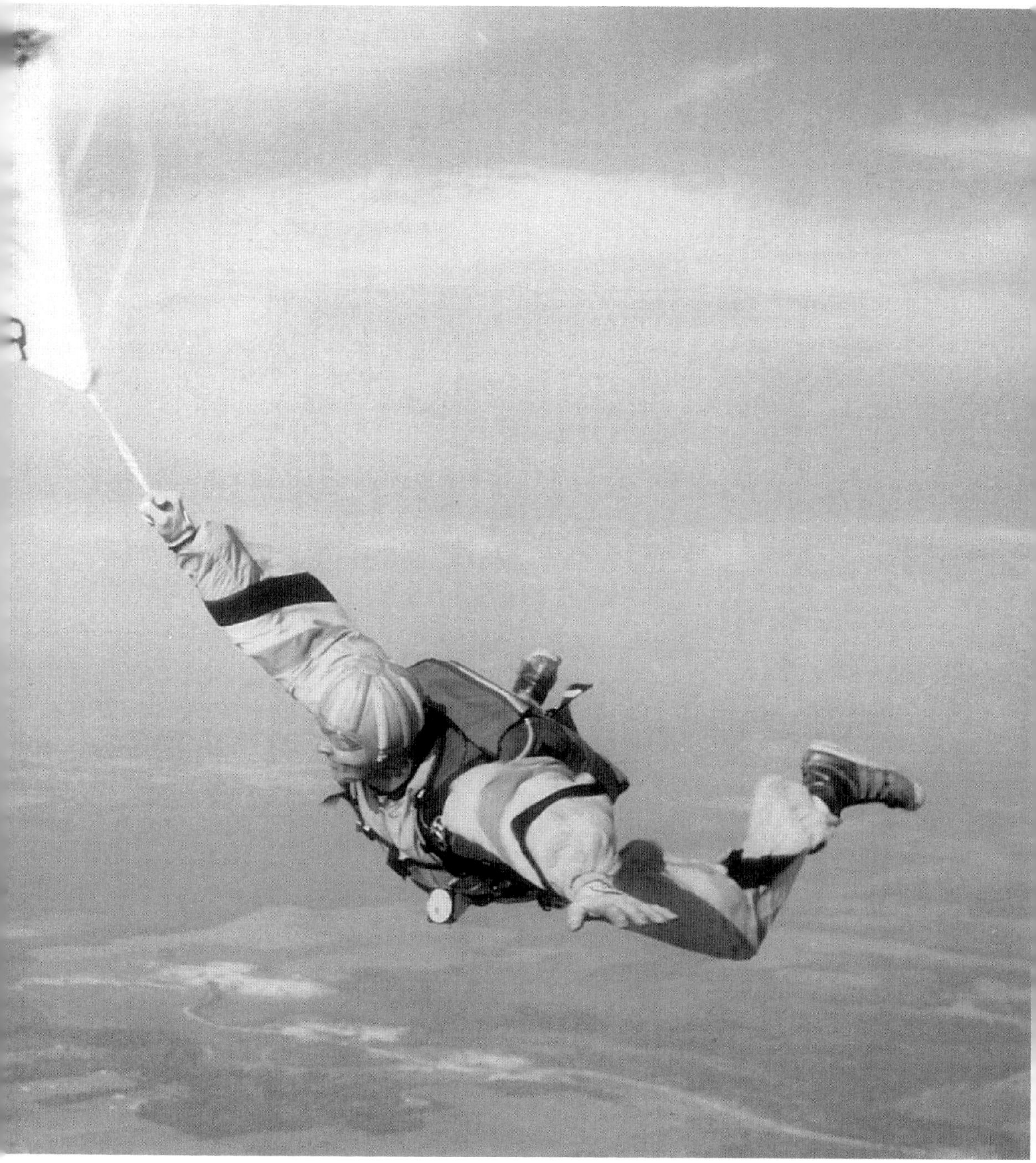

one in 1999, when he and his old friend, former president George H.W. Bush, skydived together over Houston to celebrate their 75th birthdays. In 1966, he parachuted onto the grounds of the old Simmons Elementary School dressed as Batman, and often jumped during the spectacular fireworks displays that concluded the annual Kiwanis Independence Day carnival. (Photograph by George Fray; courtesy of Thomas J. Morrison.)

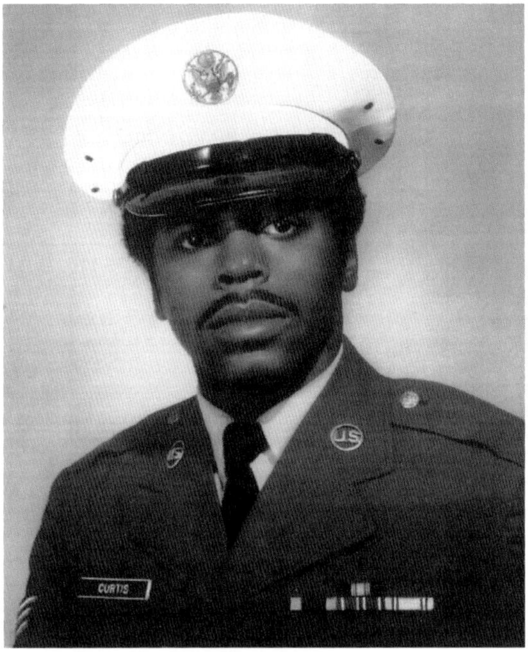

Eddie at Lackland

Like his good pal Edward "Eagle" Johnson, Ambler Borough Council member Eddie Curtis was drawn into the US Air Force. He joined the service in 1967, the year he graduated from Wissahickon High School. He is seen here in 1968, stationed at Lackland Air Force Base in Texas. (Courtesy of Eddie Curtis.)

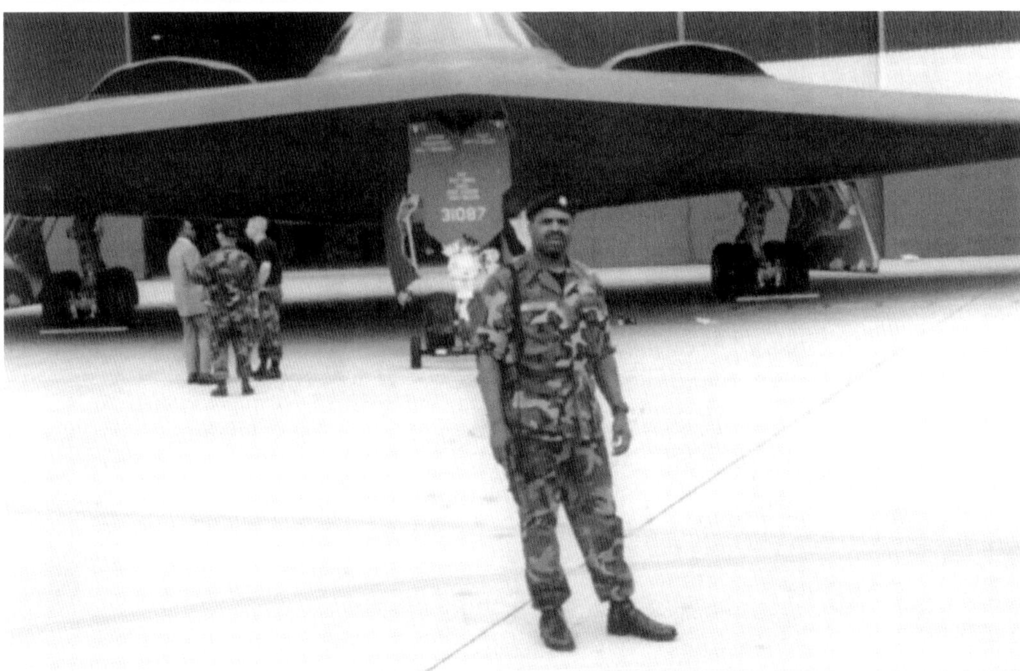

Mister Security

Eddie Curtis, seen guarding a stealth bomber at Willow Grove Naval Air Station in 1995, has made security the watchword of his adult life. After graduating from high school, he served a six-year stint in the US Air Force, where he was a security policeman. While living in his beloved Ambler home, he commuted to Riverside, New Jersey, where he served on the police force for 21 years until he retired. (Courtesy of Eddie Curtis.)

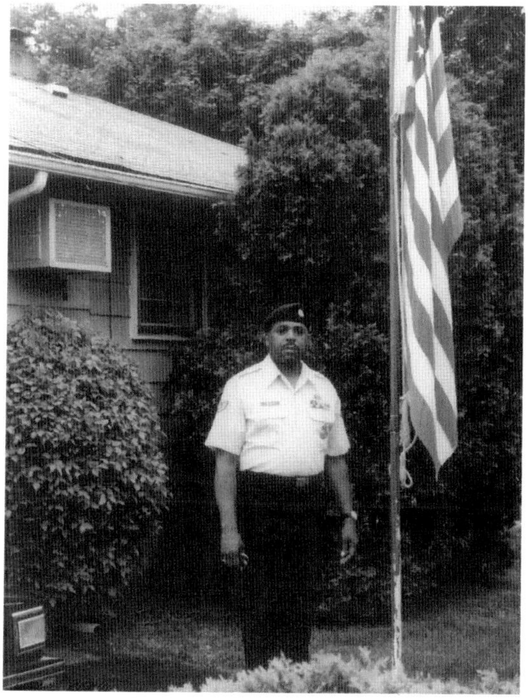

Legionnaire Nonpareil
Seen here before his longtime home in Ambler, third-generation Amblerite Eddie Curtis proudly wears his US Air Force uniform. Curtis, the commander of Daniel W. Dowling American Legion Post No. 769 for 34 of his 37-year tenure, leads the local American Legionnaires in Toys for Tots fundraisers, holds Easter egg hunts for children, and hosts community events at the post, which also serves as a safe haven for fire and flood victims. (Courtesy of Eddie Curtis.)

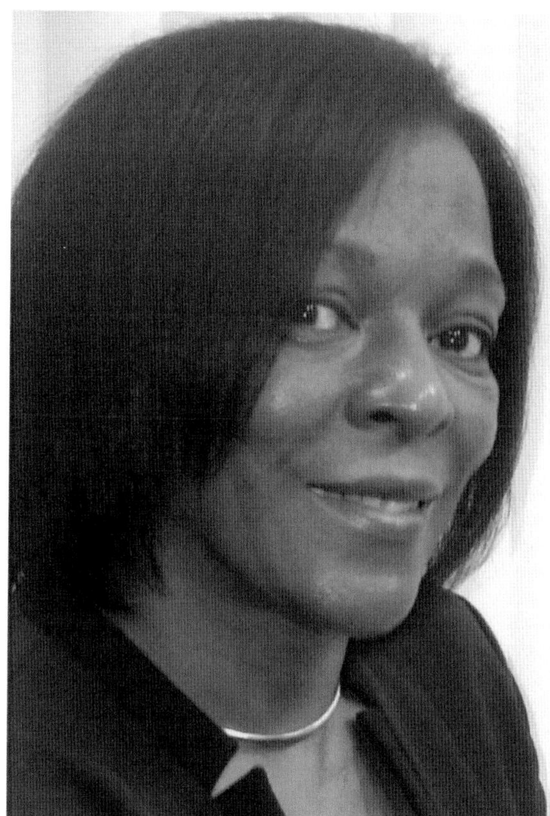

Last of the WACs
Disabled veteran Sharon Cooke-Vargas, the last member of the Women's Army Corps (WAC), retired after 20 years' service as a master sergeant E8. The only female member of Ambler's active American Legion, she has also written two published books. It seems fitting that Cooke-Vargas is now working on the University of Pennsylvania's important research project on asbestos, as her father, who worked at Ambler's Nicolet/Keasbey & Mattison asbestos factory, died from exposure to asbestos particles. (Courtesy of Sharon Cooke-Vargas.)

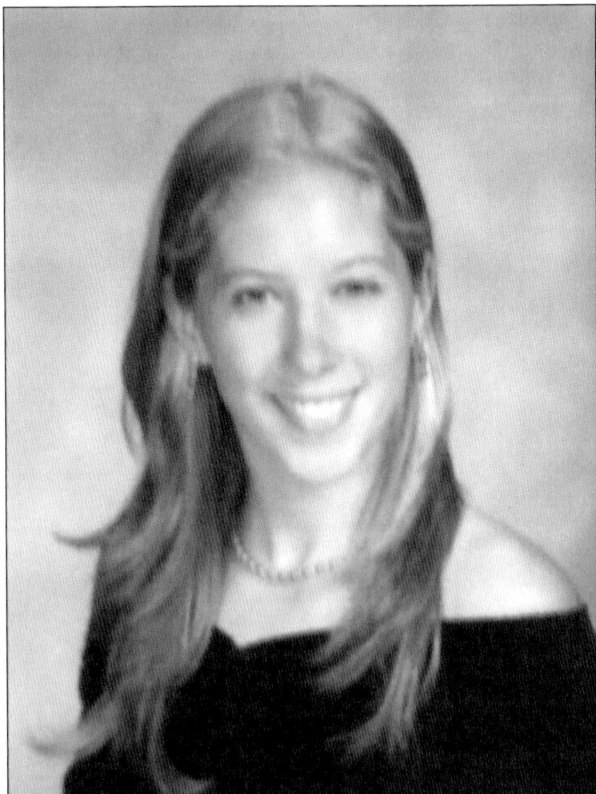

Field Hockey Supernova and Katie on Field

Pictured here in two yearbook photographs, Katie O'Donnell (class of 2007) was arguably the best athlete to don a uniform at Wissahickon High School. A varsity field hockey superstar for four years, O'Donnell was the first player to be named the *Times Herald* Player of the Year four times, and she was selected as Player of the Year twice by the *Ambler Gazette* and the *Philadelphia Inquirer.* The most decorated player in the history of the University of Maryland, where she was a member of the National Honor Society and where she returned in 2012 as a student assistant coach, O'Donnell was named National Player of the Year and Sportswoman of the Year in 2010. The youngest player ever to make the US women's national team, she played on the US Olympics Women's Field Hockey team in London in 2012. (Both, courtesy of Wissahickon High School.)

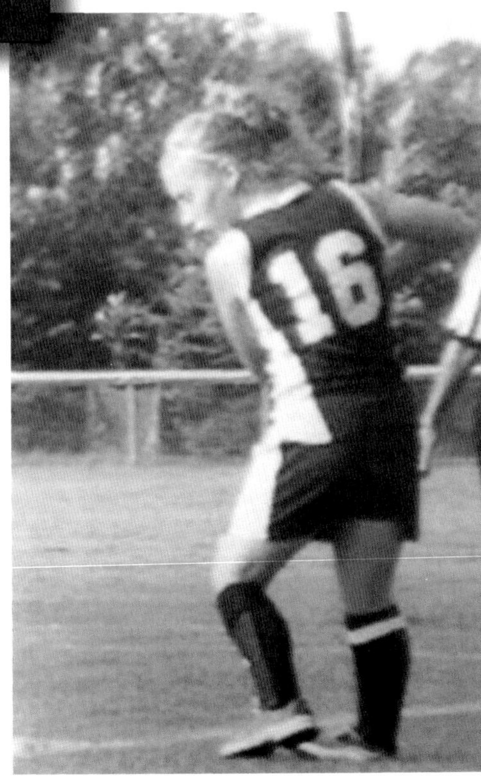

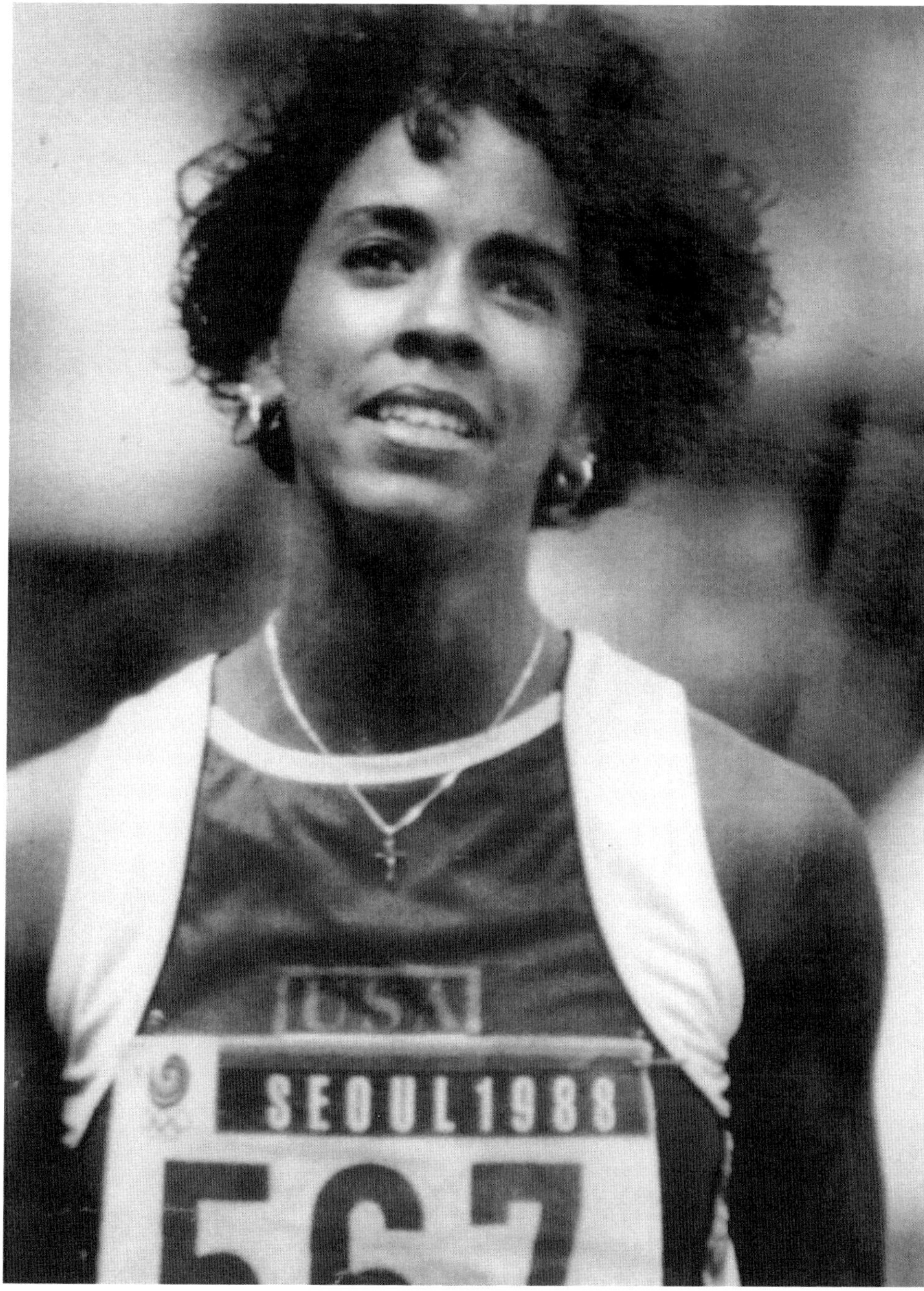

To an Athlete Dying Young

A high school All-American in track when she attended Upper Dublin High School, slim but sturdy Kim Gallagher went on to earn the silver medal in the 1984 Los Angeles Olympics and a bronze in the 1988 Seoul Olympics, both in the 800-meter race. A member of the Ambler Olympic Track Club when she was seven, Gallagher's distinguished career ended when a stroke felled her at age 38 in 2002. (Courtesy of Upper Dublin High School.)

INDEX